W9-BZJ-055

Venture Capital
due diligence

Founded in 1807, John Wiley & Sons is the oldest independent publishing company in the United States. With offices in North America, Europe, Australia, and Asia, Wiley is globally committed to developing and marketing print and electronic products and services for our customers' professional and personal knowledge and understanding.

The Wiley Finance series contains books written specifically for finance and investment professionals as well as sophisticated individual investors and their financial advisors. Book topics range from portfolio management to e-commerce, risk management, financial engineering, valuation and financial instrument analysis, as well as much more.

For a list of available titles, please visit our Web site at www.WileyFinance.com.

Venture Capital
due diligence

*A Guide to Making Smart
Investment Choices and Increasing
Your Portfolio Returns*

JUSTIN J. CAMP

John Wiley & Sons, Inc.

Copyright © 2002 by Justin J. Camp. All rights reserved.

Published by John Wiley & Sons, Inc., New York.
Published simultaneously in Canada.

No part of this publication may be reproduced, stored in a retrieval system or transmitted in any form or by any means, electronic, mechanical, photocopying, recording, scanning or otherwise, except as permitted under Section 107 or 108 of the 1976 United States Copyright Act, without either the prior written permission of the Publisher, or authorization through payment of the appropriate per-copy fee to the Copyright Clearance Center, 222 Rosewood Drive, Danvers, MA 01923, (978) 750-8400, fax (978) 750-4744. Requests to the Publisher for permission should be addressed to the Permissions Department, John Wiley & Sons, Inc., 605 Third Avenue, New York, NY 10158-0012, (212) 850-6011, fax (212) 850-6008, E-Mail: PERMREQ@WILEY.COM.

This publication is designed to provide accurate and authoritative information in regard to the subject matter covered. It is sold with the understanding that the publisher is not engaged in rendering professional services. If professional advice or other expert assistance is required, the services of a competent professional person should be sought.

Designations used by companies to distinguish their products are often claimed as trademarks. In all instances where John Wiley & Sons, Inc., is aware of a claim, the product names appear in initial capital or all capital letters. Readers, however, should contact the appropriate companies for more complete information regarding trademarks and registration.

ISBN 0-471-12650-0

10   9   8

For my father, Jerome,
who made possible all of my endeavors in venture capital

And for my wife, Jennifer,
the best thing that ever happened to me

The process of making investment decisions encompasses the heart and soul of venture capital.

—Standish H. O'Grady,
Senior Managing Director,
Granite Ventures

acknowledgments

During my final year of law school at the University of Pennsylvania, I had the opportunity to spend much of my time across Penn's campus at the Wharton School taking classes on venture capital and entrepreneurship. This book grew out of two of those courses. The first, offered jointly by the Law School and the Wharton School, was called "Private Equity Financing," and focused heavily on venture capital. It was cotaught by Steve Sammut and Frederick Lipman; the former covered the business aspects of venture capital, and the latter covered the legal. It was during this course that I first thought about how one approaches venture capital due diligence consistently and methodically. Wanting to explore further, I convinced Steve to supervise an independent study course. The objective of that course became the development of a framework with which to perform that type of due diligence. The project began as a short due diligence checklist. But, as annotations were added and its breadth was expanded, the checklist slowly matured into this book. So, I must first extend a great deal of gratitude to Steve for the opportunity to create the book. Without his willingness to supervise my project, it would never have been realized.

I also want to recognize several individuals whose encouragement and generosity in reviewing the book were terribly important: Steve, again, who was the first to read the book (in a very rough form) and suggest that I publish it; Jerome Camp, my father and partner in CampVentures, who gave me great encouragement and assistance throughout the entire writing process; Craig Johnson, whose encouragement and suggestions gave me confidence; and Richard Brandt, who caught me totally off guard with his munificence. Richard really deserves special thanks. Without his assistance and advocacy, the manuscript would still be languishing on my shelf, gathering dust.

Thanks also to my editor, Jeanne Glasser, at John Wiley & Sons (and the entire Wiley team, for that matter), for bringing the book into its final form and trusting the unconventional style of the book.

Finally, I would like to extend my deepest gratitude to my wife and best friend, Jennifer Camp. I owe her so much. The book never would have been completed without her patience, generosity, and support during the countless hours that I worked on it.

J. J. C.

contents

Venture Capital
due diligence

introduction

The phrase *due diligence* did not originate among venture capitalists, although they have certainly adopted it and use it liberally. Rather, the phrase originated in the context of public securities offerings. The federal securities laws impose rigorous obligations on companies planning to offer their securities to the public. The most important of these obligations is to provide purchasers of securities certain information, which is presented in the form of the prospectus. The phrase due diligence essentially denotes a legal obligation imposed on parties involved with the creation of prospectuses—directors, officers, underwriters, lawyers, accountants, and others—to use due diligence to ensure that they contain no material misstatements or omissions (the concept is slightly more complicated than that, but that is the general idea). The intent is to better enable purchasers of securities in the public markets to make informed investment decisions.

In the venture capital context, however, the phrase due diligence is used somewhat differently. The securities issued in this context are issued in *private* transactions, toward which the federal securities laws take a slightly more hands-off approach. Companies issuing securities privately are not required to provide purchasers (read: venture capitalists) the same level of information they would if they were selling the same securities in the public markets. Therefore, venture capitalists work hard to inform themselves regarding the companies they consider for investment. It is this informing process that has come to be called "venture capital due diligence." The venture capitalists at Woodside Fund describe it as "[t]he thorough investigation and analysis the investor makes of a prospective investment to see if it meets the investor's strategy and criteria for funding. It includes an assessment of the industry, market, business concept, management team, the company's technology, products and markets, and financials."[1] The reason that venture capitalists go to such lengths in their investigations of companies is that, by consistently and methodically doing so, they make better investment decisions, and thereby improve the returns of their overall venture capital portfolios.

The intent of this book is to provide readers with a thorough understanding of how venture capitalists perform the due diligence required to make informed investment decisions. It is certainly not performed by crunching numbers or building complex financial models; indeed, there are rarely any meaningful numbers from which to work. The essence of venture capital due diligence involves simply asking and answering specific questions. Questions are asked of many people—the founding entrepreneurs of the companies being considered for investment, the founders' fellow management team members, their former employers and colleagues, the companies' potential customers and partners, and technological and market experts—but, it basically just involves the asking and answering of questions. For that reason, the entire book is structured around carefully crafted specific questions that virtually every venture capitalist asks, in one form or another, when performing due diligence. The questions assume the reader is a venture investor doing due diligence on a particular company. They are organized logically and presented in the order that venture capitalists (generally) address them, and each question is followed with a discussion of that question and its possible answers. These discussions pull together and present the stated opinions of major players in the venture capital industry—John Doerr of Kleiner Perkins Caufield & Byers, Don Valentine of Sequoia Capital, Kevin Fong of the Mayfield Fund, Ann Winblad of Hummer Winblad Venture Partners, Richard Testa of Testa Hurwitz & Thibeault, Craig Johnson of the Venture Law Group, and many others—regarding the proper methods of performing venture capital due diligence and making venture capital investment decisions.

The first chapter of the book, "Screening Due Diligence," presents and discusses the questions generally used by venture capitalists to screen out quickly investment opportunities in which they have no interest. Venture capitalists are literally flooded with investment opportunities, and they typically use these screening mechanisms to narrow that number to a manageable few, on which they will expend significant time and effort doing further due diligence. Deals that are screened out are de facto deemed not worth such time and effort, for whatever reason: They may be in the wrong geographic area, in the wrong market space, or the deals may just be "dogs." For the deals *not* screened out, venture capitalists typically first focus their real due diligence time and effort on getting to know the management teams.

The venture capitalists at U.S. Venture Partners state that their "primary criterion" for investment is confidence that they "are backing excellent people."[2] The majority of venture capitalists share this opinion. Therefore, the second chapter of the book, "Management Due Diligence," presents and discusses the questions venture capitalists typically use to assess the quality and potential of management teams. Usually, concurrently with their investigation of management, venture capitalists focus on the targeted business opportunities. Chapter 3, "Business Opportunity Due Diligence," presents and discusses the questions that venture capitalists generally use to explore issues regarding products, business models (including markets), and competition.

Chapter 4, "Due Diligence on Intangibles," covers questions used to explore concepts that are important to venture capitalists, but that are generally difficult to measure—focus, momentum, "buzz," and "gut" feelings about management team members or business opportunities. The fifth chapter, "Legal Due Diligence," lays out the legal questions typically asked (and the legal issues faced) by venture capital investors. Legal due diligence is important for two reasons. First, the value of any investment can be greatly undermined by hidden legal problems such as inadequate intellectual property protection, and pending lawsuits. Second, legal terms can have a significant impact on the actual return venture capitalists realize from their venture investments.

The sixth and final chapter, "Financial Due Diligence," lays out the questions generally asked by venture capitalists when doing early-stage financial analysis and when negotiating company value. The issue of company valuation is critical to venture capitalists because it has a direct bearing on their financial returns. Together, these six chapters provide a clear and complete picture of the venture capital due diligence process and how venture capitalists use this process to make investment decisions.

CHAPTER 1

Screening Due Diligence

APPARENT DEAL QUALITY

Quality of Source

From what source did the deal come or by whom was the deal referred?

A simple and effective screening mechanism used by many venture capitalists is to scrutinize the routes from which deals emerge. Venture capitalists overwhelmingly tend to favor deals referred to them by trusted sources. Kevin Fong, general partner of the Mayfield Fund, states that his firm relies consistently and heavily on its network of lawyers, portfolio companies, and other respected contacts to uncover the best deals.[1] According to John Doerr, general partner of Kleiner Perkins Caufield & Byers, of the over 250 ventures in which his firm has invested, almost every one was referred by a trusted source: "a CEO, an engineer, a lawyer, friend, or another venture capitalist—known to both the founders and [the] partnership."[2] The reason that venture capitalists take this approach is that they usually know much more about the quality of the source by which a deal was referred than about the quality of the referred deal itself. It makes sense, then, for them to use the quality of the source of the deal, which is well known, as a rough proxy for the quality of the deal, which is not.

Quality of the Business Plan

What is the overall quality of the company's business plan?

As a second screening mechanism, venture capitalists often scrutinize the business plans they receive to gauge the quality of general presentation, thoroughness, clarity, coherence, and focus. These surface aspects often convey much about the quality of the investment opportunities and the entrepreneurs, themselves, underlying the surface. Says Russ Siegelman, partner at Kleiner Perkins Caufield & Byers:

> *The variations in the quality of the plans I read is amazing. Sometimes they look like the entrepreneur's dog has chewed them, and they are photocopied sloppily onto standard copy paper, with typos and coffee stains. Sometimes they are glossy, well written, with plenty of Excel generated charts and pages of financial projections. One might think that a good VC will get beyond the stains and the chewed pages and get to the business idea to make a judgment. But that isn't my view. If entrepreneurs don't present their ideas in a quality way, they probably aren't organized or professional enough for me to want to invest. I am not typically a form over substance kind of guy, but when it comes to business plans, I can't get to the substance if the form doesn't make the quality bar.[3]*

C. Gordon Bell, Digital Equipment Corporation veteran and adviser to U.S. Venture Partners, states rightly that "the ability of a CEO and his or her top-level group to write a good business plan is the first test of their ability to function as a team and to run their proposed company successfully."[4]

At a minimum, venture capitalists prefer business plans that convey a coherent and compelling story. They like plans that are clear, concise, thorough, and professional in presentation; practical, realistic, and credible in content; and that adequately explain all assumptions on which claims are made. They also like highly focused, concise plans. Venture capitalists generally prefer business plans that present a lot of information in a very few words.

As an example of what venture capitalists typically look for in business plan topic coverage, the partners at CMGI @Ventures like business plans to include the following eight categories of information:

1. The Business:
   Company's business.
   Strategy.
   Mission statement.
2. The Market:
   Historic and projected sizes in dollars.
   Market trends.
3. Product Offering:
   Product description.
   Development schedule and launch date(s).
   Product differentiation.
   Revenue model.
4. Distribution:
   Key customers.
   Customer acquisition strategy.
   Sales channels.
   Partnerships.
5. Competition:
   Key competitors.
   Competitive advantages.
   Barrier to entry.
6. Management Team:
   Roles and responsibilities.
   Background of team members.
   Board composition.
7. Financials:
   Historic and forecasted P&L (first two years by quarters).
   Projected cash flow (first two years by quarters).
   Current balance sheet.
   Projected head count by functional area (G&A, sales, marketing, product development).
   Capitalization schedule.
8. The Deal:
   Amount to be raised.
   Anticipated valuation.
   Use of proceeds.[5]

Plans addressing these topics fully (but efficiently) tend to be effective in conveying to venture capitalists the overall merits of the given investment opportunities. They also provide a solid foundation on which venture capitalists can begin their due diligence.

Additionally, most venture capital investors strongly favor business plans that contain well-thought-out, well-defined milestones. Venture capitalists use such milestones to measure and monitor companies' performance. Alan E. Salzman, managing partner of VantagePoint Venture Partners, and John Doerr explain, for venture capitalists, "early detection of deviation from the plan will indicate needed changes in the scheduled financings and help identify emerging problems in time for corrective action."[6] Business plans containing appropriate and well-defined milestones facilitate this function.

Quality of Other Equity Investors

Who are the company's existing investors, and who are the potential coinvestors?

Venture capitalists also often focus on the quality of companies' existing equity investors and potential current round coinvestors as a third screening mechanism. They do this for two reasons. First, an impressive investor list is often indicative of a good investment. Simply put, great companies attract high-quality investors. Conversely, a company's inability to find any high-quality investors suggests that an investment may not be a very promising one. Second, high-quality investors often contribute significantly to their companies' success. Depending on the particular investors, they may provide any or all of the following to their portfolio companies: general business knowledge, finance knowledge, technical expertise, entrepreneurial experience, operating experience, and business reputation. Equity investors may also bring to their portfolio companies extended networks of contacts to management recruits, service providers (law firms, accounting firms, public relations firms, etc.), customers, suppliers, strategic partners, venture capitalists, potential acquirers, and/or investment bankers.

A somewhat related point that some venture capitalists examine during due diligence is whether, and to what extent, existing equity investors will participate in the current round of financing. The failure of existing investors to support the company may dramatically reduce interest on the part of venture capitalists because existing investors often have unique information about the companies in which they hold equity. Almost surely, they have more high-quality information than that available to potential investors, even after thorough due diligence. Accordingly, if existing investors choose not to participate fully in subsequent rounds, it may quite possibly be the result of problems not visible to potential investors.

Quality of Legal Counsel

Who is the company's legal counsel?

To be successful, early-stage companies, need good legal counsel. The road from start-up through high growth to successful maturity is much too hazardous to forge ahead without a high-quality and appropriately experienced law firm on board. On one hand, law firms provide vital legal services such as creating corporate structure, addressing employment issues, and advising on contract negotiations. Companies receiving sound, quality legal advice in these areas certainly increase their likelihood of success. Regarding contracts, the venture capitalists at Accel Partners state that the "corporate contracts demanded of new companies grow geometrically—distribution agreements, employment agreements, financial agreements, patent agreements—and mistakes on any of them can seriously jeopardize a company's ultimate value. Even minor errors can require inordinate top management attention."[7] On the other hand, law firms also often provide other services to early-stage companies, such as giving advice on business plan construction and financing strategy, and making introductions to venture capital firms, bankers, accounting firms, and consultants. Receiving this assistance from experienced and well-connected lawyers can also boost a company's likelihood of success. Therefore, a fourth screening mechanism sometimes used by some venture capitalists is to evaluate the quality of companies' legal counsel.

Determining the quality of law firms is not always easy for venture investors, but, as Christopher Schaelpe, general partner of

Weiss, Peck & Greer Venture Partners, explains, there are only "on the order of 15 major law firms throughout the country with a core competence in advising private high-technology companies."[8] In Silicon Valley, this fraternity includes Wilson Sonsini Goodrich & Rosati; the Venture Law Group; Cooley Godward; Gunderson Detmer; Fenwick & West; Brobeck Phleger & Harrison; Heller Ehrman White & McAuliffe; and Gray Cary Ware & Freidenrich. In Boston, it includes Hale & Dorr; Testa Hurwitz & Thibeault; and Edwards & Angell. In New York, it includes Skadden Arps Slate Meagher & Flom; O'Sullivan Graev & Karabell; and Reboul MacMurray Hewitt Maynard & Kristol. In Seattle, it includes Perkins Coie.

Quality of Accounting Firm

Who is the company's accounting firm?

Early-stage companies also need quality accounting advice and assistance to function and grow effectively. This generally involves three basic services. First, the law requires all companies to file tax returns, and accounting firms can certainly aid in that area. And, outsourcing tax preparation often makes a lot of sense for young companies because it allows them to focus on their real task: building their companies. Second, many early-stage companies can benefit significantly from assistance with bookkeeping. Indeed, a well-designed bookkeeping system is crucial to effective early-stage management. And, third, early-stage companies will, at some point, require auditing services. Auditing services can facilitate further venture financing, bank financing, and financing in the public markets, and can often aid in forging customer relationships.

Furthermore, like their legal counterparts, venture-oriented accounting firms offer services beyond traditional accounting-type services. As Jeffry A. Timmons, professor at the Harvard Business School, points out:

> *Accountants who are experienced as advisors to emerging companies can provide, in addition to audit and taxation, other valuable services. An experienced general business advisor can be invaluable in helping to think through strategy, in helping to find*

and raise debt and equity capital, in mergers and acquisitions, in locating directors, and in helping to balance business decisions with important personal needs and goals.[9]

Therefore, a fifth screening mechanism used by some venture capitalists is to assess the quality of the accounting firms companies have chosen to retain. An appropriate accounting firm is both high quality and well qualified in working with early-stage venture-backed companies.

Quality of the Origin

Does the origin of the company conform to successful patterns?

A sixth screening mechanism used by some venture capitalists involves an examination of companies' origins. They feel much more comfortable with companies whose origins resemble those with whom they have met success in the past—that conform to successful and familiar patterns. For example, venture capitalists are used to backing companies started by well-known executives who have "spun out" of established, market-leading companies, or by well-known university professors who have developed cutting-edge innovations, or by hungry and brilliant graduate students who have happened on the "next big thing" during their studies. Companies with these origins, and others conforming to other patterns of success, tend to find venture backing relatively easily. On the other hand, companies that have questionable or unusual origins may find that venture capitalists are very tight-fisted. Recognizing patterns of success makes sense for venture capitalists, because patterns, by their nature, repeat themselves; all things being equal, companies whose origins conform to successful patterns tend to be successes themselves.

Quality of Customers and/or Partners

Has the company signed any impressive customers and/or partners?

One thing that often gets a company quickly past the screening phase of due diligence is the ability to list an impressive customer or two, or to have inked a deal with a strategically valuable partner. The venture capitalists at Oak Investment Partners state that they look for "distinctive relationships that have been formed with customers or partners that give [them] good visibility into the near future."[10] The ability to close important deals is indicative of the ability to succeed, especially in the early stages, where one key deal can make or break a company. Closing such deals also demonstrates momentum. Companies that can sign one important deal usually have a much easier time signing the next, and the next, just as a snowball builds mass quickly once it starts rolling. Therefore, venture capitalists tend to be strongly drawn to companies that can demonstrate they are just beginning to roll.

It is certainly most impressive when such deals have been finalized, but venture capitalists also are interested (though slightly less so) in those for which companies have only received letters of intent (LOIs, also referred to as memoranda of understanding or MOUs). LOIs are usually nonbinding, but they lay the foundation for final deals by spelling out their principal terms. They are often an important and necessary intermediate step toward finalizing deals, and companies that obtain them offer strong evidence that the other party is seriously interested in striking a deal.

Shopped Deal

Has the deal been shopped around to many investors, each of whom rejected it?

An eighth screening mechanism used by many venture capitalists is to determine whether deals have been "shopped," that is, whether they have been presented to and been passed over by other investors. Venture capitalists generally avoid shopped deals. Properly employed, this strategy makes a lot of sense. Shopped deals, by definition, have been reviewed and rejected several times by other venture capitalists. If a particular venture capitalist trusts the business and investment judgment of another investor who rejected the deal, there is no reason that the former should not rely on the latter's negative due diligence. However, rejecting a deal solely because it was shopped, without finding out *who* rejected the deal and *why* it was rejected, could result in the venture capitalist missing a great opportunity. Twenty venture capitalists turned down Hotmail before Draper Fisher Jurvetson invested; Hotmail was later sold to Microsoft for over $400 million.

INVESTMENT COMPATIBILITY

Market Space Compatibility

Is the market space that the company is targeting compatible with your investment strategy?

Venture capitalists invest in more than just companies, they invest in the future of a particular technology or a particular market. However, the enormous breadth of markets and the rapid pace of innovation make it impossible for them to maintain a sufficient depth knowledge across all market spaces to understand every investment opportunity. According to Robert G. McNeil, general partner of Sanderling Ventures, because of spiraling "technological complexities," the "ongoing trend in the venture community is specialization" in a few market spaces.[11] The venture capitalists at El Dorado Ventures state that they invest in only four areas: communications, enterprise software, Internet software and services, and semiconductors.[12] They add that even if a company has "a fantastic product, if it doesn't fit into one of those categories, [they] won't be interested."[13] Such investment discipline ensures, to the greatest extent possible, that venture capitalists make well-informed investment decisions.

When venture capitalists find themselves not sufficiently qualified to evaluate companies in particular market spaces, they often seek outside assistance in the form of technical consultation. For example, the venture capitalists at Draper Fisher Jurvetson state: "To evaluate technology, Draper Fisher Jurvetson does not rely on in-house expertise alone, but contacts appropriate specialists to evaluate the feasibility of developing the entrepreneur's vision."[14] Most venture capital firms actually make technical experts a part of their firms by making them venture partners or special limited partners.

Development Stage Compatibility

Is the company's stage of development compatible with your investment strategy?

Successful businesses progress through several stages of development and numerous substages. The "early stage" is generally considered to cover three substages: seed, start-up, and first stage. Venture financing is required during each, but the proceeds from such financings are used for somewhat different purposes during each substage, as William Sahlman, professor at the Harvard Business School, describes:

> Seed Financing: *Seed financing is the earliest stage of funding. A small investment (typically $25,000 to $300,000) is made to support an entrepreneur's exploration of an idea. Often there is no business plan, an incomplete management team, and little assurance that the basic technology is feasible.*
>
> Startup Financing: *Startup financing entails the commitment of more significant funds to an organization that is prepared to commence operations. A startup should be able to demonstrate a competitive advantage. Most high-technology firms should have a product in prototype form embodying a proprietary technology. A research-oriented venture, such as a biotechnology firm, might instead exhibit an impressive research staff.*
>
> First-Stage Financing: *First-stage financing is provided to ongoing businesses. A first-stage company is generally not profitable, but it normally has an established organization, a working product, and, preferably, some revenues. First-stage funds are usually used to establish a company's first major marketing efforts, and to hire sales and support personnel in anticipation of higher sales volume. Often, funds are also applied to product enhancements or product line expansion.*[15]

Venture capitalists generally have strong preferences for one or more of these substages. Some prefer earlier deals with lower company valuations and higher potential returns, but also higher risk. Others prefer later deals with higher valuations, but lower risk. Of course, such preferences are usually not set in stone. Most venture capitalists will invest in companies in less preferred substages if other characteristics of the deal are sufficiently attractive.

Keiretsu Strategy Compatibility

Does the company fit into your keiretsu *strategy?*

The *keiretsu* concept originated in the Japanese business system. Japanese *keiretsu* are groups of firms that bind themselves together in webs of obligation. They are controlled under Japanese law and are built such that cooperation between firms is virtually mandatory. The theory behind Japanese *keiretsu* is that each associated firm gains a competitive edge through the creation of a long-term strategy for the entire group, as opposed to a situation where each firm merely pursues its own strategy. The bellwether venture capital firm of Kleiner Perkins Caufield & Byers has adopted this concept and the term, but the venture capitalists there apply them in a slightly different manner than do the Japanese. Like the Japanese, the Kleiner Perkins *keiretsu* is also based on company cooperation, but they merely *encourage* their portfolio companies to cooperate.

Much of the value venture capitalists bring to early-stage companies comes from leveraging their extensive networks of potential managerial talent, advisers, customers, strategic partners, acquirers, and other sources of capital. These networks, which all venture capital firms have in varying qualities, are significantly composed of people associated with their current or former portfolio companies. A few venture capitalists actually incorporate the drive to create powerful networks into their investment strategies (they choose to invest in companies that can benefit, and benefit from, their network). It is this concept—an extensive network of carefully chosen portfolio companies—that Kleiner Perkins has captured in their adoption of the keiretsu concept. It can be a powerful and valuable approach when trying to build early-stage companies. The venture capitalists at Kleiner Perkins explain: "The companies in the KPCB Keiretsu consistently share experiences, insights, knowledge and information. This networking resource, comprised of more than 175 companies and thousands of executives, has proven to be an invaluable tool to entrepreneurs in both emerging and developing companies."[16] Doerr states that venture capital *keiretsu* "are rooted in the principle that it is really hard to get an important company going and that the fastest and surest way to build an important new company is to work with partners."[17] Venture capitalists, like those at Kleiner Perkins, who sit at the center of these *keiretsu* networks create valuable connections between members of the network, such as facilitating management hires, customer relationships, partnerships, and acquisitions. Such connections add value to each company involved, and that value translates into enhanced returns to venture capitalists.

Portfolio Compatibility

Will the company be competitive with any of your existing companies?

It is unusual for venture capitalists to invest in competing companies. Those at @Ventures state in no uncertain terms: "We have a policy against investing in new business opportunities that compete directly with our existing portfolio companies."[18] Significant legal conflicts can arise when venture capitalists invest in competing companies, particularly when they take positions on competing boards of directors. When two of Draper Fisher Jurvetson's portfolio companies became competitive (they were not truly competitive when they initially invested), the venture capitalists at the firm had to erect a Chinese wall to inhibit the flow of confidential information from either of the companies to the other. They put one managing director, Tim Draper, on one company's board and put another, Steve Jurvetson, on the other company's board, and then attempted to have them avoid speaking directly about either of the companies. This arrangement actually worked out quite well, but to minimize these awkward situations (and serious legal problems), venture capitalists in general create policies similar to that of @Ventures. So, whether new companies compete with existing portfolio companies is another widely used screening mechanism.

Investment Amount Compatibility

Is the amount of capital sought by the company compatible with your investment strategy?

Venture capitalists generally have a preferred range for the amounts they like to invest. For any given venture capitalist, Tyzoon T. Tyebjee and Albert V. Bruno, professors at the Santa Clara University School of Business, explain, the upper bound of this range is "determined by the capitalization of the portfolio and the desire to maintain an investment base that is diversified. . . . [19] Investors must make a sufficiently large number of investments to reap the risk reduction benefits of diversification. At the other end, as Tyebjee and Bruno explain, the lower bound is determined by the fact that active venture investors "cannot afford to spread [their] portfolio[s] over too many small deals because the subsequent control and consultation demands . . . are essentially the same regardless of the size of the investment."[20] William Sahlman elucidates this idea:

> *In order to realize value from their investments, the fund's managers need to commit time to board meetings, consultation with management, and other monitoring activities. Because of the number of competing opportunities for the VC to add value, there is a substantial opportunity cost (or shadow price) to the VC's time. Thus, an investment must be large enough to justify the commitment of time it entails; if the number of investments per manager becomes excessive, it will become impossible to add value to any of them. In addition, if a venture capitalist will be one of several investors, that VC will wish to have a large enough holding relative to the other major shareholders to be able to influence company policy.[21]*

The following are some examples of venture capitalists' preferred ranges: the venture capitalists at AVI Capital average an investment of $4 to $6 million in each portfolio company;[22] the venture capitalists at Benchmark Capital typically invest $5 to $7 million;[23] the venture capitalists at Sequoia Capital invest anywhere from a $50,000 seed investment to $10 million;[24] the investments of venture capitalists at

Oak Investment Partners range between $2 million and $15 million;[25] and the venture capitalists at Battery Ventures make investments of $5 to $20 million, or more.[26]

Geographic Compatibility

Is the company geographically accessible for adequate due diligence, and is the company strategically located for success?

Geography has historically been a large factor for venture capitalists during due diligence. Traditionally, many would only invest in companies that were located within two hours' drive from their offices. This actually remains largely true today. The venture capitalists at U.S. Venture Partners state that they "tend to focus on opportunities that are geographically close to [their] offices in Menlo Park. . . ."[27] Likewise, the venture capitalists at El Dorado Ventures say that they invest "only in companies that operate primarily from the West Coast."[28] They state bluntly: "We love it here in Boston" from a company would be a "sure-fire deal-killer."[29] On the opposite coast, the venture capitalists at Flatiron Partners focus their investing on the New York metropolitan area because when investing in early-stage companies they also "prefer to invest close to home."[30] Most other venture capitalists echo similar sentiments, though a few maintain a nationwide scope (e.g., Sevin Rosen Funds).

The reasons behind these geographic preferences are largely logistic. Venture investors need to be able, geographically, to do several things: (1) perform adequate due diligence, (2) monitor and periodically visit portfolio companies, (3) consult regularly with senior management on strategic decisions, and (4) attend meetings of boards of directors. To do all these things adequately while maintaining a national focus translates into an enormous amount of travel. Benjamin M. Rosen, founding partner of Sevin Rosen Funds, states that because of their national focus, when active, he was spending most of every week on the road and logging over 250,000 miles per year.[31] Most venture investors prefer to spend less time traveling and choose instead to narrow their geographic focus.

Location can also have significant ramifications for companies' long-term success, as Kevin Fong notes: "[A] big consideration is geographic location. If a company is in a place [that] doesn't have the necessary infrastructure, I'm not going to give that much time."[32] Having adequate access to the appropriate infrastructure is crucial for early-stage companies. They need access to a high-quality labor pool and leading service providers such as cutting-edge consultants, top law firms, accounting firms, and public relations firms. They also need to be in close proximity to attractive customers and strategic partners. When necessary, venture capitalists sometimes counsel (and often successfully persuade) their portfolio companies to strategically relocate in order to increase their likelihood of success.

Personal Compatibility

Is there personal compatibility between you and the company's management team?

Venture capitalists tend to maintain close working relationships with their portfolio companies during the life of their investments. Only a small percentage of early-stage venture capitalists choose to be passive investors. Spending a substantial amount of time with entrepreneurs over several years is virtually a necessity. Therefore, personal chemistry between themselves and entrepreneurs is extremely important to venture capitalists. Says John Fisher, managing director of Draper Fisher Jurvetson, "I don't care how good the concept is or the market is, if I don't like the guy I don't want to do the deal."[33] "Life," he says, "is too short."[34] The early-stages of a company's development can be extremely intense and can put great stress on all parties involved. If the participants can maintain effective working relationships in that environment, companies are much more likely to succeed. For precisely that reason, the partners at New Enterprise Associates consider the following question one of their "three key considerations" when doing due diligence: Are the entrepreneurs "people we can work with 'through thick and thin'—especially thin?"[35]

Harvest Strategy Compatibility

Is the company's projected liquidity strategy compatible with your investment strategy?

Mitch Kapor, founder of Lotus Development Corporation and general partner of Accel Partners, says that he will only invest in ventures that are targeting specific liquidity events.[36] He is not alone. Most venture capitalists scrutinize companies' harvest strategies carefully, in terms of both the type of liquidity event projected and the timing. Liquidity strategies are of vital importance to venture capitalists because they determine the schedule and the size of their harvests—when and how much they get paid. With regard to timing, Fred Dotzler, general partner of Medicus Venture Partners, explains: "The time required for an investment to turn into liquid securities or cash is important. The sooner cash is realized, the higher the rate of return."[37] For that reason, venture capitalists generally make sure that entrepreneurs fully understand that they must have the ability to liquidate their ownership positions at some point in the not too distant future. The venture capitalists at Draper Fisher Jurvetson specifically state that they prefer "an exit after a five to seven year holding period."[38]

Howard H. Stevenson, professor at the Harvard Business School, explains, "Not all ventures have the same alternatives for harvesting; some cannot be harvested at all and must simply be operated for cash."[39] Venture capitalists, however, will almost never consider investing in companies that do not have strong prospects for successfully achieving (and are not working diligently toward) events that will provide them with liquidity. Essentially, two types of events do this: (1) when companies effect IPOs that create liquid markets for their securities in the public securities markets; and (2) when companies are acquired, either for the stock of a public company for which a liquid market already exists or for cash.

Whether an early-stage company sets its sights on an IPO or an acquisition can depend on several factors. Ed Glassmeyer, a general partner at Oak Investment Partners, explains, "A lot of times a plan to sell has a lot to do with whether you are building a company or a product."[40] Companies that are projecting and working toward

IPOs, he explains, have to build "fully developed enterprises that can grow on their own with a capital infusion from a public offering."[41] Companies that are projecting and working toward acquisition may focus less on building fully developed enterprises and instead on building some sort of value (maybe a product or a product enhancement) that has the potential to attract corporate acquirers.

Traditionally, venture capitalists have tended to favor companies targeting IPOs. The venture capitalists at Hummer Winblad Venture Partners say that they "are always thrilled by IPOs, but are open to other positive strategies, such as acquisitions. . . . "[42] Acquisitions have, however, recently gained in popularity relative to IPOs, partly because many acquisition values have begun to approach IPO values. And, according to Ray Rothrock, general partner of Venrock Associates, sometimes it is just "easier to be swallowed."[43] Regardless of individual preferences toward IPOs or acquisitions, the most important thing for most venture capitalists is that companies have some sort of liquidity strategy in place. The reason is simply that, in general, companies whose investors realize the greatest capital gains from harvest are started and grown with a liquidity objective in mind.

CHAPTER 2

Management Due Diligence

MANAGEMENT RESOURCES

Quality of the Management Resources

Does the company have top-quality management resources at its disposal?

Early-stage companies rarely have complete management teams, ready to manage without assistance from day one. Such companies often must look elsewhere for management support, at least until their teams can be completely filled out. The places to which they most often look are their boards of directors, their boards of advisers, if they have them, and their equity investors. The quality of these management resources, along with the quality of management teams themselves, are an enormously large determinant of success among early-stage companies. Alan Salzman and John Doerr explain that "the very best product or technology cannot succeed without the management skills necessary to control and operate the business, penetrate the markets and thereafter compete in the marketplace."[1] Legendary venture capitalist Arthur Rock explains that venture capitalists greatly decrease the risk of portfolio company failure by investing in companies with top-quality management resources: "After all, a good idea, unless it's executed, remains only a good idea. Good managers, on the other hand, can't lose. If their strategy doesn't work, they can develop another one. If a competitor comes along, they can turn to something else. Great people make great companies. . . ."[2] For that reason, venture capitalists usually send a great deal of time investigating all of the management resources at the disposal of companies.

Furthermore, management resources are also often scrutinized by venture capitalists to ensure that they are great at recruiting other top-quality people. This will ensure that as the management team is filled out, it will continually recruit top-quality talent. Kevin Fong claims that this usually can be accomplished merely by ensuring that the people already affiliated with the company are top-quality: "good people tend to attract more good people. So eight good people attract eight more good people. . . .[3] Therefore, he simply looks for "A-players."[4] Regardless of how the task is accomplished, perhaps the most important responsibility for venture capitalists in all of due diligence is to make sure that companies have, and will continue to have in the future, top-quality management resources at their disposal.

MANAGEMENT TEAM

Quality of the Management Team

Is the management team made up of top-quality managers?

With the possible exception of Don Valentine ("I don't even care about the people. Give me a huge market"), venture capitalists generally place an enormous amount of weight on the quality of management teams.[5] Kevin Fong states that he and his partners at Mayfield clearly "rank people first."[6] Jim Swartz, founding partner of Accel Partners, states that for him, "the most important factor in a decision to invest in a company is the quality of the people."[7] He explains, "In real estate, the three biggest criteria are 'location, location and location.' The venture capital axiom is people, people and people."[8] Arthur Rock shares this opinion:

> *Over the past 30 years, I estimate that I've looked at an average of one business plan per day, or about 300 a year, in addition to the large numbers of phone calls and business plans that are not appropriate. Of the 300 likely plans, I may invest in only one or two a year; and even among those carefully chosen few, I'd say that a good half fail to perform up to expectations. The problem with those companies (and with the ventures I choose not to take part in) is rarely one of strategy. Good ideas and good products*

are a dime a dozen. Good execution and good management—in a word, good people—*are rare.*

That is why Rock says that he "generally pay[s] more attention to the people who prepare a business plan than to the proposal itself."[9] John Doerr claims to take a slightly different tack by focusing not on people, but on entire management *teams:*

> *In the world today, there's plenty of technology, plenty of entre-preneurs, plenty of money, plenty of venture capital. What's in short supply is great teams. I always turn to the biographies of the team first. For me, it's team, team, team. Others might say, people, people, people—but I'm most interested in the team as a whole.*[10]

The reason venture capitalists place so much importance on the quality of management teams is that the returns they realize on their investments depend heavily on the thousands of decisions, big and small, that the management teams make during the time that investors hold equity. Regarding his firm, Kevin Fong says "We feel that if we back the right people, they're going to do the best job at making the inevitable mid-course corrections that will be necessary in any start-up business."[11] John Fisher explains, a "business is nothing but a collection of people."[12] "Those people are your assets, and if those aren't the highest quality people, then you're not going to have the highest quality results."[13] According to Arthur Rock, however, finding people who are great at successfully making "the day-to-day and month-to-month decisions required to manage a business" is not easy.[14] Successful venture capitalists, therefore, learn well how to become good judges of people.

Two primary investigation methods provide the information for making judgments: the direct method, whereby venture capitalists interact directly with entrepreneurs, and the indirect method, whereby venture capitalists question those who have themselves interacted directly with particular entrepreneurs in the past. The most obvious approach to the direct method involves face-to-face meetings between venture capitalists and entrepreneurs. Such meetings generally consist of an initial presentation to venture capitalists by entrepreneurs, followed by several concentrated question-and-answer sessions.

According to the venture capitalists at Accel Partners, unless a company has worked with a particular firm previously, venture capital firms usually require "a number of intensive meetings with the firm's principals. . . ."[15] Venture capitalists also usually require meetings at companies' places of business. Venture capitalists usually like to observe entrepreneurs in their environments. In these direct interactions, venture capitalists generally listen to and watch managers closely. In doing so, they can pick up subtle signals that convey valuable information—sometimes more information than is obtainable through direct verbal communication. Venture capitalists, therefore, tend to be keenly aware of what is going on in their peripheral vision and are able to pick up little hints about entrepreneurs during due diligence. According to C. Kevin Landry, managing director at TA Associates, a good venture capitalist often "looks very relaxed and casual," but really has "got all these antennae out" constantly seeking information about the entrepreneurs.[16] Many venture capitalists also supplement their own judgment by asking trusted contacts to assist them in directly assessing entrepreneurs. Ruthann Quindlen, founder and partner of Ironweed Capital (formerly partner of Institutional Venture Partners), explains:

> IVP, like many partnerships, sends entrepreneurs to meet with executives or employees in our own portfolio companies. Because we've worked with these people in building their companies, we know and understand their thinking and trust their technical judgment. These meetings are completely confidential—these entrepreneurs don't reveal information given to them. We make sure that there is no competitive overlap. Their assessments are an important element in helping us to decide whether to fund a new company.[17]

Ann Winblad, founder and general partner of Hummer Winblad Venture Partners, takes another approach to the direct method. She is known for requiring entrepreneurs to prove themselves by what she calls "Excalibur tests." She gives entrepreneurs individually designed tests and asks that they bring her proof that they passed the test—that they bring her "Excalibur." Venture capitalists generally design Excalibur tests by identifying important risk points that can be overcome in the short term. Entrepreneurs "bring back Excalibur" by actually overcoming these risks. Winblad tells entrepreneurs that they will move forward with the investment process when and if they can, for example, sign up a crucial customer, land an important management recruit, or forge a key alliance with a significant strategic partner. "We don't necessarily require them to complete the Excalibur test," says Winblad, "but we want to throw them in the thicket . . . and see if they can come back out with the sword, vs. all beat up and scratched from the bramble bushes."[18] Excalibur tests provide venture capitalists with perhaps a more realistic opportunity to observe entrepreneurs in action.

Venture capitalists also pursue information about entrepreneurs through the indirect method. The primary approach under the indirect method involves checking entrepreneurs' references. Venture capitalists usually obtain a great deal of valuable information taking this approach, and thus most pursue it zealously. Generally, they turn first, to the extent possible, to their own trusted contacts. Such references are considered the most reliable. For this purpose, the venture capitalists at Draper Fisher Jurvetson have carefully developed a network of "intelligent, hard working, influential people" whom they can tap when they need to check a particular reference.[19] Additionally, venture capitalists generally require from entrepreneurs a list of references for key management team members, with names, addresses, and phone numbers. The Draper Fisher Jurvetson venture capitalists state their requirements as follows:

> *Draper Fisher Jurvetson requires each entrepreneur to supply a list of references in order that the General Partners may get a better sense of the entrepreneur's past experience, strengths, weaknesses, and work habits. Draper Fisher Jurvetson makes it a point to get references outside this list as well, in order to avoid only "cherry-picked references."*[20]

Cherry-picked references are a problem because they inhibit venture capitalists from gaining a true and complete picture of entrepreneurs. James Bergman, general partner of DSV Partners, offers another solution to this problem: "In a reference check, most people do not want to say anything bad about a person. However, if you give them the opportunity, they are often willing to name someone who might have something unfavorable to say."[21] Even though such aggressive reference checking is some of the most difficult work venture capitalists do—it is time-consuming and often frustrating—those that have the patience and discipline to check references creatively and rigorously have a great advantage over those who do not, and are often able to avoid costly mistakes. Venture capitalists typically average 50 due diligence telephone calls per deal, many of which are reference checks.

The following list supplied by Arthur Lipper, former editor of *Venture* magazine, is an example of a set of questions venture capitalists often ask references when performing reference checks:

1. When did you first meet _____ and under what circumstances?
2. What was the nature and quality of the relationship?
3. Are you still in contact with _____ and with what frequency?
4. What bad things can you tell me about _____'s performance under pressure?
5. Does he seem to seek stressful or comfortable situations?
6. How does he handle failure or situations that do not develop as he planned or would have liked?
7. In instances of failure or problems, does he tend to blame himself, others, or circumstances beyond his control?
8. When he fails to succeed, how long does it take him to bounce back with alternative means to accomplish the same goal or with another new idea? Does he get "frozen" into one approach?
9. What can you tell me about the family relationships of _____ ?
10. Can you think of anyone who might question his integrity?
11. Do you know any people who dislike or have disagreements with _____ ?
12. Other than the names of such individuals, can you tell me anything about the problem or disagreement?
13. What are the best things or strongest points you can tell me about from the perspective of a future partner or investor?
14. Have you been able to observe how _____ works with other people? Does he work better with peers or those he is supervising? How does he relate to superiors?
15. Does he complete projects undertaken or does he become distracted?
16. Whom do you know who is closest to _____ or in a very good position to provide insights about him?

17. Did you expect this contact and have you had others of a similar nature? If so, from whom? Did you tell them the same as you are telling me?
18. What do you think _____ will be doing 10 years from now? What do you think he really wants to be doing 10 years from now?
19. If you had the opportunity to invest, alone or with others, in a business to be managed and possibly controlled by _____, would you invest?[22]

Another common component of the indirect method is to conduct background checks, through firms specifically offering such services. These background checks often consist of examinations of any criminal records, including both felony and misdemeanor records at the county, state, and federal levels, and any outstanding criminal warrants. Certainly, no venture capitalist wants to back someone with a history of embezzlement or securities fraud. Background checks can also include examinations of civil court records, searches for any bankruptcies, judgments, and/or tax liens, examinations of credit histories, and examinations of motor vehicle records. All of these are simply tools through which venture capitalists can confirm that entrepreneurs are reasonable, dependable, responsible, trustworthy people.

Completeness of the Management Team

Is the management team complete and functional in each critical area (marketing, business development, operations, finance, and any other areas specifically critical to the particular business)?

Venture capitalists almost universally prefer team-led ventures. Kevin Fong explains, "One person can't do it all."[23] He says, "You need a team."[24] Karl Vesper, in his book, *New Venture Strategies,* provides six reasons that lie behind this preference:

(1) Teams make available larger labor effort, and (2) teams can provide a more complete balance of skills and other resources with which to start. With a team, (3) the departure of any given

member is less likely to be disastrous for the venture than with a lone entrepreneur. (4) With a team, the venture should be able to grow further before having to expend valuable management effort in seeking out and recruiting additional key talent. (5) A willingness and ability on the part of the initial entrepreneur to assemble and work with a team can be symptomatic of ability to attract and manage people, whereas inability or disinclination to work with a team may signal, particularly to potential investors, a lack of managerial capacity for growth. Finally, (6) the attempt to recruit team members can be a preliminary stage of checkout of the venture idea. Their willingness to join can be indicative of its merits as well as the founder's.[25]

That said, most venture capitalists, such as those at Hummer Winblad Venture Partners, generally do not consider the fact that an early-stage company is centered around a solo manager as necessarily a large problem: "We recognize that strong teams aren't built overnight, and are always excited to work with individuals intent on surrounding themselves with excellence. Many Hummer Winblad companies began with two people and a strong vision."[26] Such beginnings are actually very common. According to C. Richard Kramlich, cofounder and general partner of New Enterprise Associates, every company with which he has been involved initially "looked like a piece of Swiss cheese up close."[27] So, the consensus among venture capitalists is that, although you certainly need a great team to succeed, you do not have to have that team in place from the beginning. It is, however, a common misconception among entrepreneurs that they must have a complete team when approaching venture capitalists. According to Kevin Fong, inexperienced or mediocre managers are often placed in management positions by companies just to complete the team before seeking venture capital funding:

One typical mistake is entrepreneurs think they have to have a complete team when they approach us. They'll place people in the holes just to have a name in each spot. In the early stages, no one really cares about that. You can have placeholders or you can just say, hey there's an empty spot here that we need to fill.[28]

In fact, many times venture capitalists prefer to fill holes in the team *after* they have established a relationship with the company. Then, venture capitalists can use their experience and their networks to drive the management searches. Few entrepreneurs have the same level of experience in recruiting and team building or the same access to extensive networks of potential management recruits that most venture capitalists have.

Adult Supervision

Can and should top-quality managers be brought in to fill out the management team?

Venture capitalists are famous for requiring companies to agree to bring in what they call "adult supervision"—seasoned managerial talent—before they will invest. This usually involves replacing founding CEOs with CEOs who have more experience. Whether they will have to do that (and whether they will be able to do that) are things that venture capitalists like to examine carefully during due diligence. Despite the extensive networks of managerial talent to which many venture capitalists have access, it is still relatively much more difficult for them to search out the right managerial talent than it is to simply back qualified founders. Says Don Valentine:

> If in fact you have founders that can grow with the opportunity, it is monumentally easier for us to stay with them and augment them where they modestly need augmentation. It's monumentally hard to hire John Morgridge when you're looking for him. It's much easier to finance a company where you have all of these people in place. That almost never happens. But it is very desirable. We finance companies both ways.[29]

It is also relatively more risky. There is never any certainty that venture capitalists and their portfolio companies will be able to locate the right individuals in time, or that they will be able to convince them to drop everything they are doing, relocate their families, and join their risky start-up companies. When venture capitalists determine that for particular opportunities to be viable investment opportunities, they will have to find adult supervision, it significantly increases both the time and effort they must contribute to the companies and it significantly changes their risk profiles. So, whether they will have to do this is something most venture capitalists want to know and take into consideration before committing any capital.

Also, beyond the question of whether companies will *need* adult supervision, another vital consideration for venture capitalists is whether they will *accept* adult supervision. If founders are unwilling to do so, it is typically difficult for venture capitalists to do much about it—at least not without a nasty fight. This is generally true even when venture capitalists hold board control. Therefore, venture capitalists usually attempt to ascertain up front whether entrepreneurs will be amenable to bringing in adult supervision. Floyd Kvamme, general partner at Kleiner Perkins Caufield & Byers, explains:

> *One of the questions we ask every CEO before we back them is, "Is it more important for you to be CEO of this company or for this company to succeed?" That's always a tough question for a person who wants to be the long-term leader of any enterprise. But we frankly will not enter into an investment situation with someone who answers the question the way that doesn't lead to the success of the enterprise."*[30]

Management Team Diversity and Efficacy

Is the management team diverse in its composition and do the members of the management team complement each other and work together effectively?

Venture capitalists usually favor management teams that are diverse in composition. Diversity in this context means diversity in terms of skills, backgrounds, personalities, and perspectives. Diverse management teams are generally stronger and more effective than homogeneous management teams. Diversity enables management teams to address a wider range of issues than would otherwise be possible, and to approach such issues from several perspectives, which generally results in fundamentally stronger decisions. Furthermore, because of the importance to early-stage companies of strategic partnering and deal making, diverse management teams provide companies with more opportunities to strike such deals and stronger platforms with which to close them. An ability to forge important relationships can be important to start-up success. Diversity is not, however, by itself, enough. Management teams also should possess complementary skills and backgrounds. Essentially, venture capitalists like to see that each management team member adds value to the particular company and fits well with the other team members, but is not redundant. Management teams that achieve this standard, whose members have skills, backgrounds, personalities, and perspectives that are both diverse and complementary, are likely to create a strong and effective synergistic force.

Venture capitalists also prefer to back management teams that are cohesive and effective in their decision-making processes as well as in their actions. Discord among management team members is a primary cause of venture failure. Armed with this knowledge, the venture capitalists at Draper Fisher Jurvetson require that any management team they back "work well together."[31] Venture capitalists prefer teams that feel they are all "in this thing together" and have the mentality that "if the company wins, everyone wins." Kevin Fong explains that one thing he and his partners really look for is "the fact that the team generally likes each other."[32] Says Fong:

> [A]s a final step, before a team comes in and we decide to invest, we have them come together and give a presentation to our entire partnership, so all of my ten partners and I sit there and get a presentation from the team. And we look for signs of cohesiveness, even little things like how they split up the presentation, and how each of them delivers certain parts. And then, during the question and answer period, how they interact with each other.
>
> I mean, it's not unusual to have a team sit there and argue in front of us, as well, when they don't agree on a point. Or if a team absolutely, each of the people has to have a say in terms of how they see it or something like that, there're just little things that just tell us that, boy, this team's not getting along.[33]

Teams that get along, are cohesive and work well together, and are effective in their decision making and their actions, have a much higher likelihood of success than those that are otherwise.

It is not always a simple task, however, for venture capitalists to determine how well a team works together or to gauge its effectiveness or cohesiveness. John Doerr offers a method by which he and his colleagues at Kleiner Perkins assess teams:

> *We want to understand who they are, how they will work together. For example, I'll ask them to sell me their product. I'll ask them to recruit me to join your team. I'll ask practical questions about how they'll live and breathe the business: "If I were on your team, I might qualify to be your vice president of business development, or sales. How will you manage me and the other team members? How will we agree on priorities? How will we measure whether or not we're getting the right job done? What's your instinct about process versus results? How will you stay ahead of competition? What will you do when someone isn't working out?"* [34]

By simply interacting in this way with entire management teams together for sufficient periods of time, venture capitalists usually can obtain fairly clear pictures of a team's true character and nature.

Past Success of the Management Team

Has this management team met with success in the past, as a team?

Management teams that have met with success in the past are particularly attractive to venture capitalists. The venture capitalists at Norwest Venture Partners state that they specifically look for management teams that have been previously successful.[35] This preference, widely shared among venture capitalists, is a sound one. The best method of predicting whether a team will be successful together in the future is to determine whether they were successful together in a previous endeavor.

Commitment of the Management Team

Are the members of the management team committed to the long-term success of the company?

Arthur Rock will not invest in any company whose management team is not fully committed to the company's long-term success.[36] Venture capitalists, in general, attempt to measure the management team's level of commitment. Making such measurements, however, is not always easy. Although valuable information is obtained simply from watching and listening to the members of the management team, venture capitalists attempt to *ensure* the commitment of all members through equity ownership. Venture capitalists often feel more confident about the management team's dedication if the members are financially committed to their company's success. In some situations, it is not necessary for investors to disturb the entrepreneurs' existing equity positions, especially when they have each contributed significant personal capital. Many times, however, investors will find it necessary to use such legal mechanisms as *vesting provisions, repurchase provisions,* and *drag-along provisions* to properly motivate entrepreneurs and ensure a certain level of commitment. (These provisions and others are discussed in detail in Chapter 5.) Venture capitalists are usually careful, however, not to be too heavy-handed when utilizing these mechanisms. In the opinion of the venture capitalists at Draper Fisher Jurvetson, entrepreneurs "must know that the company is still their company."[37] They add that "keeping sight of an entrepreneur's incentives is one of the most important jobs of the venture capitalist."[38]

Management Team's View of Investors

How does the management team view you and your involvement with the company?

According to the venture capitalists at Hummer Winblad Venture Partners, "The relationship between the entrepreneur and the venture capital firm should be one of mutual respect and understanding, one of true teamwork."[39] Says Kevin Fong:

> We want to try and enter in—at least in Mayfield's approach to venture capital, we want to approach investment as a partnership. Having a partnership means open communications, and open communications means that everybody should have all of their cards face up on the table as they sort of go and try and grow a company."[40]

The relationship should be a relationship built on trust, where neither side is trying to "get the upper hand," and where both are simply working together to make money. The large majority of relationships between venture capitalists and entrepreneurs are exactly thus. However, an unfortunate few venture capitalists view success as foisting unfair and lopsided deals on entrepreneurs. On the other side of the coin, a small minority of entrepreneurs take the view that venture capitalists are merely a necessary evil, to be tolerated and, if at all possible, ignored after their money comes in. Such entrepreneurs may or may not be successful, but venture capitalists find working with them difficult and unnecessarily risky. Says Ruthann Quindlen, "If the founders mistrust the investors, the difficult business of starting a company is made much more difficult unnecessarily."[41] There are plenty of opportunities for entrepreneurs to harm the interests of venture capitalists during the life of their relationship, and legal remedies are costly and usually inadequate. There is the distinct danger that entrepreneurs who hold venture capitalists in low esteem will not be fully forthcoming during the due diligence process. Because any failure to disclose material information will create significant risk to venture capitalists, openness on the part of entrepreneurs is of vital importance for the due diligence process to function properly.

CHARACTERISTICS OF THE MANAGEMENT TEAM MEMBERS

Quality People

Is each individual member of the management team a high-quality person?

Venture capitalists, across the board, seek to invest in people they deem to be of high quality. The specific characteristics they look for vary, but most venture capitalists agree on a few general characteristics of high-quality people:

- *Integrity* Venture capitalists generally look for entrepreneurs with high integrity. Tommy Davis, founding partner of the Mayfield

Fund, is quoted as saying, "I'm looking for people with very high ethics. I'm looking for people who take great care in their involvement with other human beings."[42] The reasoning behind this preference is twofold. Integrity is an important quality of great leaders. Early-stage employees will generally be more loyal to, and tend to work much harder for, leaders with high degrees of integrity. Says Ann Winblad, "In this market good guys don't finish last, they finish first."[43] Additionally, venture capitalists must be able to trust completely the entrepreneurs they back, as there are many opportunities during the life of the investor/entrepreneur relationship for entrepreneurs to harm the interests of venture capitalists. Therefore, as Jim Swartz explains, "[j]udging an entrepreneur's integrity is crucial."[44]

■ *Intellectual Honesty*   Most venture capitalists also require that the entrepreneurs they back are "ruthlessly, absolutely intellectually honest," as Doerr puts it.[45] George Quist, cofounder of Hambrecht & Quist, stated that he looked for "intellectual honesty above all," which he defined as "a willingness to face up to facts rigorously whether they prove you right or wrong."[46] Tommy Davis explained, "Some people have built-in filters that filter out the boos and amplify the hurrahs."[47] "That's not the guy," Davis explained, "who will know when he's in trouble."[48] Arthur Rock echoes his former partner:

[T]he issue I set the most store by is whether they are honest with themselves. It's essential to be totally, brutally honest about how well—or how badly—things are going. It is also very difficult. Too many business people delude themselves. They want so much to believe, that they listen only to what they want to hear and see only what they want to see. Failure to be honest with yourself is a problem in any business, but it is especially disastrous in an entrepreneurial company, where the risk-reward stakes are so high. As an entrepreneur, you can't afford to make mistakes because you don't have the time and resources to recover.[49]

■ *Intellectual Brilliance*   Virtually all venture capitalists look for entrepreneurs who are intellectually brilliant. Says Rick Burnes, founder and partner at Charles River Ventures, "You look for people who are smarter than the average bear."[50] Intellectual brilliance is a trait that is consistently positively associated with entrepreneurial success. On one hand, brilliant entrepreneurs are generally able to outmaneuver and overpower their competition. John Doerr explains that "really smart people" clearly give any early-stage company an advantage.[51] On the other hand, Jeffry Timmons explains that entrepreneurs must be able to create "clarity out of confusion, ambiguity, and uncertainty," all of which are constantly present in early-stage companies.[52]

■ *People Smarts*   Venture capitalists also tend to be drawn to entrepreneurs who have great interpersonal skills or "people smarts," as David Beirne, general partner of Benchmark Capital and noted headhunter, calls them.[53] Leaders with people smarts find it much easier to forge crucial relationships with fellow management team members, employees, customers, suppliers, strategic partners, financiers, and the media. People rally around those with people smarts.

Real Entrepreneurs

Are the members of the management team "honest to goodness bona fide real entrepreneurs"?

Kevin Fong explains the importance of this attribute to venture capitalists:

> *Every great startup has a driven entrepreneur—an absolutely honest to goodness bona fide real entrepreneur—someone who will walk through walls to make their vision a reality. Companies fail when you have what I call entrepreneur wannabe's. They like the glamour and the potential wealth creation at a startup, but they're not willing to put in the hard work, really don't know their way, or need a lot of help in order to be successful.[54]*

Because they have such a strong interest in avoiding an entrepreneur wannabe and in locating real entrepreneurs, venture capitalists generally look for several key qualities associated with these types of entrepreneur:

- *Driven Intensity* Venture capitalists are strongly drawn to people who are driven and are willing to work extremely long hours. Arthur Rock states that "[h]ard work alone doesn't bring success . . . , but all the effective entrepreneurs [he has] known have worked long, hard hours."[55] Rock also adds that "there's something more than the number of the hours: the intensity of the hours."[56] Rock's point about intensity is not lost on other venture capitalists. Venture capitalists, in general, like to invest in highly motivated entrepreneurs who get a lot of things done simultaneously. Early-stage companies require people who move quickly to stay ahead of the competition. Because they believe quick movement is so vital to the success of early-stage companies, the venture capitalists at Sequoia Capital look for entrepreneurs who demonstrate to them a "sense of urgency."[57] They like to back entrepreneurs who "know that a combination of speed and stealth will usually help them beat large companies" and who understand, too, that other early-stage companies, that are no doubt also moving quickly, "pose the greatest threat to their existence."[58] As a related note, the venture capitalists at Draper Fisher Jurvetson state that the entrepreneurs they back must be "stable enough to handle a high degree of stress," which the long, intense hours in early-stage companies inevitably produce.[59] Early-stage companies are cauldrons of stress and pressure, and venture capitalists cannot afford to become involved with entrepreneurs who do not thrive in such environments.
- *Bold Self-Confidence and Willingness to Take Risks* Venture capitalists are generally obsessed with finding entrepreneurs who are obsessed with finding great opportunities, and who will not shrink from seizing such opportunities when they present themselves. Therefore, they tend to seek entrepreneurs with high self-confidence. Successfully launching and growing an early-stage company is a daunting enterprise. It is, therefore, imperative for venture capitalists to back entrepreneurs who have the guts and fortitude to undertake enormous risk and fully commit themselves to achieving incredibly lofty goals, and who also have a strong belief in their own ability to achieve those goals. "Entrepreneurs do things that are unnatural acts, things that shouldn't

happen," says Rick Burnes.[60] "They just make things happen. They will them to happen."[61] Venture capitalists are careful, however, to avoid individuals who are merely reckless, who set goals too lofty, or who undertake unnecessary risks. Furthermore, because even the smartest risk takers will encounter failure in some measure, venture capitalists look for individuals who may be disappointed by failure, but are not apt to become discouraged. They also look for individuals who are able to look critically at their own role in any given failed objective and can learn from the experience—and who do not simply seek to assign blame to others.

Sense of Vision and Ability to Execute The most successful entrepreneurs consistently demonstrate an astonishing ability to see clearly years into the future. Therefore, a characteristic commonly sought by venture capitalists is extraordinary vision. Says Kevin Fong, "You want them to have a vision of what the world will be when they bring their product or service to market."[62] They seek individuals with this characteristic because vision enables entrepreneurs to anticipate what markets will deem valuable years ahead and to maintain course during the inevitable frustrations that arise during the start-up process. Furthermore, venture capitalists generally look for entrepreneurs who, along with extraordinary vision, can execute on their vision—they are able to accomplish all the intermediate objectives necessary to successfully realize their vision. They also try to back entrepreneurs who prioritize intermediate objectives and to focus their efforts on achieving objectives in their proper order, the most important and necessary objectives first. The venture capitalists at Draper Fisher Jurvetson consider the "ability to prioritize and focus" a key trait that has "been associated with entrepreneurial success."[63] One of the most frustrating things for venture capitalists to realize is that a portfolio company has lost precious time, energy, and money because the entrepreneurs failed to prioritize and became distracted by less-important objectives.

Ability to Solve Problems Entrepreneurs in the process of starting and growing a new company face an almost constant barrage of problems, both large and small. Therefore, venture capitalists usually like to back individuals with powerful abilities and determined desires to solve those problems, whether by head-on confrontation or skillful circumvention. Fred Dotzler provides some examples of problems often encountered in the early stages: "product bugs, sales that are below forecast, manufacturing glitches, cash shortfalls, budget allocation decisions, distribution channels, and so on."[64] He says that the best entrepreneurial managers are able to "identify the key problems needing attention" and to "select and implement optimum solutions."[65]

- *Ability to Adapt*   Entrepreneurs must be able to adapt. Market and competitive conditions are constantly shifting and changing. To respond effectively, entrepreneurs must be able to adapt their business models, their competitive strategies, their products, and their people. The inability to adapt to constantly changing market and competitive conditions will almost surely doom early-stage companies to failure.

- *Ability to Use Resources Effectively*   Because of the severe limitations on resources—most importantly financial and human resources—to which most early-stage companies have access, success requires that entrepreneurs employ resources efficiently and effectively. From the perspective of venture capitalists, entrepreneurs must be willing to spend their financial resources conservatively, and only in ways that will contribute the absolute greatest value to their venture. The venture capitalists at Sequoia Capital "have discovered that founders and entrepreneurs clever enough to develop a large return from a small investment will frequently build significant companies."[66] Entrepreneurs must also be willing to continually identify and employ the best possible people who will contribute the most value to their respective companies. Kevin Fong says that the type of entrepreneurs he seeks are those who say "'I'm very good at what I do, but I am always willing to hire people who can help me.'"[67] "Those are the people," says Fong, "who will always be very successful."[68] The venture capitalists at Draper Fisher Jurvetson add that successful entrepreneurs must be "willing to hire the best people for the task even if it means dilution of their stock or authority."[69]

One point of which venture capitalists are wary, however, when they locate honest to goodness bona fide real entrepreneurs possessing these six qualities is that such individuals are often extremely persuasive when pitching their ventures. It is easy for investors to get caught up in the entrepreneurs' enthusiasm and optimism, to ignore the risks, and to fail to view the pitch rationally.

The Business Judgment Standard

Do the members of the management team have solid business judgment?

It is crucial to venture capitalists that the entrepreneurs in whom they invest have sound business judgment. It is on such judgment that thousands of important decisions will be made during the time that venture capitalists hold equity. For most venture capitalists, sound business judgment means that the person has the ability to make rational decisions, supported by extensive, relevant business experience. Therefore, when assessing a given entrepreneur's business judgment, venture capitalists usually attempt first to assess whether the entrepreneur tends to make rational decisions based on logical thought, and not based on habit, prejudice, or emotion. The market has no patience for decisions based on illogic. Rather, says William Davidow, founding partner of Mohr, Davidow Ventures, the market "rewards rational decisions executed with precision and conviction."[70]

Second, venture capitalists gauging business judgment usually attempt to assess the extent and the relevance of an entrepreneur's business experience. Venture capitalists generally adhere to the principle that the more business experience an entrepreneur has, the better: Seasoned businesspersons with years of experience in the business world tend to be better equipped for entrepreneurial success than people with relatively little business experience. Additionally, venture capitalists almost universally require that entrepreneurs have business experience relevant to their new venture, to help ensure that they have a clear and solid understanding of the business environment in which they will operate—the competitive landscape, market trends, technological trends, and so on. A combination of strong, relevant business experience and an ability to make decisions based solely on logical thought will satisfy most venture capitalists regarding a particular entrepreneur's business judgment.

Background

Does each member of the management team have an impressive and relevant background?

One of the most sought-after entrepreneurial characteristics among venture capitalists is an impressive and relevant background, in terms of both education and experience. The partners at Kleiner Perkins Caufield & Byers claim to care "more about the résumé of the proposer than the proposal" itself.[71] This position actually makes a lot of sense. According to Karl Vesper, "Prior mental programming in the form of both formal education and experience in the particular line of work of the new venture repeatedly crops up as correlated in generally positive ways with the odds of success in studies of startups."[72]

Educationally, venture capitalists generally prefer to back entrepreneurs who hold distinguished academic credentials, usually graduate level degrees from top colleges or universities. They also strongly prefer that such credentials are in areas highly relevant to each particular entrepreneur's position in a given company and to the market space where the company operates. Experientially, venture capitalists typically look for a couple of things. First and foremost, they strongly prefer that entrepreneurs have industry experience. Kevin Fong states bluntly that the "business plans that get the least attention are ones where the team has never even participated in the space that they are proposing to get into."[73] Though speaking specifically about CEOs, Fred Dotzler provides several reasons for this preference for industry experience, each of which applies equally to all entrepreneurial management team members:

> *The individual hired to be CEO of a start-up company must have experience in the same industry [his or her] company is pursuing. One who has worked in the industry will understand customer needs and how to influence their purchasing decisions. He or she will understand the strategic positioning of competitors and know their strengths and weaknesses. He or she will be able to identify the most effective selling and distribution channels. In addition, a CEO with industry experience will know others in the industry who may be candidates for future management*

positions, and will have contacts that may be valuable when establishing corporate partnerships.[74]

An entrepreneur with solid industry experience will generally have a strong advantage over one who is a relative newcomer, and venture capitalists thoroughly recognize this tendency.

Venture capitalists also like to back entrepreneurs who have at least some entrepreneurial experience. Some, like Jennifer Gill Roberts, general partner of Sevin Rosen Funds, prefer "serial entrepreneurs," who have been involved with several previous start-ups.[75] Taking the complete opposite (and probably minority) position, the venture capitalists at Draper Fisher Jurvetson believe that "[o]ften the best entrepreneurs are young and *inexperienced.*"[76] There is also some disagreement among venture capitalists over whether prior entrepreneurial forays should ideally have been successes or failures. Some venture capitalists favor entrepreneurs who have been "seasoned" by being affiliated with failed ventures. They prefer entrepreneurs who made many mistakes in previous ventures, and who have learned from those mistakes. "[S]car tissue is good," Roberts says.[77] Fong also subscribes to the view that entrepreneurs who have failed are wiser entrepreneurs: He states that such entrepreneurs have often "learned the best lessons."[78] Douglas Leone, general partner of Sequoia Capital, on the other hand, says that he likes "seasoned" entrepreneurs, not because they are wiser, but because they are highly motivated:

> *Sequoia enjoys nurturing . . . the experienced entrepreneur who failed miserably the first time out and wants to show the world that the defeat was a fluke. We don't do as well with people who have built successful companies before. They tend to worry about their golf handicap. They've forgotten what it's like to work six and seven days a week.*[79]

Michael Moritz, also a general partner of Sequoia Capital, echoes his partner:

> *Two guys walk through the door. Give us a choice between the one who's built two successful companies and has a house in the*

hills—or the one who's got a mortgage up to the chimney tops and who can't afford to fail—we'll always finance the hungry guy if we can only write one check."[80]

At the other extreme, many venture capitalists, such as those at Chase H&Q Venture Capital, prefer to back entrepreneurs with prior entrepreneurial successes under their belt.[81] Fred Dotzler takes this view. He explains that "candidates who've worked for successful companies usually have had experiences that enable them to create a mental model of how the start-up should look in five years. This helps them position the company for success."[82]

Motivation

Does each member of the management team have the proper motivation in being part of the company?

According to Ruthann Quindlen, venture capitalists must often play the role of "unofficial psychologist."[83] Says Quindlen, the "skills of a psychologist—mainly, the ability to discern and understand people's motivations—are some of the most valuable tools in investing."[84] According to Kevin Fong, "[W]e spend a lot of time, both in a business setting, and sometimes in a more casual setting to understand . . . the motivation behind someone that really wants to start a company."[85] Venture capitalists do, however, tend to have wide-ranging opinions as to what the proper motivations should be (see the earlier quotes from Douglas Leone and Michael Moritz). In general, most agree that entrepreneurs should be motivated by their vision and their desire to build great companies—not simply their desire for wealth. Quindlen explains:

> *Motivation is everything in building a company. A few founders are motivated purely by the goal of creating wealth. This can be an excellent incentive, but if it is the sole reason the founder creates the company, it does not usually produce the best results. In general, founders who are motivated purely by wealth often have a short-term view, leading them to make tactical rather than strategic decisions. Their companies may succeed in producing*

substantial short-term payback, but they generally do not de-velop into the kind of large and successful companies that create the greatest value for founders and investors over time.

At the same time, a healthy desire for wealth creation is a nec-essary goal. Otherwise, the investment is dominated solely by the psychological needs of the founder—needs that can be as diverse as personal achievement, a desire for power, or even a search for purpose in life. The company that becomes the personal sandbox of the founders almost never becomes hugely successful. "[86]

Kevin Fong holds a similar opinion. He states that the entrepreneurs he looks for "usually are driven, obviously, by financial and value creating, you know, getting wealthy, basically. But they're also driven, usually, as they would like to make an impact on the world, they would like to change the world. So having that sort of dual pur-pose is important."[87]

Discerning motivations and determining whether those motiva-tions are proper and healthy is tricky business. True motivations are often easy to conceal, especially when multiple motivations exist, as is usually the case. Also, it is rarely a "black and white" issue whether a particular motivation is a good one or not. But, by and large, through sufficient contact with the entrepreneurs they are considering backing, venture capitalists usually get an adequate feel for the moti-vations driving those entrepreneurs, and then simply use their best judgment as to whether those motivations will be beneficial or detri-mental to the companies and their interests.

The Peter Principle

At what point will the members of the management team bump up against the Peter Principle?

The Peter Principle, developed by Laurence J. Peter and Raymond Hull in their best-selling satirical work on organizational theory, captures the concept of that point at which employees reach their capacity, the point beyond which they cannot and should not advance.[88] This con-cept and the term, *Peter Principle,* have been adopted by some venture capitalists to describe that point in a particular company's growth at which entrepreneurs reach the limit of their capacity to manage a rapidly growing and quickly changing enterprise. "People run out of head room," says Bill Kaiser, general partner at Greylock.[89] "They run out of gas at some point along the line."[90] Therefore, venture capitalists usually scrutinize each member of a given management team to determine whether and when he or she will bump up against the Peter Principle. They simply cannot afford to sink funds into a company and realize a short time later that it lacks the management talent to continue moving forward. And, if they do sink funds, they want to make sure that they are ready and able to pull in qualified talent to replace any management team members who have hit the Peter Principle.

CHIEF EXECUTIVE OFFICER: THE LEADER

General Considerations

Does the company currently have a chief executive officer (CEO)?

Venture capitalists almost uniformly agree that the presence of a strong and lasting CEO is a key ingredient of success. Says Seth Neiman, managing partner with Crosspoint Venture Partners,

> *When I first got involved in the venture capital business, I did an analysis across Crosspoint's portfolio, trying to answer the question: All right, how does this work? I learned that the only high correlation with the success of a business was the quality of the CEO. Even if they had great markets and great technology, there were no successful companies that didn't also have a great CEO.*[91]

According to Fred Dotzler, "With a good CEO, a company flies; with an average CEO, it languishes; with a poor CEO, it usually disappears."[92] Therefore, with the possible exception of the chief technology officer, the CEO is perhaps the most scrutinized member of any given management team. Venture capitalists must satisfy themselves that a particular CEO will make his or her company (and their investment) fly. Some early-stage companies approach investors while still lacking a CEO. Venture capitalists generally view the lack of a CEO as a problem, but not an overwhelming one. Dotzler explains, "Some venture capitalists will fund a company that lacks a CEO, but only if the founding team has an agreed-upon plan for hiring this critical executive."[93] And that plan must be a solid one, targeted at finding the best possible CEO, and usually must allow for substantial participation on the part of the venture capitalists in the search process.

CEO Skills

Does the CEO have the right skills?

Good CEOs come in all shapes and sizes. There is certainly no model for the perfect CEO. History does show that experienced CEOs tend to be more successful than those with little or no CEO experience. That, however, is only a tendency. A great many first-time CEOs have been incredibly successful. Beyond simple experience, most effective CEOs also have several other essential skills:

■ *Leadership Ability* Every start-up needs a great leader. Strong leadership by a CEO significantly enhances any early-stage company's chances of success. Ruthann Quindlen compares a company without adequate leadership to "a headless body that flails around and injures itself in the process."[94] On the other hand, a good CEO is able to lead, manage, and motivate an entire company. That ability is crucial. Speed and precision are often key to entrepreneurial success, and it takes a great leader to get an entire organization to work together and work hard enough to achieve these goals. Christine Comaford, general partner of Artemis Ventures, states that great leaders "have the uncanny ability to make their mission everybody else's. A great leader can inspire and motivate people to do anything."[95] That is why venture capitalists are always on the lookout for great leaders. The strong leadership ability for which they look comes almost without exception from experience in leadership positions. Therefore, according to Fred Dotzler, "venture capitalists don't like to back individuals who haven't run a company, a division or at least a department—the risk of failure is too great."[96] Often the most popular CEO candidates among venture capitalists come from the executive ranks of larger, proven companies.

■ *Strong Communication Skills* Early-stage CEOs must also be great communicators. They are the faces (and the voices) of their respective companies. Therefore, it is generally imperative that they have the "[a]bility to communicate effectively and clearly, both in speech and in writing, to the media, the public, customers, peers, and subordinates," according to Alexander L. M. Dingee, Brian Haslett, and Leonard E. Smollen, venture capitalists and cofounders of Venture Founders Corporation.[97] Also, a large component of that communication skill, often considered vital by venture capitalists, is the ability to sell. Kevin Fong explains:

Roger McNamee at Integral Capital Partners has a famous line. He asks if the entrepreneur gives good roadshow? That's a test of whether the person can sell their company? Not only do they have a vision, but they can impart that vision to others. They have to do that when they are recruiting, when they are raising money, when they're approaching Wall Street.[98]

■ *Decision-Making Ability* Entrepreneurial chief executives face many important decisions, on an almost daily basis. A great percentage of the most important decisions made at early-stage companies fall most heavily, if not sometimes entirely, on the shoulders of CEOs. Not surprisingly, therefore, venture capitalists prefer to back CEOs who have strong strategic decision-making ability. Because of the significant uncertainty that characterizes the early stage, however, strategic decisions must often be made without compete information. Therefore, venture capitalists also look for CEOs who are able to make decisions on incomplete data. The last thing venture capitalists can accept is a CEO that cannot make decisions under those conditions. Says Ruthann Quindlen:

Analysis paralysis is a common problem in large companies with rigid bureaucratic structures. Indecision may slow a large company down, but it is death in a start-up. In a small company a manager should not be fired for making the wrong decision so much as for making no decision at all. At least from the wrong decision the manager and the company can learn which is the

*more correct path to take. Indecision results in no information
at all, and the results can be disastrous as a wrong decision.*[99]

Furthermore, despite the scarcity of information, venture
capitalists look also for CEOs who, nonetheless, constantly and
aggressively seek to obtain as much information as they possibly
can before making important decisions. Ruthann Quindlen asks,
if a CEO "shows himself incapable of absorbing input and making decisions based on more, rather than less, information, how
can he hope to create a successful company?"[100] According to
Jim Swartz, "great entrepreneurs are continuously taking input
from everyone around them . . . ."[101] Arthur Rock adds, however, that the best CEOs are also discerning regarding the
sources of input:

*[An] essential characteristic for the entrepreneur is to know
whom to listen to and when to listen, and then which questions
to ask. Some CEOs listen only to what they want to hear because
of fear of the truth; in other cases, it's because they are arrogant
or have surrounded themselves with yes-men/women. A lot of
managers simply will not accept criticism or suggestions from
other people; they demand absolute loyalty from their subordinates and call disloyal anybody who tries to tell them something
they don't want to hear.*[102]

Venture capitalists generally attempt to avoid the type of
CEO that Rock describes, and instead they look for CEOs who
obtain, filter, and make smart use of any information they can
access to make sound decisions.

■ *Administrative Skill* Great CEOs are also able to effectively
manage their companies from an administrative perspective.
Probably the most important administrative role of an early-stage
CEO is that of building quality personnel ranks. According to
John Doerr, great entrepreneurial managers are "great re-
cruiters."[103] Therefore, the CEOs that venture capitalists seek are
able to recruit other high-powered management team members
and many high-powered employees.

While sometimes able to locate CEOs possessing *all* of these attributes, venture capitalists generally accept that if a particular CEO

lacks one or more of them the missing attributes can sometimes be compensated for in other members of the management team.

CHIEF TECHNICAL OFFICER: THE VISIONARY

General Considerations

Does the company currently have a chief technology officer (CTO)?

The CTO is often the *real* entrepreneur in a given company, the visionary who created the concept on which the company is based. Therefore, the CTO is usually considered by venture capitalists, at least initially, to be the most important person in any early-stage company; indeed, without a concept and without a vision, there can really be no company. John Doerr explains:

> *Just as important as the leader is the technical genius. At the heart of every great technology company is a technical genius. Apple had its Steve Wozniak, Sun had Andy Bechtolsheim and Bill Joy, Netscape has Marc Andreessen, @Home has Milo Medin. A great marketing company like Intuit has Scott Cook.*
>
> *These founding geniuses are the heart and soul that represents the real reason for doing the startup. Its more than, "Lets build a big business and get a lot of stock and make money." The idea is, "Let's do something that's technically excellent. Let's make a difference." Sooner or later as the venture grows we can help the founders find someone like Netscape's Jim Barksdale, Intuit's Bill Campbell, or @Home's Tom Jermoluk."[104]*

Because of the importance of the CTO, Gordon Bell states that a "company should have selected its CTO by the end of the seed stage, and if it is tackling a technologically difficult product, the CTO must be on board from the start."[105] Bell explains that funding a venture without a CTO "is extremely risky because he or she is the individual responsible for ensuring that the product is really feasible at the price, quality, schedule, and resource level specified in the business plan."[106]

CTO Skills

Does the CTO have the right skills?

Venture capitalists generally seek CTOs who possess several specific skills, as outlined by Alexander Dingee, Brian Haslett, and Leonard Smollen:

- *Ability to Manage Applied Research* CTOs should be able "to distinguish and keep a prudent balance between long-range projects at the frontiers of [the company's] technology, which attract the most creative individuals, and shorter range research in support of current product development activity."[107]
- *Skill in Managing Development* They should also be able "to plan and direct work of development engineers and to use time and cost budgets so that perfectionists do not ruin [the company] and yet product performance, appearance, and production engineering needs can be met; ability to distinguish between breadboard, field and pre-production prototype programs."[108]
- *Skill in Managing Engineering* They should be able "to plan and direct engineers in the final design of a new product for manufacture and in the engineering and testing of the production process to manufacture that new product."[109]
- *In-Depth Knowledge of Relevant Technology* Lastly, they should be able "to contribute personally to research, development, and/or engineering because of up-to-date in-depth knowledge of the technologies in which [the] company is involved."[110]

CHIEF FINANCIAL OFFICER: THE MISER

General Considerations

Does the company currently have a chief financial officer (CFO)?

Most venture capitalists categorize the CFO position as a crucial component of any early-stage company's management team, and every bit as important as the other team roles. Though opinions vary somewhat on this issue, most feel this way, including Arthur Rock:

I am especially interested in what kind of financial people [a start-up] intend[s] to recruit. So many entrepreneurial companies make mistakes in the accounting end of the business. Many start shipping products before confirming that the orders are good, or that the customer will take the product, or that the accounts are collectable. Such endeavors are more concerned about making a short-term sales quota than about maximizing the long-term revenue stream.

Granted, the pressure on new businesses to make sales quotas is strong. And that's precisely why the company needs a very, very tough accounting department. Otherwise, it will get into trouble. I always ask what kind of chief financial officer the entrepreneurs plan to bring on board. If they understand the need for someone who will scrutinize the operation closely and impose the appropriate controls, they are more likely to be able to translate their strategy into a going concern.[111]

According to Ann Winblad, a "CFO needs to be there on day one."[112] It is not unusual, however, for early-stage companies to seek venture funding before they have filled the CFO position. In such instances, venture capitalists are usually quick to ask companies precisely the question Rock asks: "What kind of CFO do you plan to bring on board?"

CFO Skills

Does the CFO have the right skills?

Alexander Dingee, Brian Haslett, and Leonard Smollen outline some of the skills often required of CFOs by venture capitalists:

- *Skill in Raising Capital* They should be able "to decide how best to acquire funds for start-up and growth; ability to forecast the need for funds and to prepare budgets; familiarity with sources and vehicles for short- and long-term financing."[113]
- *Skill in Money Management* They should also be able "to design, install, maintain, and use financial controls; familiarity with accounting and control systems needed to manage; ability

to set up a project cost control system, analyze overhead/contribution/absorption, prepare profit and loss and balance sheets, and manage a bookkeeper."[114]

■ *Solid Command of Financial Concepts* They should have a strong working knowledge of general financial concepts such as "[c]ash flow analysis, break-even analysis, contribution analysis, budgeting and profit-planning techniques, profit and loss, balance sheet, and present value analysis of return on investment and payback."[115]

BUSINESS DEVELOPMENT OFFICER: THE WHEELER-DEALER

General Considerations

Does the company currently have an officer in charge of business development?

Regis McKenna, chairman of the McKenna Group and venture partner of Kleiner Perkins Caufield & Byers, is well known for stressing that companies live and die by the quality of the strategic relationships they are able to forge. For precisely that reason, venture capitalists generally agree that early-stage companies must be open to strategic relationships and, in fact, should aggressively seek out the most strategically valuable relationships possible. Such relationships come in many forms: customer relationships, supplier relationships, manufacturing relationships, joint ventures, technology exchanges, equity positions, and—perhaps most important to venture capitalists—relationships with possible merger or acquisition candidates. One or two of these key strategic relationships can mean the difference between greatness and mediocrity (or greatness and complete failure) for early-stage companies.

Although strategic relationships are important, building them takes considerable time and effort on the part of management teams. Therefore, venture capitalists like to see that companies have a management team member specifically designated to forge these relationships. Such individuals typically carry the title of vice president of business development or director of business development. Floyd Kvamme explains that if companies simply rely on other management team members to forge such relationships—those already focusing on technology, marketing, sales, operations, and finance—then business development "just plain won't happen."[116] Therefore, venture capitalists prefer that companies have someone focusing entirely on business development as early as possible.

Business Development Skills

Does the officer in charge of business development have the right skills?

Venture capitalists tend to look for a few general skills in business development officers that facilitate the successful building of strategic relationships:

- *Strong Communication Skills* Effective communication is central to relationship building. Therefore, they should be able to communicate effectively both in speech and in writing.
- *Interpersonal Skills* They should be able to deal effectively with people. They should be charismatic, confident, forceful, and frank, but also friendly, courteous, cooperative, and always aware and mindful of the interests of others.
- *Negotiation Skills* They should have a full understanding of the principles of negotiation. They should operate effectively in negotiation situations, to aggressively and appropriately represent the interests of their companies.
- *Ability to Close* Last, they must have the ability to close deals—to bring negotiations to a close and to reach final agreements.

MARKETING AND SALES OFFICER: THE EVANGELIST

General Considerations

Does the company currently employ an individual able to offer top-quality marketing and sales expertise?

Top-quality marketing and sales expertise is a fundamental component to the success of early-stage companies. Fred Dotzler points out that the "viability of many companies is determined by customer acceptance of the first product. So it is imperative to make the right commercialization decisions long before market entry."[117] He says: "Ideally, every effort should be made during the product development process to thoroughly evaluate product features and benefits, to determine how they stack up against offerings already in the marketplace or under development by others, and to plan ways to make the company's products stand out."[118] Therefore, it is vital that early-stage companies have top-quality marketing and sales expertise to address these issues early in their development. Many times, existing founding team members will have the marketing and sales expertise to fill initial early-stage requirements, for example, a CEO or a vice president of business development with a solid marketing background. Alternatively, Dotzler suggests, "If the founding team does not have the experience or resources to perform early market analysis and product positioning, the company may temporarily enlist the services of a consultant. It is possible to find at least one qualified strategic consultant in most market segments."[119] Eventually, however, Dotzler explains, all early-stage companies "need to hire senior executives for both marketing and sales."[120]

Marketing and Sales Skills

Does the company's officer in charge of marketing and sales have the right skills?

The following skills, according to Alexander Dingee, Brian Haslett, and Leonard Smollen, are generally required by venture capitalists of any marketing and sales officer they back:

- *Skill in Market Research and Evaluation* They should be able "to design and conduct market research studies and analyze and interpret study results," and should have "familiarity with questionnaire design and sampling techniques."[121]
- *Ability to Strategically Plan* They should have "[e]xperience in developing marketing strategies and establishing forces and then planning appropriate sales, advertising and promotional programs and setting up an effective network distributor or sales representative organization."[122]

- *Skill in Sales Management*   They should have "[a]bility in organizing, supervising, motivating and providing merchandising support to a direct sales force; analyzing territory and sales potential; and managing a sales force to obtain a target share of the market."[123]
- *Skill in Direct Selling*   They should have "[e]xperience in identifying, meeting and developing new customers" and a "demonstrated success in closing sales."[124]
- *Understanding of Service Provision*   They should have "[e]xperience in identifying service needs of particular products and in determining service and spare parts requirements, handling customer complaints, and managing a service organization."[125]
- *Skill in Distribution Management*   They should be able "to organize and manage the flow of the product from manufacturing through distribution channels to the ultimate customer, including familiarity with shipping costs, scheduling techniques, carriers, and so on."[126]

CHIEF OPERATING OFFICER: THE PRAGMATIST

General Considerations

Does the company currently have a COO?

Whether and when an early-stage company needs a COO is generally judged by venture capitalists on a case-by-case basis. Some companies need an executive who can take full responsibility for day-to-day operations and can free the other management team members to focus wholly on their own core competencies (strategy, technology, marketing, sales, finance, etc.). Such is the function of a COO—to make sure, from a nuts-and-bolts perspective, that all the parts of a particular company are working properly and working together. The COO is particularly helpful when a CEO is more of a "big picture" strategist or a relationship builder than a hands-on operational manager. Often, however, day-to-day operations in an early-stage company can be handled easily by the CEO and the other management team members. Therefore, whether venture capitalists prefer to see a COO really depends on the composition and the internal dynamics of each particular company's management team.

COO Skills

Does the company's COO have the right skills?

According to Alexander Dingee, Brian Haslett, and Leonard Smollen, venture capitalists tend to look for the following characteristics in COOs:

- *Manufacturing Management Ability*   They should have "[k]nowledge of the production processes, machines, manpower, and space requirements to produce the product; experience in managing production to produce products within time, cost, and quality constraints."[127]
- *Skill in Inventory Control*   They should also have a "[f]amiliarity with techniques of controlling in-process and finished goods inventories of materials."[128]
- *Quality Control Ability*   They should be able "to set up inspection systems and standards for effective control of quality in incoming, in-process and finished materials."[129]
- *Purchasing Skills*   Lastly, they should be able "to identify appropriate sources of supply, the amount of material in inventory, familiarity with economical order quantities and discount advantage."[130]

THE BOARD OF DIRECTORS

Quality of the Board of Directors

Does the company have a strong, diverse, and balanced board of directors?

A corporation, the business form which virtually all early-stage companies take, is required as a matter of corporate law to maintain a board of directors. The legal function of a board of directors is to represent shareholders—the owners of the company—in the oversight of the management of the company, rather than to participate in actual day-to-day management. Early-stage boards, however, may find it necessary to reach beyond their legal function—sometimes to the extent of essentially assuming the role of interim CEO. It is a widely held view among venture capitalists that, in the early stages, boards are simply extensions of their management teams. This most often occurs when a management team is inexperienced or when a company has yet to build a complete management team. Regardless of whether boards are integrated into day-to-day management, or serve in more traditional capacities, venture capitalists generally view high-quality boards as crucial to the success of early-stage companies.

Early-stage boards are typically composed of company founders, management team members, representatives of any venture capital investors, representatives of any significant angel investors, and ideally some outside directors—usually executives from established, complementary companies in the same or related market space. According to the venture capitalists at El Dorado Ventures, the "ideal size is five directors, not so big, that the board is unmanageable, and large enough to include all the needed perspectives."[131] "An ideal composition," they state, is:

- Two investors' representatives.
- One or two management representatives.
- One or two outsiders.[132]

And, just as with early-stage management teams, venture capitalists like board members to have diverse and balanced skills, backgrounds, personalities, and perspectives, and to be appropriately experienced and well-connected. Gordon Bell elaborates on the concept of diversity:

> *A homogeneous board should be avoided, since this type of board is unlikely to have the perspectives that a new company needs in such diverse areas as operations, finance, technology, marketing and consulting. In contrast, a heterogeneous board is the ideal (although heterogeneity should not be carried to the point where board members cannot work together harmoniously or communicate effectively).*[133]

With regard to balance and experience, the venture capitalists at Advanced Technology Ventures advise that early-stage companies should have boards that include individuals with "experience in [the company's] market segment" and at least "one director with a strong financial background and another who is the CEO or VP of Marketing of a successful company in a complementary business segment."[134] They explain, such "people can provide insight not only on issues specific to your company, but also provide a broader perspective on industry trends, etc."[135] Venture capitalists also strongly prefer to back companies with directors who can supply broad, high-quality networks of strategic contacts. The venture capitalists at Advanced Technology Ventures say that an ideal board member should have "a wealth of contacts," whether those contacts are "potential customers, partners or additional investors."[136] Because of the importance of partnerships and alliances to early-stage companies, such contacts can prove extremely beneficial.

Independence of the Board of Directors

Is the company's board of directors an independently functioning body?

It is generally important to venture capitalists that the early-stage companies they finance have boards that are independently functioning. Those at Advanced Technology Ventures warn: "One of the most common mistakes by entrepreneurs is to 'stack' the board with members friendly to their cause."[137] They explain, "A board with too many representatives from management . . . is far less effective" than one composed of outside members.[138] The most obvious reason to avoid such boards is that they are usually unable to provide rational, unbiased appraisals of company strategy. Jeffry Timmons and Harry Sapienza, professors at the Darla Moore School of Business at the University of South Carolina, explain:

> *Having someone to discuss and critique [management's] plans and ideas before [the company] is firmly committed can help avoid costly mistakes. [A] savvy outsider can provide that insight to a management team. Venture teams come to work together so closely and intimately that they begin to think alike. New product ideas, strategies and directions, can emerge as if*

out of one mind. The dangers of this tendency are obvious, and the outside investor, because of a reasonably removed and objective view, can better assess the rationale of plans, ideas and initiatives.[139]

Another important reason to avoid stacked boards is that they are usually unable to provide rational, unbiased appraisals of the performance of management teams. One of the main functions of any board is to appraise management performance and to take corrective action if performance is poor. Boards are hindered in this objective if they comprise the very management team members they are supposed to be reviewing (or those friendly to the management teams), who cannot be expected to provide rational and unbiased assessments of their own performance. An independent board is in the best position to judge in a rational and unbiased manner both company strategy and the performance of a management team.

Attention and Intensity of the Board of Directors

Does each of the company's directors have the ability to devote the appropriate amount of time and attention to their directorial duties?

Venture capitalists prefer to back companies with directors who are able to devote significant time and attention to their directorial duties. According to the venture capitalists from Advanced Technology Ventures, however, "Too many companies view their board as window dressing and board meetings as a nuisance in which the management gives carefully rehearsed 'dog and pony shows.'"[140] Companies often seek directors with impressive credentials, but also often without the time for significant, long-term commitments to helping their companies succeed. Venture capitalists generally view such directors negatively. Early-stage companies need all involved persons to pull their weight, directors included. The venture capitalists from Advanced Technology Ventures state, "If board members are unable or unwilling to spend the time necessary to help the company and/or CEO, they shouldn't be on the board in the first place."[141] Such directors will contribute little to the success of their company. Says Gordon Bell, "[A] start-up should select board members who can spend the time necessary to learn about the company's business, its products, its competitors, and its customers. They should understand the business well enough to detect danger signs and recognize opportunities."[142]

THE BOARD OF ADVISERS

General Quality of the Board of Advisers

Does the company have a strong, effective, balanced board of advisers?

Darlene Mann, general partner of Onset Ventures, found in a study done by her firm that one of the major reasons early-stage companies fail is due to "a lack of a mentor . . . someone who had been there and done it before. . . .[143] Therefore, successful early-stage companies usually have strong advisory boards composed of those who *have* been there and done it before. Gordon Bell explains why such advisers are crucial to early-stage companies:

> *Every company needs an appropriate review mechanism to help direct its efforts. In the case of an established firm, customers automatically provide such a review through the marketplace. In contrast, a start-up is like a newly launched missile, in that it must be aimed in the right general direction and its trajectory must then be continually corrected midcourse if it is to reach the intended destination.*[144]

Advisory boards are often able to provide intelligent suggestions regarding possible midcourse corrections. For that reason, venture capitalists generally prefer companies that have built impressive advisory boards, composed of members who add considerable value to their companies, such as leading technology experts, who can review technology issues and product development, or seasoned entrepreneurs or executives, who can provide advice on company strategy.

OTHER EQUITY INVESTORS

General Quality of the Other Equity Investors

Can your coinvestors materially aid in the success of the company?

Early-stage companies are generally able to derive substantial value from their investors, whether they are venture capitalists, corporate venture investors, or sophisticated angel investors. For that reason, venture capitalists generally become interested in companies in whom other top quality investors have already invested or are about to invest. It is common to see two or three (or sometimes more) investors—institutional venture capital firms, corporate venture funds, angel groups, or individual angels—agree to coinvest to take advantage of their combined value contribution.

The specific contributions that investors can make vary by investor and investor type. Venture capitalists can, according to those at Accel Partners, "bring a broad perspective of experience," that enables them to recognize patterns of success and failure.[145] Based on such knowledge, venture capitalists usually can provide significant and valuable counsel to early-stage companies. The venture capitalists at Oak Investment Partners explain that, in providing counsel to their portfolio companies, they rely on their "years of experience with companies that have faced similar challenges."[146] Many venture capitalists also can give entrepreneurs access to impressive networks. Most venture capital firms have made dozens and dozens, if not hundreds of portfolio investments, and continue to make new investments all the time. In the process of making those investments, they cultivate all sorts of valuable relationships: with seasoned entrepreneurs, leading technologists, top executives, and many quality service providers, not to mention the portfolio companies themselves, all of which are possible customers, suppliers, partners, and acquirers. These powerful networks can prove vital to the success of early-stage companies.

Corporate venture investors are generally much less active investors than venture capitalists; nevertheless, corporate venture investors can also contribute significant value to their portfolio companies. They are often able to provide the type of assistance that they might provide to one of their divisions, for example, guidance on technology, advice on company strategy, and assistance with marketing and distribution. Furthermore, the imprimatur of an established market player in the form of a significant equity investment can greatly help to position an early-stage company as a market segment leader like no other type of investment can.

Last, sophisticated angel investors are generally able to offer their portfolio companies solid and practical "been there, done that" advice, based on previous start-up experience and/or operating experience. Because angels are typically previously successful entrepreneurs and executives, they are usually sufficiently experienced; indeed, their experience is typically what enabled them to be angelic. Angels also can provide companies with valuable strategic contacts. They too have typically cultivated many relationships potentially valuable to early-stage companies.

However, not all investors have the capacity to contribute equally. The venture capitalists at Accel Partners state bluntly that there is "a wide range" among venture capital firms in terms of "industry expertise," "business experience," and ability to contribute value.[147] Similar wide ranges exist among corporate venture investors and angel investors. Investors can either add value beyond their money (smart money) or just add money (dumb money). Most venture capitalists investigate thoroughly their coinvestors (including those who have made prior investments, those investing alongside them, and those who have committed to invest in the future) to determine whether they fall into the former category and can contribute significant value.

CHAPTER 3

Business Opportunity Due Diligence

IDENTIFICATION OF PRODUCT TYPE: EVOLUTION OR REVOLUTION?

Evolutionary Product

Is the company's product evolutionary in nature?

There are essentially two routes early-stage companies may successfully take with product type. The first is the revolutionary route (or the "Brave New World" route, as it is sometimes called by venture capitalists), whereby companies create paradigm shifts through the development of revolutionary technologies embodied in revolutionary products. This route involves the creation of *new* markets. Apple, Netscape, and Yahoo! are examples of companies that have successfully pursued this strategy. The second route is the evolutionary route (or the "Better, Faster, Cheaper" route), whereby companies identify more narrow and as yet unaddressed market segments of existing markets and seek to dominate those segments by developing evolutionary technologies embodied in evolutionary products. Regis McKenna explains that evolutionary technologies are "changes in technology—enhancements of it."[1] They are not, he continues, "inventions like the light bulb or the first automobile."[2] This second route is the one most often available to entrepreneurs because true paradigm shifts are difficult to initiate. Two examples of companies that have successfully pursued the evolutionary route are Cisco Systems and CrossWorlds Software.

Focusing on the domination of narrow market segments in existing markets can prove a successful strategy for early-stage companies.

In fact, according to William Davidow, early-stage companies that pursue this strategy have a much greater likelihood of survival than those that "attack too broad a market."[3] The primary reason is that companies do not have to wait for (and hope for) target markets to develop—they already exist. By pursuing this strategy, companies can quickly build profitable businesses. Kevin Fong and his partners at the Mayfield Fund prefer to back this type of company, and have found it to be a lucrative approach: "[W]e like existing markets. Every startup doesn't have to be the next Netscape to be a success. Being the ninth player in a space is great if you're going to be acquired by Cisco. Most of these companies make money for their investors and founders."[4] Although the upside potential may be somewhat smaller than the upside potential of companies taking the revolutionary route, there is often much less risk for investors and the time from investment to harvest is often much shorter. Therefore, returns to venture capitalists who fill their portfolios with investments in evolutionary companies tend to be strong.

The point about which venture capitalists are generally wary when evaluating evolutionary companies is that, to be successful, their innovations must be *significant*. They must not be innovations that do little or nothing to enhance a product's value to the customer. According to Benjamin Rosen, there is a saying in the venture capital industry that "'slightly better' is dangerous."[5] Therefore, explains Davidow, successful evolutionary products "are not just a *little* bit better in a few ways, they are significantly better in one or more ways that are important to the customer."[6] Products that fill that bill are certain to draw customers away from existing product offerings, and that is the key to success for companies taking the evolutionary route.

Revolutionary Product

Is the company's product revolutionary in nature?

"We're looking for people willing to think big, who want to take over the world," states Ann Winblad boldly.[7] In contrast to the venture capitalists previously discussed, some venture capitalists, like Winblad, "are more eager to invest in a company that they think can own a brand-new market than in one that offers an improved version of an already-existing product."[8] They prefer investing in companies taking the revolutionary route. The obvious attraction of investing in such companies is that the upside potential to investors for any given investment is generally much greater than with a similar investment in a company taking the evolutionary route. One only need glance at the examples quoted earlier of companies that successfully created revolutions (Apple, Netscape, Yahoo!) to realize the enormous upside potential for companies pursuing this route. The key to this tremendous potential is that companies that successfully open brand-new markets usually, at least for a while, have those markets all to themselves.

Opening a new market, however, usually takes a great deal of work, time, and money, and is fraught with risk. Companies developing evolutionary technologies and products stand on the shoulders of other technologists, building on their work and their dollars spent to enhance existing technologies and products. Companies developing revolutionary technologies and products must do all the work themselves and pay for it themselves. Furthermore, companies hoping to open new markets face significant risk that the target markets may not yet be ready to be opened or that they might never open, at all. And, to add to that risk, when companies locate markets that are ready to be opened, they tend to quickly draw powerful competitors. Therefore, targeting revolutionary opportunities usually makes little sense unless tremendous value is being created. Says Michael Moritz, "[T]he difference between a good company and a great company begins with the product and the services that you provide to the customers. You don't become a great company if you don't have a product or service that really does a tremendous amount for your customers."[9]

Finding such enormous value is not a simple task. In fact, it is one of the most elusive objectives venture capitalists pursue. It is difficult to spot companies with the potential to create enormous value before they actually do so, and in those rare cases with easily recognized potential, competition among venture capitalists to land deals with them can be fierce. Still, it is precisely because of this great value that so many venture capitalists are constantly on the lookout for the next "grand slam home run" that will turn millions into billions.

ALSOP'S FORMULA: WILL ANYONE BUY THE PRODUCT?

Product Description

What is the company's product?

According to Stewart Alsop, general partner at New Enterprise Associates, companies find success most fundamentally by simply "designing products that people want."[10] At first glance, Alsop's statement might seem ridiculously simple; however, the most successful venture capitalists always keep in the back of their minds the question of whether companies will do just that. John Doerr puts this question into casual venture capital parlance: "Will the dogs eat the dog food, or will the fish jump out of the tank?"[11] This is as fundamental a question for venture capitalists as those regarding the quality of management teams. Fred Dotzler goes as far as saying that "[n]othing is more important for a start-up company than developing a product that customers want and will buy."[12]

Alsop offers the following formula as a simple rule of thumb to assess the probability of people actually buying a particular company's product:

$$Q + I + S + M - P^2 = \text{success}$$

The Q in the Alsop equation stands for quality. Assessing quality, according to Alsop, essentially requires venture capitalists to ask, "Does the product work?"[13] Or, sometimes, "*Will* the product work?" The I in the equation stands for innovation. Venture capitalists assessing the degree of innovation embodied in a given product should ask, according to Alsop, "Does it do something that people want that they couldn't do before?"[14] The S stands for smarts. Assessing smarts involves asking, "Does management understand the process of delivering and communicating with the customer?"[15] The M stands for money, which simply requires venture capitalists to write checks. And finally, the P in the Alsop equation stands for pain. This is perhaps the most important element of the equation—hence the exponent. Assessments of the degree of pain associated with a particular product require venture capitalists to ask, according to Alsop, "What [is the company] asking the customer to go through for [their] product to work?"[16]

Quality

Does the company's product work?

According to the venture capitalists at Accel Partners:

> *Venture firms approach the venture business as much from the standpoint of "risk reduction" as from opportunity maximization. That is, the operating assumption is that opportunities can be realized by eliminating the risks (impediments) to their achievement. Almost by definition, the companies in which venture firms invest will be standing in the middle of enormous opportunities. The practical problem then becomes how to eliminate the impediments to achieve this success.*[17]

John Doerr shares this view, and states that the "way to succeed" is to "ruthlessly evaluate the risk" that will be encountered by each particular company.[18] During the due diligence phase, the task venture capitalists generally seek to undertake, therefore, is to determine whether the risks that will be encountered can be overcome. One type of risk that venture capitalists concentrate on heavily is *technical risk*—the risk that companies will not be able to actually develop viable technologies as planned, or will not be able to convert technologies into viable commercial products that can be sold at sufficient levels with sufficient profit margins. Says Ruthann Quindlen, making sure that products are technically feasible is one of the "most cherished principles" in the venture capital industry.[19] Whether technical risk can be overcome can usually be determined with some level of certainty by venture capitalists through sufficient due diligence, often including significant expert consultation. Such assessments are much easier if products are nearing the end of, or are beyond the development stage, such as when companies are *beta* testing (testing with customers, after the lab or *alpha* testing) or are in production. If near the end of or beyond the development stage, venture capitalists generally simply ascertain from companies themselves whether their technologies and their products are functioning well and as intended, without major problems, and that those products can be produced in sufficient quantities with sufficient profit margins. Then, venture capitalists attempt to independently verify the information received.

When products are still in the development stage, the question of technical feasibility becomes more difficult to answer. In such situations, venture capitalists must dig deeply into the backgrounds of the technologists. Certainly, venture capitalists tend to feel fairly confident in a product's feasibility, though not yet fully proven, if the personnel developing the product—the company's technologists and marketing personnel—are top-quality personnel. Also, it has become standard practice in the venture capital industry to consult with technical experts. The venture capitalists at Draper Fisher Jurvetson explain their approach: "Draper Fisher Jurvetson does not rely on in-house expertise alone, but contacts appropriate specialists to evaluate the feasibility of developing the entrepreneur's vision."[20] Many venture capital firms actually make expert consultants partners of their firms (e.g., venture partners or special limited partners) to have ready access to their technical expertise. To further facilitate their technical due diligence through experts, venture capitalists also like to see companies prepare a list of references who can be contacted regarding the technology, perhaps members of their technical advisory boards or experts in the field.

Another question implicitly embedded in the "will the product work?" query is asked and investigated by venture capitalists at the same time: "Will the product work *on time?*" It is easy for companies to proceed with product development more slowly than planned or to begin their product development entirely too late, and to miss their product's market window. Market opportunities only exist for finite periods, and according to Regis McKenna, those windows tend to close quickly, especially if they are particularly attractive opportunities.[21] To be successful, therefore, early-stage companies must generally get their products to their customers as early as possible. Furthermore, venture capitalists generally do not like to back extensive research efforts. The partners at ComVentures state: "We do not want to invest in a couple of years of R&D. In general the company should be within one year of a prototype."[22]

Of course, it is possible to bring a product to market too soon. Venture capitalists generally try to avoid funding companies that seek to introduce products into the market before other products or services (and any other necessary infrastructure) that will support the products are completely ready. Support from such infrastructure is crucial to product success. If the supporting market infrastructure that is required for a company's product to be successful has not yet developed, then it will be difficult for the particular entrepreneurs to convince venture capitalists that their target market is ripe, and that people are ready to buy the product. The venture capitalists at Sequoia Capital state bluntly that they "cannot afford to wait for markets to develop" and "do not have the money or inclination to educate customers to buy products they don't know they need."[23] Says Michael Moritz, one of the Sequoia partners: "The two most horrifying phrases for venture capitalists are 'market education' and 'market development.' We don't want to have to think about either."[24]

To do proper due diligence for product timing, venture capitalists typically investigate two things. First, so that they may fully understand companies' product development schedules, and exactly when the companies' products will actually hit the market, venture capitalists usually insist that companies provide a full explanation of "where [product development] stands and what will be necessary to complete development, including time and cost schedules for achieving both the entire project and various significant interim milestones," according to Alan Salzman and John Doerr.[25] Second, they also work very hard at understanding the existing and future market conditions for companies' products, and corresponding trends in technology. Understanding these things sufficiently is crucial for venture capitalists.

Innovation

Does the company's product do something that people want that they couldn't do before?

As stated, venture capitalists generally work hard to understand market conditions and technology trends. They attempt to maintain what is commonly called in the venture capital world, a "30,000-foot view" of both the technological landscape and the market landscape, typically by consulting with analysts at investment banks and market research firms, attending trade shows and industry conferences, reading industry journals, and talking with anybody and everybody—entrepreneurs, technologists, executives, industry experts, other venture capitalists. What such a view lacks in depth (venture capitalists leave the serious technical depth to the entrepreneurs), is made up for in breadth. A 30,000-foot view allows venture capitalists to keep abreast of innovations being developed across many technologies, and helps them predict which of those innovations the market will consider valuable and avoid those it will not. Jim Hynes, formerly with Fidelity Ventures, explains: "If you're not following what's going on, you can say, 'that looks like the greatest thing in the world.' But there might be something being worked on over here that's going to leap-frog it."[26]

When making such predictions, venture capitalists, such as those at Accel Partners, recognize well that to be deemed valuable by the market, innovations must be targeted at solving as yet unmet customer needs:

> *It may seem self-evident to say that a new company must make a true contribution to prosper, but attention to this fundamental discipline of a free market system is often lost in the enthusiasm to start a new company in a growth market. Unfortunately, despite that growth, market share will only go to a new company if it is adding value by solving unmet customer needs.*[27]

Additionally, venture capitalists generally prefer that the unmet customer needs targeted are dire ones. An instructive metaphor among those in the venture capital business is that they prefer innovations that are painkillers, not vitamins. Vitamins are certainly beneficial, but people may or may not take them—in good health or in bad. But, a person who is lying awake in the middle of the night with a horrendous headache is likely to swallow a painkiller. The same is true of customers. When companies develop innovations that target customers' most basic needs, they are relatively more likely to have customers lining up to buy their products. It is the difference, Ruthann Quindlen explains, between building products that are "must haves" or "nice to haves."[28] Not surprisingly, venture capitalists are strongly drawn to companies targeting dire customer needs and building "must have" products.

Some early-stage companies, however, fail to target any unmet customer needs, and are instead afflicted with what has been termed *mousetrap myopia*. Mousetrap myopia occurs when entrepreneurs become irrationally attached to their sophisticated or elegant technologies and fail to focus solely on the needs of potential customers. Albert Bruno explains: "Engineers and scientists employed by high-technology firms have an inclination to design products that attract the admiration of their technical peers in other companies often to the detriment of the needs of the marketplace."[29] Venture capitalists tend to avoid backing companies that cannot demonstrate that their innovations were created with customers' needs in mind, and whose products, therefore, do not squarely address those needs. Venture capitalists also tend to avoid companies that only *partially* address customers' needs. Ruthann Quindlen explains:

> *Another manifestation of "vitamins vs. aspirin" is the tendency of companies to develop a "point," or partial, solution to a customer problem, as opposed to a "total" solution. In these cases, a company may have a product that satisfies a customer's need— but only part of it. The company will need to expand its focus to address the larger problem, or else will have to depend on other companies—through partnerships or even by being bought—to become a necessary "aspirin" product.*[30]

Smarts

Does the company's management understand the process of delivering and communicating with the customer?

This ground was largely covered in Chapter 2; however, it is worth reiterating what venture capitalists tend to look for among entrepreneurial management teams, this time from the *product* perspective. As Alsop's question reveals, venture capitalists generally look for management teams that collectively understand two things: delivering products to customers and communicating with customers regarding those products. Surprisingly, despite the importance of these two functions, many management teams fail to do either effectively. Delivery and communication are the key components of what Guy Kawasaki, founder of Garage.com and former chief evangelist for Apple Computer, calls *churning*: getting products to customers (maybe even just in beta form), communicating with customers about those products, improving the products based on customer communication, and getting the improved products back to customers to start the process again.[31] Churning allows companies to continually understand the needs of their customers and to meet those needs on an ongoing basis. When management teams have the smarts to do this effectively, the results can be tremendous.

Pain

What is the company asking the customer to go through for your product to work?

Often an early-stage company's success hinges on its ability to sell some sort of change to its target customers. Almost inevitably, customers are required to change their behavior in some way to use a new company's product. And, there are nearly always costs to customers related to such changes. Successful early-stage companies must, therefore, convince customers to buy their products despite these costs. Sometimes the costs are small, but often they can be significant. Some examples of these costs are expenditures on training in the use of the products, expenditures on necessary additional equipment and/or accessories, and, if customers are businesses, integration costs.

Venture capitalists are usually careful to take these costs into account when attempting to determine whether the market will find a particular company's product valuable. If such costs approach or exceed the potential benefit of a given product, customers will not be receptive. Says Darlene Mann, if products "create greater pain or even marginally equal pain" to the pain being addressed, then those products will surely fail.[32] The last thing venture capitalists want to find out is that, although they have backed an otherwise great product, the costs associated with using it are so high that no one is willing to buy it.

Empirically Testing Alsop's Formula

Will customers actually be receptive?

Even after using something like Alsop's formula to determine a particular product's potential for success, venture capitalists almost always attempt to test their determinations empirically. They try to find out whether the dogs will *really* eat the dog food. "In the end," says G. Bradford Jones, general partner of Redpoint Ventures, "a company will not be very successful if there is not a market—a big market—that wants what the company has to offer."[33] Entrepreneurs tend to foist on venture capitalists reams of market data churned out by the major market research firms for this purpose; venture capitalists rarely find such information helpful. If a company is developing a revolutionary product, by definition, little if any meaningful market data will exist for the targeted market or market segment. Alternatively, if a company is developing an evolutionary product, where market research may exist for the larger market in which the targeted market segment resides, it is still unlikely that any meaningful data will be available about the specific targeted market segment. Where data is available about a targeted market segment, then that segment is probably too mature for early-stage companies to enter.

So, rather than rely on the predominantly quantitative market research prepared by market research firms, the most successful venture capitalists take instead what Regis McKenna terms a "qualitative approach" to market research.[34] This approach, McKenna explains, involves using "a combination of intuition and keen sense for changing attitudes" to "develop a feel for the market."[35] Such a feel for the market is developed by living and breathing the market itself—by interacting with customers and other market participants on a regular and continuing basis. "That doesn't sound as scientific as statistical analysis," says McKenna, "but the fact is, it works better."[36] He explains that "conversations with market participants often provide more insights than do a long list of statistics or a set of sophisticated theories."[37]

Darlene Mann is a venture capitalist who uses the qualitative approach. According to Mann, her firm, Onset Ventures, has "a strong focus on anecdotal data, using real world data" to understand markets and market segments.[38] She states that she is "more interested in talking to five customer references . . . than in looking at 300-page research reports."[39] The venture capitalists at Draper Fisher Jurvetson also use the qualitative approach. They say that they make "it a practice to call a number of prospective customers to get a sense of how they might respond to the envisioned product."[40] Venture capitalists such as those at DFJ and Onset—and really those at most major venture firms—are likely to be persuaded if they can contact several customers who can state clearly why they will purchase a particular product and why that product is relatively better than anyone else's product. According to Ruthann Quindlen, this kind of due diligence, "talking with potential customers to gauge interest in the product or service," is the most important type for venture capitalists.[41]

If companies' customers are large and few, empirical market due diligence is relatively easy. Venture capitalists usually simply contact customers directly to gauge their receptiveness to the particular products. The following list is an example of a set of questions venture capitalists often ask of companies when making such calls:

1. What is your role at _____ (in order to understand the context of the comments)?
2. How long have you been working at _____?
3. What is the business relationship between _____ and the company, if any?
4. How do you expect this relationship to evolve over time?
5. What business needs drove you (or might drive you) to work with the company?
6. What other competitors have you evaluated as potentially addressing these business needs?
7. What is your impression of the company's product?
8. Are you satisfied with the company's product?
9. How does it compare with competing products?
10. Who is your primary contact at the company?
11. How responsive is this person?
12. What is your overall impression of the company?

Such calls by venture capitalists are common. To facilitate them, venture capitalists usually require companies to provide lists of their actual customers, beta customers, and/or potential customers who can confirm their need for the product and attest to the product's value. If customers are small and many, as is usually the case for consumer products, then venture capitalists may still attempt to verify their judgments about potential product success through contact with customers, but the task becomes more difficult. They are typically only able to contact a small sampling of the total customer base, which they do through such mechanisms as focus groups and polls, or sometimes even more informal mechanisms, such as casual conversations with potential customers.

MANN'S FOUR COMPONENTS OF A BUSINESS MODEL

The Business Model

Does the company's business model make sense?

The venture capitalists at Bay Partners highlight a simple question that is absolutely vital to venture capital due diligence: "Does the business model make sense?"[42] Business models are an aspect of due diligence over which venture capitalists obsess, and rightfully so. According to Darlene Mann, a business model is "a description of how a firm is going to make money once the business is operating" and how it will "maintain sustained growth over time."[43] The reason for the obsession is that there is a direct correlation between the amount of money portfolio companies are able to make, on one side, and the returns venture capitalists are able to harvest from their investments in those companies, on the other.

As Mann explains, any business model has four components: "markets and customers, products and services, channels of distribution, and the financial engine that's going to run the business."[44] Regarding markets and customers, a business model defines who will buy a particular company's product and/or service. Regarding products and services, a business model defines what product and/or service will be sold. Regarding distribution channels, a business model defines how those products and/or services will be connected with markets and customers. And finally, regarding the financial engine, a business model defines how money will be made from connecting products and services with markets and customers; that is, how revenues from products and/or services sold will consistently and sufficiently exceed the costs of producing and distributing those products and/or services.

Venture capitalists scrutinize companies' business models to ensure that their four components fit together in a way that makes sense and is sustainable. According to Quindlen, "if the business model is correct, often other mistakes can be fixed. But if it's wrong, there's usually no way to prevent ultimate failure."[45] It is not an easy task, however, to discern whether business models are correct. "Most start-ups do not have believable business models unless the business under consideration is highly analogous to an existing and proven business," explains Mann.[46] Therefore, venture capitalists most often test business models by comparing them with models employed by existing companies. They tend to have confidence in models that have been proven viable by successful companies, and are wary of models that have been tried and have failed. When companies propose to employ new and as yet untested business models, venture capitalists are also wary. Most also recognize, however, that it is sometimes necessary to go out on a limb and back new and untested business models. According to Ruthann Quindlen, business models "that break new ground—ones that have never been thought of before—are often the most successful."[47]

Markets and Customers

Who will buy the company's product?

Who will buy a particular company's product is actually a fairly complex question for venture capitalists. It has several subparts, the answers to each of which have significant implications. The place where most venture capitalists start their exploration of this question is to ask entrepreneurs directly for a description of exactly to whom they intend to sell their products. One of the most important things for venture capitalists is that entrepreneurs have a good, solid understanding of their customers. Says Yogen K. Dalal, general partner of the Mayfield Fund:

My favorite question is, "What is a typical day in the life of your customer?" The customer can be a consumer, a technologist, anyone. The reason I ask that is because if you don't understand what your customer does at 8:00 in the morning, 4:00 in the afternoon, or 8:00 at night, you don't know how your product fits into their life.[48]

It is a huge red flag when entrepreneurs are unable to adequately describe their target customers; for example, when they have become blinded by mousetrap myopia or make the outrageous claim that *everyone* is a target customer. Lacking sufficient knowledge of the specific, individual customers to whom they hope to initially sell their products, entrepreneurs will never be able to meet customers' needs and will ultimately be doomed to failure. As a result, venture capitalists are constantly on the lookout to avoid such types. Instead, venture capitalists are generally drawn to entrepreneurs who have targeted specific customers for specific reasons, and who know and thoroughly understand those customers. Companies that base their business plans on their knowledge of specific customers tend to be most successful. Conversely, companies that lack adequate knowledge of their customers tend to fail.

Therefore, venture capitalists are drawn to entrepreneurs who have segmented their respective markets and have targeted the most attractive segments. Segmentation and targeting are crucial. Geoffrey A. Moore, venture partner of Mohr, Davidow Ventures, explains that segmentation begins with entrepreneurs "divid[ing] up the universe of possible customers into market segments."[49] Market segments are groups of customers sharing common desires, needs, and buying patterns. By performing segmentation, Gordon Bell explains, companies come to understand precisely who their customers are, "including their educational backgrounds, demographics, buying motivation and patterns, etc."[50] Armed with this understanding, companies are much more likely to design products that truly meet their customers' needs. On the other hand, according to Moore, targeting happens when entrepreneurs "evaluate each segment for its attractiveness" narrowing them down to a small number of "finalists."[51] And finally, he says, companies simply "pick one and go after it."[52] Targeting the most attractive market segments means targeting those customers

who "value [the] offering the highest compared to the competition,"
according to Leonard M. Lodish, professor at the Wharton School,
Howard L. Morgan, Vice Chairman of idealab!, and Amy Kallianpur, professor at Michigan State University.[53] If a company is able to
do that, they explain, "it has many benefits including better pricing
and higher margins, more satisfied customers, and usually a better
barrier to potential and actual competition."[54]

The next thing venture capitalists usually examine in their customer due diligence is the total number of customers that reside in
(or potentially, in the future, could reside in) the targeted market.
They overwhelmingly prefer to invest in companies aimed at very
large markets—"monster" markets, as Don Valentine, founding
partner of Sequoia Capital, refers to them. Valentine, famous for his
position, goes so far as saying, "I don't even care about the people.
Give me a huge market."[55] Also a big fan of monster markets, Ann
Winblad says: "We're market real estate investors first and foremost."[56] There are multiple reasons for this strong preference. First,
Ruthann Quindlen explains, large markets are "very forgiving."[57]
Says Quindlen, "If the market is large enough, even a mediocre team
and a mediocre execution can still produce a big win."[58] Second,
Fred Dotzler explains, monster markets "hold the promise of high
sales and earnings, as well as a high return to investors."[59] Therefore, simply put, the potential reward is much greater when companies target monster markets. Market size is actually one of the
most important aspects of due diligence for venture capitalists—so
much so that they will generally accept much more risk with regard
to other aspects when they locate companies targeting monster markets. Ruthann Quindlen explains:

> If the potential opportunity is large enough, an investor will take
> on more risk. If not, more of the pieces of the puzzle have to be
> nailed down and in place. This weighing applies to management
> teams, the maturity of the technology, the amount of money to be
> raised, the number of unanswered questions, the business
> model—to just about everything, really.[60]

Monster markets are not without their perils, of which venture capitalists tend to be acutely aware. John Van Slyke, Howard Stevenson,
and Michael Roberts explain:

The raw size of the market is naturally a critical dimension, because it has a direct bearing on potential sales volume and, thus, financial returns. All things being equal, of course, bigger is better. But, things are not always equal. Large markets often attract large, powerful competitors, making smaller niches more hospitable to the entrepreneur.[61]

Therefore, venture capitalists, when doing due diligence on companies targeting monster markets, usually attempt to calculate the likelihood that the targeted market segment might attract such competitors. This aspect of due diligence is covered more fully later in this chapter.

Along with the raw size of targeted markets, venture capitalists also usually examine the rate at which markets are growing and will continue to grow. Venture capitalists universally prefer very high-growth markets; early-stage companies thrive in that environment. Bob Zider, president of the Beta Group, a Menlo Park-based technology incubator, explains:

One myth is that venture capitalists invest in good people and good ideas. The reality is that they invest in good industries— that is, industries that are more competitively forgiving than the market as a whole. Growing within high-growth segments is a lot easier than doing so in low-, no- or negative-growth ones, as every businessperson knows. In other words, regardless of the talent or charisma of individual entrepreneurs, they rarely receive backing from a VC if their businesses are in low-growth market segments.[62]

Early-stage companies have an easier time in high-growth market segments because, in them, demand temporarily exceeds supply and therefore companies are able to escape the pressures of competition, at least for a time. Says George S. Day, professor at the Wharton School, "[R]ivals in the market are preoccupied with building capacity to meet demand and are less likely to react to losses in their share."[63] Therefore, companies are usually able to maintain relatively high profit margins, as there is little pressure on them to lower their prices. High-growth market segments are able to cover many of the mistakes made by early-stage companies. George Middlemas, managing general partner of Apex Investment Partners, explains, "If you have a market that is growing at 30 percent a year, a venture company can . . . make a couple of mistakes and still come out on top."[64] It is the "momentum," according to Darlene Mann, that high-growth markets provide which allows companies to succeed despite "mistakes in execution, organization, product or technology directions," which in early-stage companies are "inevitable."[65]

Karl Vesper states in his work *New Venture Strategies* that companies can pursue at least five strategies to participate in high-growth markets: (1) found new industries, (2) participate in expanding industries, (3) innovate in backward industries, (4) break into established industries, and (5) improve standards of service.[66] Venture capitalists generally only back companies if they are pursuing one of these strategies.

The last thing venture capitalists usually explore during customer due diligence is the percentage share that companies are striving to obtain in their targeted market segments. When thinking about market share, many entrepreneurs become afflicted with what venture capitalists call the *China Syndrome*. William Sahlman explains that the China Syndrome is based on the idea that "if the potential market is defined to include all the people in China, then great riches can be forecast based on a tiny market share."[67] Entrepreneurs tend to take this approach because they want to appear to investors as conservative in their financial projections, but also because they want it to appear that the opportunity they are targeting is enormous, and that they cannot lose with it, no matter how small a share of the market they obtain. The venture capitalists at El Dorado Ventures state that, for them, this approach is a "sure-fire deal killer," and they tell entrepreneurs that up front:

> *"All we need is one percent of a billion-dollar market." That may sound like $10 million to you, but in reality, only one or two top companies in a market can make money. Unless you believe that your company has what it takes to be a market leader, you'll need to look elsewhere for financing.*[68]

According to William Davidow, this view of entrepreneurs afflicted with the China Syndrome is well founded:

Many companies enter businesses planning to capture only a small percentage of the market. Such plans are not conservative; they are extremely dangerous. They are strategies for failure. The only good plans . . . are those aimed at dominance, backed by sufficient resources to achieve it, and executed with precision.[69]

For that reason, venture capitalists tend to invest only in companies that are striving for dominance of their market segment by gaining a certain percentage market share. Companies able to obtain greater than 30 percent market share are almost always profitable, and companies unable to obtain greater than 15 percent market share almost always fail. Venture capitalists, therefore, often use the 30 percent threshold when looking at early-stage companies: If companies are not shooting for a percentage share of their market segment greater than 30 percent (or cannot realistically hope to gain more than that percentage), they are rarely interested. And, venture capitalists are almost universally uninterested in companies shooting for shares less than 15 percent.

Products and Services

What is the company going to sell?

When looking at the subject of products and services from the business model perspective, the issues are not materially different than those issues explored in the discussion of Alsop's formula. One additional question comes to light, however, and that is "What comes next?" As discussed, business models define how companies make money and grow *over time.* Therefore, venture capitalists, in their business model due diligence, often explore if and how companies plan to evolve and expand their product offerings going forward, to continually generate revenue and sustain growth. Says Darlene Mann, there is "great concern in the venture capital community and probably even more so on Wall Street, about the one-trick pony company."[70] Venture capitalists much prefer companies whose business models are *platform* models. Platform models allow companies to deliver products and services beyond their initial offerings, for example, follow-on products, follow-on services, and new products. Such companies can sustain growth over the long term and often offer investors the highest returns on their investment.

Distribution Channel

How will the company connect its product with its customers?

Distribution channels define exactly how companies put their products into the hands of customers. Large, more established companies tend to focus heavily on their distribution channels. Early-stage companies, on the other hand, tend to completely overlook them, focusing instead primarily on product development. According to Ruthann Quindlen,

> There's one critical component of the business model that entrepreneurs generally fail to consider until it's too late: the distribution model, or how exactly you plan to sell your product or service. Oh, entrepreneurs are able to figure out the target customer just fine. It's the problem of getting the product to the customer in an economically efficient way that suffers from neglect.[71]

But, no matter how great a product, no matter how great the potential of a product to meet the needs of customers, it cannot hope to succeed without equally great distribution channels. Therefore, distribution channels often prove to be the Achilles' heel for many early-stage companies. Scores of companies with great products fail regularly because of poor channel selection, poor channel development, or poor channel maintenance—these three key channel functions are typically referred to collectively as *channel management*. For obvious reasons, venture capitalists tend to consider channel management as an extremely significant due diligence issue. Yogen Dalal views channel management as *the* "make-or-break issue" for early-stage companies.[72]

It is vital that channels fit the products to be distributed. Venture capitalists like to back companies that have built (or are planning to build) distribution channels that employ the optimal means for getting their particular products into the hands of customers. To determine whether a particular channel is an optimal channel, venture capitalists generally focus on three things. First, the channel must be the right *length*. According to Hirotaka J. Takeuchi, professor at the Harvard Business School, questions of distribution channel length involve a choice "between selling directly to customers or selling through inter-mediaries."[73] This choice is heavily influenced by the trade-off be-tween needing to control channel functions and having the financial and/or human resources necessary to exercise that control. Because early-stage companies tend to be characterized by few financial and few human resources, they are often forced to cede control over chan-nel functions to intermediaries. Leonard Lodish, Howard Morgan, and Amy Kallianpur explain, "Distribution intermediaries (e.g., wholesalers, jobbers, retailers, value-added resellers) possibly can be used to perform some of the required functions more efficiently and/or more profitably to the entrepreneur."[74] Distribution intermedi-aries can help companies get to market quickly and economically, so that they may begin generating revenues much earlier than otherwise. This is crucial for early-stage companies. Therefore, most venture cap-italists very much like to see that companies have established such re-lationships. Todd Dagres, general partner at Battery Ventures, tells entrepreneurs: "Before you approach the venture firm, it helps if you can show that large companies with established distribution channels are willing to work with you to deliver the product."[75]

Next, venture capitalists usually seek to ensure that the distribu-tion channels selected have the right *breadth,* which Takeuchi defines as the "relative intensity of distribution coverage."[76] Optimal breadth depends on the types of products to be channeled and the types and sizes of the markets targeted. Some products and some markets (for example, products to be sold in the consumer market) require wide channels. Companies must choose and develop channels that provide them with sufficient coverage to reach an adequate number of cus-tomers. Others, such as products to be sold in the industrial market, require narrow channels. In such markets, there tend to be relatively few customers. So, companies must choose and develop narrow chan-nels to target those customers effectively and efficiently.

Last, venture capitalists usually attempt to make sure that the channels chosen are not too *costly* (in terms of both time and money) to develop and maintain. The costs to construct and main-tain distribution channels are often high. When these costs are too high, companies' business models cannot work effectively. Says Ruthann Quindlen, many early-stage companies have "run onto the rocks" because the costs to develop and maintain distribution channels prohibited them from being able to make any money.[77]

Distribution channels that are the wrong length or breadth or are too costly will almost surely doom the distributed products (and most likely the companies distributing them) to failure. On the other hand, distribution channels of optimal length and breadth, which are not too costly, usually provide companies with strong advantages over competitors. Early-stage companies can sometimes leapfrog earlier entrants to particular markets and/or larger, more established competitors by selecting and developing such channels. Not surprisingly, venture capitalists tend to be drawn to companies that can demonstrate a dedicated focus on channel management, especially those that have a solid strategy for the selection and development of *optimal* distribution channels.

Financial Engine

Will the company make money?

Venture capitalists need to know that, ultimately, the companies in which they invest will make money. Darlene Mann explains:

> *Now, obviously, start-ups don't make money the first day they start or they wouldn't need venture capitalists. But what we do want to believe is that in the long run, as we've primed the pump, so to speak, . . . we're going to see the ability to make profits. . . .* [78]

It is on such profits (or at least the realistic promise of future profits) that venture capitalists realize returns on their investments. As previously discussed, venture capitalists look first and foremost for companies attacking monster markets. Monster markets offer the potential for large revenues and large earnings. The partners at Sequoia Capital state that they "like investments with the potential to blossom into markets over $1 billion."[79] But, venture capitalists also tend to spend a great deal of time and effort examining that part of the companies' business models that Darlene Mann calls their "financial engines."[80] They want to make sure that companies are armed with strong financial engines; without strong financial engines companies cannot hope to realize that large revenues and large earnings that monster markets offer. John Barry, managing general partner of Prospect Street Ventures, explains: "While many early-stage concepts appear to present attractive market opportunities, a closer examination of the key revenue drivers and associated expenses often reveal an unsustainable or unworkable business model: fixed costs too high, margins too thin, and so on."[81]

Venture capitalists primarily focus on two components, both of which indicate strong financial engines. First, they look for the potential for high gross profit margins. Jeffry Timmons explains that the "potential for high and durable gross margins (i.e., the unit selling price less all direct and variable costs) is important" for early-stage companies.[82] He states, "Gross margins exceeding 40 percent to 50 percent provide a tremendous built-in cushion that allows for more error and more flexibility to learn from mistakes than do gross margins of 20 percent or less."[83] Furthermore, and most important to venture capitalists, businesses built on high gross margins tend to make "the best candidates for superior return on equity invested," according to the venture capitalists at Draper Fisher Jurvetson.[84]

The second component venture capitalists look for when examining financial engines is the potential for recurring revenue streams. Venture capitalists like recurring revenue streams because they are predictable. Predictability, says Kevin Compton, general partner at Kleiner Perkins Caufield & Byers, is something to which he and his partners are strongly drawn: "We don't like companies that have to reinvent themselves every year. We are attracted to companies that have recurring revenues. . . ."[85] Companies that do not enjoy recurring revenue streams—companies that are focused to reinvest themselves—face the very real (and quite large) risk that they will not be able to do so, at least not viably.

Companies with financial engines that combine both of these elements—high gross profit margins *and* recurring revenue streams—are well suited to support the rapid growth sought by venture capitalists.

COMPETITIVE STRATEGY

Existing and Future Competitors

Who are the existing and possible future competitors to the company?

According to the venture capitalists at Hummer Winblad Venture Partners, successful entrepreneurs—those in whom it is worth investing—have "a clear understanding of the competitive marketplace, and the strengths and weaknesses of each potential competitor."[86] Many entrepreneurs, however, fail to acquire an adequate depth or breadth of understanding before approaching venture capitalists. In fact, the venture capitalists at Accel Partners say, "The absence of good analysis and lack of appreciation for the competition are probably the most common mistakes made by new entrepreneurs."[87] Such mistakes can be costly, both for entrepreneurs and for the venture capitalists who back them. Therefore, for the venture capitalists at El Dorado Ventures, it is a "sure-fire deal-killer" when a company claims, "We have no competition."[88] They explain that even if that were true, "that blissful state of affairs won't last forever," and companies that ignore their competition, existing or future, will not get far.[89] However, as bad as ignorance of competition is, it is equally dangerous for entrepreneurs to be preoccupied with their competition. When companies are focused on weakly defined new markets, entrepreneurs must concentrate first and foremost on their own growth and development and somewhat less on competitive positioning. They should focus on building great companies, not simply besting their competition. Companies cannot win their races while constantly looking over their shoulders.

For their own competitive due diligence purposes, therefore, venture capitalists by and large attempt to do two things. First and foremost, they attempt to make sure that entrepreneurs fully understand the competitive marketplaces in which they operate, including the strengths and weaknesses of each of their competitors, but not to the extent that they focus myopically on those competitors. Second, venture capitalists seek to educate themselves about companies' competition. Such information is vital to their ability to determine how companies are likely to fare in the marketplace. And, they generally must be comfortable with all of this—companies' competitive knowledge, as well as their own—before they will make any investment decisions.

Accurately mapping competitive landscapes is no easy task. But, through conversations with company executives and with experts in the field, venture capitalists usually acquire a fairly good sense of the existing terrain. More and more, however, early-stage companies operate in "stealth mode"; they grow in secret to avoid tipping off competitors about their existence or plans. So, until all such stealth companies formally announce themselves, venture capitalists cannot be sure that they are perceiving accurate competitive landscapes. Even more difficult than identifying existing competitors is forecasting potential *future* competitors. According to Michael Porter, professor at the Harvard Business School, the way to make such predictions is through an "assessment of present and future barriers, coupled with the attraction the industry will hold to various types of firms and their ability to hurdle the barriers cheaply."[90] Therefore, identifying existing and future competitors is imprecise work, and venture capitalists are forced to make the best guesses they can. Having done so, they also generally attempt to determine the degree to which such competitors might pose serious competitive threats.

"Venture capitalists prefer to invest in companies that have little competition," says Fred Dotzler.[91] The reason for this preference is that such companies are not forced to face the harsh downward pressure on profits that competitive forces exert. Early-stage companies generally find it much easier to survive and grow in markets lacking such competitive forces—"markets that the competition has overlooked," in the words of Elton Sherwin, managing director of Ridgewood Capital.[92] In such markets, profit levels tend to remain relatively high, as do returns to investors. Many venture capitalists, however, like to see *some* competition because it validates the particular market—the targeting of the same market by others reassures venture capitalists that it is a real market opportunity. Also, competition can be an incredible motivating factor for early-stage companies. For both of these reasons, Floyd Kvamme says of himself and his partners at Kleiner Perkins Caufield & Byers:

> [W]e like competition in our companies. I think we've convinced ourselves that if there's no one competing with you,

maybe there's no market. Competition is an important aspect of business and it can hone you and it can cause you to do better. I don't think anybody would have run a sub-four minute mile if someone hadn't been pushing at it and once somebody did, somebody else did it and got it faster and faster and faster. I think those are very important concepts. We like to look at competition as an important entity and judge ourselves by our competition in a very aggressive way.[93]

What venture capitalists do not want to see are overly crowded competitive landscapes or landscapes dominated by one or two powerful and ferocious competitors.

Proprietary Advantage

Does the company have any proprietary advantages?

Venture capitalists almost universally cite strong proprietary advantages as a critical investment criterion. The partners at Trinity Ventures state that they "look for products or services that offer a clear and sustainable advantage over the competition."[94] Elton Sherwin explains:

Venture capitalists take large financial risks and expect large returns. They look for opportunities to create a unique product that can maintain its uniqueness over time. If it can be copied too quickly, the financial return will be low and the venture unattractive. A unique defensible competitive advantage . . . is foremost in a venture capitalist's mind.[95]

Proprietary advantages allow companies to offer unique products— truly *differentiated* products—that their competitors cannot. Product differentiation is critical to early-stage companies. The venture capitalists at Hummer Winblad Venture Partners list, along with market and management, "differentiation of the company's products and ideas" as a primary "determinant of success."[96] Product differentiation is only important, however, if products and/or services are different from those of the competition in ways that are important to customers. According to Leonard Lodish, Howard Morgan, and Amy Kallianpur, "Every product or service idea has to be wanted by some market segment more than competitive products or services in order to obtain sales."[97]

Venture capitalists also prefer that proprietary advantages be sustainable. The venture capitalists at H&Q Venture Capital explain that when they are considering companies for investment they "want to understand why they will be able to maintain their success through continuing stages of corporate growth."[98] Sustainable proprietary advantages allow companies to do so. By making sure that companies are likely to maintain their success through continuing stages of corporate growth, venture capitalists increase their own likelihood of earning significant returns. Say Lodish, Morgan, and Kallianpur, "If a way can be found to continually be ahead of the competition, then the venture will probably return higher than normal returns to its owners."[99]

Successful venture-backed companies typically build their proprietary advantages around the following:

- *Technology Advantages* Technological innovations can provide proprietary advantages because competitors often find it difficult to replicate those innovations, at least in the short term. Therefore, technology advantages can be crucial to the success of early-stage companies. A competitive advantage based solely on technology is usually not enough. Early-stage companies relying exclusively on technology advantages often find out that after a surprisingly short time, competitors are able to catch (and often surpass) them in technological sophistication. Therefore, venture capitalists prefer companies that can demonstrate an ability to innovate technologically on an ongoing basis.
- *Legal Advantages* Early-stage companies often develop proprietary advantages by legal means. Intellectual property protection—patents, copyrights, and trade secrets—can be a robust shield from competitive pressures. (These protections are discussed more fully in Chapter 5.)
- *Access Advantages* Preferred access to resources or to customers is a particularly attractive proprietary advantage for early-stage companies. Access advantages protect companies

from competition because competitors are generally reluctant to enter into competition with the holder of a true access advantage; if they did, they would necessarily suffer. Two conditions must exist, however, for access advantages to be true advantages. First, access must be secured under terms that are more favorable than those available to competitors. Indeed, if access cannot be secured under better terms, then there is no advantage. Second, access must be enforceable on a long-term basis. Enforceability can derive from "ownership, binding contracts, or self-enforcing mechanisms such as switching costs," according to Pankaj Ghemawat, professor at Harvard Business School.[100] He warns, however, that enforceability can be a "two-edged sword."[101] If conditions change and access can be gained through other channels under even more favorable terms, a company that once enjoyed preferred access may be saddled "with worse terms than those available to its rivals."[102]

Leonard Lodish, Howard Morgan, and Amy Kallianpur provide some additional sources of proprietary advantage:

- Other companies may rely on excellent design, perceived high quality, or continual innovation as distinctive competencies.
- Others will use excellent customer service by loyal employees who have adopted corporate service values. Southwest Airlines is an excellent example of a venture that differentiates itself from competitors with both excellent customer service and technology for scheduling and turning flights around. Many customers fly Southwest, not only because it is economical, but because it is fun. Many other airlines have tried to imitate Southwest and have been unsuccessful.
- Reputations and other differences in customer perception of products, services, and companies can be extremely valuable sources of sustainable advantage. If customers perceive you as being a preferable source, they will be more likely to choose your products or services. Dell's service reputation as well as its business-to-business salesforce have succeeded in getting many customers to perceive them as a trustworthy, reliable resource for

computers and related equipment and services. As a result, Dell has also been difficult to compete with.[103]

First-Mover Advantage and Market Share

Will the company be able to exploit a first-mover advantage and garner a large market share?

In some markets, companies cannot develop strong proprietary advantages or differentiate their product and/or service offerings; or, at least, they can only briefly *maintain* the differentiation they are able to achieve. Therefore, other factors typically determine early-stage competitive success in such markets. The following discussion by the venture capitalists at Sequoia Capital highlights two such factors in successful early-stage products:

> *The products that fuel start-ups fall into two categories. The first are difficult to duplicate and contain a lot of proprietary know how. The second type do not contain tremendous science or technological know-how but have a first mover's advantage and allow a company to start rolling very quickly, garner a large market share and turn that position into a powerful competitive weapon.[104]*

Therefore, when companies lack proprietary advantages, and when the barriers keeping others from competing with them are low, venture capitalists are reluctant to invest in them unless they become satisfied with two aspects of the given opportunities. First, they must have a strong "first-mover advantage," meaning that the companies are the first ones to enter their respective market segments. Says Ann Winblad, the "first-mover advantage is very, very important."[105] First movers have the opportunity to reach customers before anyone else is competing for them and can lock in many customers quickly, before competitors can emerge. But, to do this, companies have to be *ready* to do so. Therefore, the second thing venture capitalists generally want to understand is whether the companies have the ability to go out into the market and quickly gain significant market share, because market share becomes their competitive weapon. The primary challenge, however, to companies hoping to win significant market share, Steve Jurvetson and Tim Draper explain, is "scalability."[106] Scalability refers to a company's ability to rapidly grow its operations to the level necessary to reach a large number of customers, without sacrificing the quality of the product and/or service delivered to each customer. According to Winblad, these companies either "scale or die."[107] If they cannot scale, they will be unable to gain sufficient market share and will be left without competitive weapons of any kind. Essentially, therefore, when looking at these companies, venture capitalists generally just want to know that they have the ability to be the first and biggest out there, in their respective market segments.

Competitive Positioning

Does the company have a good positioning strategy?

It is usually not sufficient that companies develop sustainable proprietary advantages and achieve real product differentiation. Companies must also make sure that customers understand fully the differences between their products and competitors' products and perceive those differences as valuable. Leonard Lodish, Howard Morgan, and Amy Kallianpur explain:

> *It is obvious that people make decisions based only on what they perceive. Many entrepreneurial firms are happy when they have developed products or services that are actually better than competition on characteristics that they know should be important to people in their target market(s). What they forget is that the job is not done until the targeted people actually perceive the differences between their product and competition.[108]*

Therefore, companies need to develop effective positioning strategies very early in their development. Competitive positioning, according to Leonard Lodish, Howard Morgan, and Amy Kallianpur, determines "how the product or service is to be perceived by the target market compared to the competition."[109] Companies usually position their products and/or services based on their proprietary advantages because it is precisely those advantages that make them and their product or service offerings different (and valuable) to customers. Venture capitalists typically want to understand completely and become comfortable with companies' position strategies. Therefore, many venture capitalists make an examination of such strategies a key part of their due diligence.

CHAPTER 4

Due Diligence on Intangibles

COMPANY INTANGIBLES: FOCUS, MOMENTUM, BUZZ

Focus

Does the company have focus?

An aspect that many venture capitalists examine during due diligence is the extent to which companies are focused. "Focus," according to Eugene Kleiner, "is essential."[1] Too many entrepreneurs fail to maintain their focus in the early stages. They try to be all things to all people, instead of focusing solely on those things that add the most strategic value to their companies: maximizing their distinctive expertise and developing the skills that will put the companies at the leading edges of their market segments and enable them to provide products that their competitors cannot match. Such a lack of focus is dangerous because resources—human, financial, and time—are incredibly scarce during the early stage. Companies cannot afford to waste any of the resources to which they have access. And without focus, each of these resources is inevitably wasted. Says Ruthann Quindlen, "Without focus, nothing else matters: the troops scatter in all directions, efforts are wasted, and crucial time is lost."[2]

Momentum

Does the company have momentum?

Venture capitalists are drawn to companies that have built significant momentum, and they tend to be especially drawn to companies for whom that momentum is continuing to increase. The venture capitalists at Oak Investment Partners state that "demonstrating consistently growing momentum" is very important.[3] Momentum in this context connotes the energy that companies build when they begin to hit their major milestones, doing such things as signing top-notch management team members, obtaining impressive outside directors and advisers, establishing significant customer and partner relationships, generating favorable "buzz." When companies begin to build that energy, it tends (though, not always) to be somewhat easier for them to hit their next major milestone, and then even easier to hit the ones after it. So, in general, it is a much more difficult task to build that energy from scratch than it is to maintain it, or even increase it. Therefore, companies that have already built significant momentum by the time they approach venture capitalists tend to be most successful afterward, compared with those that have yet to build momentum or have lost momentum, for example, those that are floundering because of a lack of focus or that have lost momentum because of a key employee's departure.

Buzz

Has the company been able to generate any buzz?

The ability to generate favorable buzz can be critical for early-stage companies. *Buzz* is generally defined as word-of-mouth public relations (PR) generated by credible sources outside companies—customers, partners, experts, and the media, especially those in the media who are perceived as trustworthy. Says Oliver Curme, general partner of Battery Ventures, "Increasingly, promotion and buzz are what define an industry leader."[4] Being perceived as an industry leader can be a huge boost for early-stage companies. It generally makes signing customers, forging partnerships and alliances, and obtaining financing much easier. Therefore, companies greatly increase their chances of success by, as Ann Winblad is famous for saying, "declaring victory" very early in their development. Companies cannot, however, declare victory alone, at least, not credibly. They must be able to convince and persuade other credible sources, such as those mentioned earlier, to do it for them. That is no easy task, and companies that do so effectively are particularly attractive to venture capitalists. According to the venture capitalists at Oak Investment Partners, "Word of mouth 'buzz' from credible sources" is important.[5] In fact, the ability to generate buzz has become so important to venture capitalists that some firms, such as Battery Ventures and Sequoia Capital, have hired professionals to assist their portfolio companies in generating it effectively.

INVESTOR INTANGIBLES

Gut Feeling

What does your gut tell you about the company?

Perhaps the most important thing that separates good venture capitalists from the rest of the pack is a dependable gut. Good venture capitalists can consistently rely on their gut feelings to tell them which management teams are likely to be successful or which markets are likely to be most attractive. Mediocre and bad venture capitalists either do not or cannot. All venture capitalists must ask certain fundamental questions during due diligence (such as those questions presented in this book), but the answers to those questions rarely provide concrete information on which investors can make decisions with absolute objective certainty. Such questions do, however, usually result in a great deal of data about the management team, their backgrounds, their personalities, their abilities; about the technology, whether it will work, whether it solves real, unmet customer needs; about the potential market, whether it will be a monster market, whether it will grow at a sufficient rate, whether the companies can obtain sufficient market share. Venture capitalists must sort through all this information before making their investment decisions. To complicate the decision-making process even further, most companies have strengths in some areas, but weaknesses in others. Says Kevin Fong:

> *I think the real art of venture capital has to do with how you judge each of those factors. It'd be great to have . . . a plus in every category, but, of course, you can't always get that. And so*

the real key is to judge between those things, and understand how one offsets another.[6]

Without concrete information, however, it is fairly difficult to do this. The imprecise nature of due diligence means that venture capitalists cannot analyze the information obtained the way investment bankers analyze investment opportunities, by simply crunching numbers. Instead, venture capitalists must rely largely on gut feeling. They cannot use analytics; they must instead use their instincts. "There's no way you can say with certainty [whether a particular investment] is a great deal or . . . a dog," explains Jonathan A. Flint, principal of Burr, Egan, Deleage & Co.[7] "You have to accept that the process . . . involves facts and gut feeling."[8]

CHAPTER 5

Legal Due Diligence

PREINVESTMENT LEGAL ISSUES

GENERAL CONSIDERATIONS

Business Form

What is the company's business form?

Of the various business forms available to entrepreneurs, virtually all early-stage companies are organized as either C corporations, S corporations, or limited liability companies. Which one of these forms entrepreneurs choose to employ—even among this subset—is an important piece of information to any venture capitalist considering backing them. That choice determines what the venture capitalists will actually own after they do invest: A share of stock is very different from an ownership interest in a limited liability company; and a share of stock in a C corporation is very different from a share of stock in an S corporation. The reality, however, is that companies hoping to raise venture capital almost universally choose to organize as C corporations because venture capitalists unanimously prefer to invest in C corporations. Entrepreneurs are generally loath to do anything that might give potential investors a reason to decline investment.

The C corporation gains its name from Subchapter C of the Internal Revenue Code, which covers the general taxation of corporations. The C corporation is the market standard among business forms. It has been the dominant business form in the United States for more than a century. Most significant U.S. companies, venture-backed and otherwise, are organized as C corporations. Several advantages (over other business forms) characterize the C corporation and make it the most popular business form; these include being a distinct legal entity and having easily transferable ownership interests, unlimited life, and limited liability for shareholders. However, one particularly important disadvantage also characterizes the C corporation, and that is double taxation—corporate profits are taxed twice—once at the corporate level and once at the shareholder level when they are distributed to shareholders. Despite this potentially burdensome characteristic, venture capitalists still overwhelmingly prefer to invest in C corporations.

The S corporation (named, not surprisingly, for subchapter S of the Internal Revenue Code, which covers the taxation of this special corporate subtype) was introduced to ease the onus of double taxation for small, closely held corporations. (A closely held corporation is one with very few shareholders.) All early-stage companies start out small and closely held. Therefore, many entrepreneurs initially assume that utilizing this tax-efficient entity is the right course of action. For companies hoping to raise venture capital, however, such entities are essentially off-limits, due to several narrow restrictions imposed on such entities. Most importantly, to maintain S corporation status, the Internal Revenue Code mandates that companies can only have shareholders that are classified as either individuals or certain types of trusts. That restriction makes it impossible for venture capital firms to invest in S corporations; such firms are nearly universally organized as limited partnerships and, less commonly, as LLCs or corporations. Indeed, if a venture capital firm were to invest in an S corporation, it would be immediately and automatically converted into a C corporation. The restriction likewise thwarts investment by corporate venture capital funds, which assume all sorts of business forms, none of which fit within the S corporation restrictions. Therefore, S corporations (at least those that wish to maintain their S corporation status) may only obtain venture backing from angel investors, who typically invest as individuals or through trusts.

Even those angels who are able to invest in S corporations, however, tend to strongly disfavor them. The primary reason for this aversion is another restriction imposed by the Internal Revenue Code: S corporations are allowed to issue only one class of equity.

The upshot of this restriction is that S corporations may issue only plain vanilla common stock. They cannot issue *preferred* stock, which has long been the favored investment vehicle among venture investors, including angels. (Preferred stock is discussed more fully later in this chapter.) Therefore, while it is not entirely unheard of (occasionally a company is able to convince a group of angels to take common stock), companies eager to raise venture capital rarely organize as S corporations.

The limited liability company (or LLC) is a relatively new business form, a creation of state statutory law. Similar to S corporations, LLCs are generally not subjected to double taxation, but LLCs do not have to contend with the severe restrictions imposed by the Internal Revenue Code on S Corporations. Therefore, according to John Steel, partner of the law firm of Gray Cary, "By organizing a venture-stage business as an LLC rather than as a corporation, significant tax savings could be achieved upon a sale or distribution of its assets, or through distribution of profits resulting from its operation as a privately-held 'cash cow.' "[1] Despite these potential tax advantages, however, there are several legal, tax, and practical reasons for the C corporation remaining the chosen business form among venture capitalists. These reasons are discussed in the following subsections.

Familiarity to Venture Capitalists and Public Markets   A major reason that venture capitalists prefer to invest in C corporations is simply that they have become accustomed to doing so. The C corporate form, with both common and preferred stock, is the market standard in the venture capital industry. Every venture capitalist is familiar with the issues and the documents surrounding investments in C corporations. By contrast, explains John Steel, "an LLC's organizational documents typically must include extensive details on governance, accounting and tax matters," which he says "can be unfamiliar or confusing to investors used to dealing with corporate documentation."[2] Although by their very nature, venture capitalists are willing to take great risks, they are generally reluctant to take chances on issues such as the choice of business form.

Another reason venture capitalists favor C corporations is that they facilitate the IPO (initial public offering) process. As Cole and Sokol explain, " 'C' corporations present . . . the preferred vehicle (in fact, practically the exclusive vehicle) for an initial public offering."[3] It is the preferred vehicle because investment bankers generally find it much easier to market and sell shares in C corporations to investors in initial public offerings—primarily, institutional investors— than to market and sell interests in other entities, such as LLCs. Indeed, lengthy and cumbersome disclosures must be added to IPO prospectuses if an LLC structure is maintained. These additional disclosures, coupled with the general unfamiliarity on the part of institutional investors with entities other than C corporations, are typically sufficient to deter many investors from participating in such offerings. Therefore, venture capitalists generally prefer to invest in C corporations in part because they perceive that their shares are relatively more likely to become liquid in the public markets.

Companies can convert into C corporations prior to their IPOs. Such conversion is not, however, always an easy task. In fact, it is generally a very complicated task unless conversion was carefully planned for from initial founding. Furthermore, no matter how much planning goes in it, conversion is costly and can often significantly delay the IPO process. Therefore, whereas some companies are able to pull off successful pre-IPO conversions, the added complication, especially when coupled with several other considerations to be discussed, is generally still sufficient to frighten off most venture capitalists (or at least to get them to request that companies convert to C corporations prior to their investment).

Stability of Legal Treatment   Venture capitalists invariably impose numerous legal controls and restrictions on companies to protect their investments and usually insist on investing with the C corporate form because with it such controls and restrictions have been tried and tested in the courts. A substantial and established body of law exists governing corporations, and that body of law is unlikely to yield many surprises for venture capitalists. It is relatively easy for a C corporation to create a preferred series of securities (preferred stock) that will meet the needs of venture capital investors without sacrificing its ability to offer attractively priced options (common stock options) that will attract employees.

The laws governing LLCs (and governing the use of similar controls and restrictions in the LLC context), on the other hand, are relatively new and untested. There exists relatively little judicial guidance about their interpretation. Also, because LLC statutes vary from state to state, some venture capitalists (and their LLC portfolio companies) may encounter difficulties when attempting to achieve liquidity through mergers or acquisitions. Some states still make it difficult (and sometimes impossible) for LLCs to merge into corporations, and venture-backed companies that cannot be merged into, or acquired by, other corporations lose an important path to liquidity. Venture capitalists shy away from anything that will at all hamper a company's ability to achieve liquidity. Therefore, such possible complications are an additional reason venture capitalists prefer not to invest in LLCs.

Tax Considerations for Investors   The most advantageous tax treatment available to venture capitalists for gains realized from liquidity events—mergers, acquisitions, and IPOs—is that afforded by Section 1202 of the Internal Revenue Code. Under Section 1202, noncorporate taxpayers are permitted to exclude 50 percent of the gain from the sale or exchange of "qualified small business stock," if such taxpayers have held their stock for more than five years. Qualified small business stock is generally defined under Section 1202 as stock acquired directly from an issuing corporation after August 10, 1993, if the issuer, among other things, (1) is a domestic C corporation and (2) has aggregate gross assets of no more than $50 million at all times prior to and immediately after the issuance of the stock. Section 1202 effectively reduces the normal long-term capital gains rate of 20 percent to 14 percent for venture capitalists. This results in a tax savings of 6 percent on their gain from liquidity events. Section 1202 is phased out when such gains exceed $10 million (or 10 times their basis in the stock), but such savings can still be significant. Additionally, Section 1045 of the Internal Revenue Code allows venture capitalists to continuously defer gains from the sale or exchange of qualified small business stock that would otherwise be taxable by reinvesting (within a certain period of time) the proceeds in new companies meeting the requirements of the section. The section also allows taxpayers to tack holding periods—to add together all holding periods (initial investment holding periods plus any rolled-over investment holding periods) when attempting to meet Section 1202's five-year holding period requirement. These tax benefits are, however, only available to equity holders in C corporations, not to equity holders in LLCs.

Another tax benefit available only to equity holders in corporations is that of the deferral of the recognition of gain resulting from certain mergers and acquisitions, where such equity holders exchange their shares in one corporation for that of another. Transactions where deferral treatment is obtained are called "tax-free reorganizations." In a tax-free reorganization, neither the acquiring corporation, the target corporation, nor the shareholders of either recognize gain as a result of the merger or acquisition. Tax-free reorganizations can offer another valuable tax deferral opportunity to venture capitalists, but not if their portfolio companies have organized as LLCs. Furthermore, the Internal Revenue Code mandates that such companies may not simply convert into a corporate form right before a merger or acquisition to attain eligibility. Such conversions would have to be accomplished significantly before (and not in contemplation of) the transactions intended to be considered tax-free reorganizations.

Tax Considerations for Companies Another benefit for venture capitalists is that venture-backed companies organized as corporations can achieve attractive tax advantages. First of all, venture-backed corporations typically find it considerably less difficult to compensate and reward their employees than do venture-backed LLCs. Steel explains why this is true:

> *Because LLCs are governed largely by partnership tax rules, traditional corporate employment contracts and stock options have to be structured and drafted in a more complex fashion to achieve roughly the same business results for a venture-stage LLC and its employees. Even then, some of the tax effects that can be achieved in a corporate setting may not be available at all with an LLC. For example, the significant tax advantages afforded by granting "incentive stock options" to employees of a venture-stage corporation are not available to an LLC and its employees. As a result, venture-stage LLCs may find themselves at a competitive disadvantage in attempting to hire key employees without being able to offer the most tax-advantageous form of options.*[4]

The last thing most venture capitalists would ever want to do is to back any companies that might be at all hampered in their ability to hire the very best people possible. In fact, venture capitalists commonly agree that companies with the ability to attract the best quality people—management team members, technologists, and other key employees—overwhelmingly have the highest likelihood of success; settling for employees of lesser quality inevitably will greatly diminish a company's chances of success.

Another advantage enjoyed by venture-backed C corporations over venture-backed LLCs is that they are typically more able to conserve their operating capital during their early years of profitability. Before achieving profitability, investors in LLCs are able to use company losses—of which early-stage companies are virtually guaranteed—to reduce their own federal tax liability, due to the pass-though tax treatment given to LLCs and their members. Investors in C corporations are not allowed to take such losses. However, once companies become profitable, C corporations are allowed to use those losses to shelter operating capital. Steel explains:

A C corporation is usually able to offset its prior tax losses against its early taxable income for some period of time, thus sheltering the company's precious cash while it remains in the development stage. By contrast, equity holders in an LLC typically demand distributions of cash to enable them to pay taxes on their allocated portions of the LLC's taxable income. Overall, during the first few years of profitability, when venture-stage companies typically wish to reinvest as much of their earnings as possible into their continued expansion, they are normally able to conserve considerably more operating capital if they are organized as C corporations rather than as LLCs.[5]

Capital conservation is a serious issue for venture capitalists. The more their portfolio companies conserve their capital, the less danger they will face of finding themselves not yet profitable and having to shut down because they are unable to raise additional money. Also, the more they are able to conserve capital, the less money those companies will need to raise in future rounds of financing—and, therefore, the less dilution their venture capital backers will have to face with regard to their equity holdings. Dilution is an unpopular concept among venture capitalists. In fact, the venture capitalists at Sequoia Capital call it their "greatest enemy."[6] So, venture capitalists typically favor anything that protects them, even slightly, from dilution. (The concept of dilution is discussed in greater detail later in this chapter.)

State of Incorporation

Assuming the company is organized as a C corporation, in what state did it incorporate?

Most first-time entrepreneurs simply organize their companies in their home states, and there are sometimes real benefits to doing so; ordinarily, it minimizes the expenses associated with incorporation, corporate maintenance, and taxes. Certain states, however, are viewed by venture capitalists as more attractive for initial incorporation (e.g., Delaware) even when the particular companies are actually headquartered in other states. The reason behind this preference is that most of the laws governing corporations exist at the state level, and as a result they vary (sometimes substantially) across the different states. The bodies of law governing corporations in Delaware— both case law and statutory law—are much more substantial and much more stable that those in other states, and the legal processes in that state are more streamlined. According to Joseph W. Bartlett, partner of the law firm of Morrison & Foerster:

> [T]he Delaware corporate statute is well drafted and contains few of the anomalies one finds, on occasion, in the general corporation laws of certain other states. Moreover, the Delaware state secretary's office is well staffed and Delaware bureaucrats process papers at a high rate of speed. It is often frustrating to attempt to merge two New York corporations because the personnel in the secretary of state's office get around to clearing the paperwork only in their sweet time. Further, Delaware maintains a separate court system—the Court of Chancery—to adjudicate (without the nuisance, for corporate practitioners anyway, of jury trials) issues involving the structure and governance of domestic corporations. Moreover, a modern statute such as Delaware's is generally per-

missive; the glitches which can frustrate counsel attempting to close on a financing have been ironed out.[7]

Furthermore, venture capitalists general prefer to invest in companies that have incorporated in states whose laws are generally known to lawyers practicing in other states. Doing so facilitates transactions that are important to venture capitalists. Bartlett explains:

> [L]aw firms around the country are willing to give opinions on matters involving Delaware law because of the general familiarity on the corporate bar with the Delaware statute and the cases interpreting it. The ability of counsel to opine on an issue is no trivial matter. Without the requisite opinion of counsel, no public stock offering or merger will go forward. Loan agreements routinely require comfort from the company's counsel in the form of opinions. Incorporating in Delaware gives the founder [and the venture capitalists that back the founder] assurances that counsel will be able to render and/or appraise the necessary opinions to underwriters, lenders, merger partners, and others to enable business aims to be accomplished.[8]

For these reasons, many venture capitalists prefer to invest in C corporations organized in Delaware. This is not to say that they do not invest in C corporations organized in other states, such as California. In fact, many early-stage venture-backed companies have been (and continually are) organized in California. Such companies just plan to convert to Delaware C corporations when and if they do their IPOs.

Organizational Documents and Governmental Filings

Are the company's organizational documents and related governmental filings complete, correct, and current?

Venture capitalists are usually wary about walking into situations that are legally problematic when they become involved with early-stage companies. To avoid such occurrences, most build into their due diligence review a routine examination of several items, often accomplished with the assistance of legal counsel. First, they typically require an inspection of companies' organizational documents—certificates of incorporation, charters, by-laws, minutes of board meetings, minutes of shareholders meetings, and written consents—to make sure that they are complete, correct, and current. They do this to make sure that the companies have been properly organized and properly maintained. Venture capitalists also prefer strongly to see that companies have been organized for the specific purposes stated in their current business plans and that there is nothing abnormal about their past histories since organization. Jonathan Cole and Albert Sokol explain:

> *[The] legal entity to be used as the vehicle for the investment and the conduct of the business should have no unusual prior history. For example, the company should not have been engaged in a prior business that was closed or sold. These situations present too many opportunities for unknown risks or unasserted claims. In most cases, the equity interests should be held by the entrepreneur and the key management team and a small group of people who have made investments in the company to support the early development of the business described in the business plan.[9]*

Additionally, regarding equity holdings, venture capitalists also generally require an inspection of "[a]ll prior issuances of equity interests (including not only common or preferred, but also options or warrants to acquire stock, or if applicable, partnership interests or limited liability company interests)" to make sure they are properly documented and in compliance with applicable securities laws, according to Cole and Sokol.[10] Lastly, it is common for venture capitalists to also require a review of all prior tax returns and other tax filings, as well as any other required regulatory filings, permits, licenses, and/or certificates to ensure that they are also accurate, complete, and up-to-date. Researching each of these issues is usually a fairly simple task, especially for lawyers who perform such due diligence on a regular basis, but it is also a critical task for venture capitalists to avoid unnecessary legal difficulties.

Litigation

Is the company involved in any litigation of a material nature?

Another situation that venture capitalists want to avoid is any already existing legal difficulties. They even tend to be wary when legal difficulties are only a possibility. The reason for their unease is that litigation of a material nature is nearly always damaging, if not fatal, to early-stage companies. Serious litigation is disruptive, usually necessitates significant commitments of time and energy by senior officers, and is extremely expensive. Young companies typically need to move quickly to execute their business plans and gain market share, but are at the same time characterized by a general lack of resources—most importantly human and monetary resources—to do so. Early-stage companies cannot afford to waste their precious resources on anything that distracts them from executing their business plans. Companies whose resources are devoured by the high costs of litigation greatly diminish their chances of success. Precisely for that reason, venture capitalists will generally think twice about backing companies with legal problems. In fact, according to Frederick Lipman, professor of venture capital law at the University of Pennsylvania Law School and the Wharton School, litigation—existing or potential—is very often simply a "deal killer" for venture capitalists.[11]

INTELLECTUAL PROPERTY PROTECTION

General

What are the company's intellectual property assets and how important are such assets to the success of the company?

Intellectual property is generally defined as a commercially valuable product of human intellect that can be protected by such legal mechanisms as patents, copyrights, trademarks, and trade secret rights. Venture capitalists tend to pay particular attention to the intellectual property held by the companies they consider for investment. According to David J. Byer, partner of the law firm of Testa, Hurwitz & Thibeault, as venture capitalists "attempt to analyze the potential value of a start-up company, an intellectual property due diligence investigation . . . should play a critical role in the analysis."[12] It should play a critical role because often much of an early-stage company's value is embodied in the intellectual property developed by its founders. This is especially true of technology companies. Therefore, only by including a thorough investigation of companies' intellectual property assets (and the measures taken to protect them) can venture capitalists fully understand the upside potential of those companies.

Upside potential is a function of the ability to offer something valuable to a market combined with the ability to keep others from impinging on that former ability. It is generally through the development of some intellectual property that companies are able to offer something valuable and through several legal mechanisms—patent protection, copyright protection, and trade secret protection—that they keep others from doing so in exactly the same manner. Therefore, venture capitalists seek to understand precisely what companies consider their intellectual property assets and how important those assets will be to the success of the companies. They then typically seek to estimate how successful they will be in protecting that intellectual property. Additionally, venture capitalists endeavor to judge the potential legal problems that those companies might face with such protection efforts. Protection of intellectual property is an area of the law fraught with complexities and potential problems, and (as stated earlier) the last thing venture capitalists desire is that their investment become jeopardized by costly litigation. Therefore, venture capitalists generally consider the costs of intellectual property due diligence, even very thorough due diligence accomplished with the assistance of legal counsel, much less costly than the potential costs of overlooking such matters.

Intellectual Property Competence

Has the company gained a sufficient understanding of its intellectual property positions and its intellectual property potential?

Most venture capitalists feel much more comfortable investing in companies that have worked hard to understand completely the strengths and weaknesses of their intellectual property positions, and have formulated solid plans for fully exploiting the strengths and shoring up the weaknesses. Companies that fail to achieve such an understanding and fail to formulate such plans increase their risk of failure—either by missing opportunities for creating additional competitive advantages or by unnecessarily opening themselves up to the possibility of damaging and disruptive litigation. Early-stage companies universally require the assistance of top-quality intellectual property counsel to avoid such risks. Therefore, venture capitalists prefer strongly that companies have secured such counsel and have worked extensively with them.

Support for the Development of Intellectual Property Assets

Did the company receive support from governmental organizations, industry organizations, or nonprofit organizations in the development of its intellectual property?

Savvy venture capitalists quickly learn if any third parties have rights to a company's intellectual property, and what possible restrictions exist, if any, on the company's use of that property. Some potential sources of such third-party rights and restrictions are governmental and nonprofit organizations (e.g., the Defense Advanced Research Project Agency [DARPA], the National Science foundation, and SRI International), and research universities (e.g., Massachusetts Institute of Technology, California Institute of Technology, and the University of California). It is not entirely uncommon for entrepreneurs to receive support from such entities for the development of their technology, usually in the form of grants or awards for specific research. Sponsoring entities sometimes require, however, that the commercial rights to any intellectual property arising out of the sponsored research be licensed or assigned to the sponsor, or impose "dedicate to the public" requirements, whereby no intellectual property protection may be sought by the researcher for any intellectual property developed. When sponsors require that intellectual property be assigned to them, however, they often allow entrepreneurs to license back the rights to the intellectual property in return for royalty payments or equity in resulting companies, or allow them to acquire the

intellectual property outright. Regardless of how such arrangements are actually structured, venture capitalists tend to be quick to
spot them in their due diligence investigations, as they can cause
real difficulties for investors and for the companies themselves, and
usually seek to understand them fully before committing funds.
Venture capitalists generally dislike arrangements where sponsors
require cash payments. Such payments drain precious capital out of
early-stage companies when capital is particularly precious. Venture capitalists prefer that sponsors take equity, instead. However,
they do not like to see that equity grants that are too large, as they
can cause problems with companies' capital structures. According
to Michael Lytton, attorney with the law firm of Palmer & Dodge,
companies usually grant sponsors "a minority interest, typically
ranging from a few percent to no more than 20 percent."[13] And,
he says, "Most grants of equity in early-stage companies are in the
5 percent range."[14]

"Spun-Out" Intellectual Property Assets

*Were any of the company's intellectual property assets "spun-out" of
another company?*

It is increasingly common for established companies to "spin-out"
some of their intellectual property assets (along with some of the employees who developed them or were responsible for them) into new
start-up companies. Jeffry Timmons explains that many companies
are started this way, "with products or services, or both, based on
technology and ideas developed by entrepreneurs while they were
employed by others."[15] Spin-outs typically occur when employees of
existing companies have developed valuable intellectual property assets that do not quite fit into their employers' existing product lines
or marketing plans, or do not represent sufficiently large markets for
such companies. When that occurs, established companies still seek
to extract value from the developed intellectual property assets, but
they do so through licensing them, selling them outright, or exchang-
ing them for equity in new companies started specifically to exploit
the market opportunities created by the intellectual property. Many
companies have their origins in such arrangements and most venture

capitalists are familiar with them. The questions they typically ask of them, though, revolve around the exact terms of the arrangements and whether there are any issues that might adversely affect the companies or their potential investments in them such as weak licenses or problematic equity structures. (Intellectual property licenses are discussed in more detail later.)

Patents

Are any of the company's intellectual property assets protected by U.S. patents?

Patent protection is often a source of significant competitive advantage for early-stage companies, and is therefore an extremely important topic for the venture capitalists considering investments in them. Patents afford their owners (or licensees of the owners) the right to exclude all others from making, using, selling, offering for sale, or importing the claimed subject matter for a period of 20 years from the patent filing date. In effect, they allow companies to create 20-year monopolies. They can also cover a wide range of subject matter. U.S. patent law recognizes any new and useful process, machine, manufacture, or composition of matter, or any new and useful improvement thereof, as patentable subject matter. The following are some examples of patentable subject matter relevant to early-stage companies: electronic hardware, electronic devices, computer systems, computer software and algorithms, mechanical devices, instruments, compounds, chemical formulas, medicines and drugs, and business methods. Inventions must simply be novel, useful, and nonobvious to one of ordinary skill in the field of the invention.

Because patents are generally considered the strongest form of intellectual property protection available, they can be valuable and potent weapons in the marketplace. Companies can use them to lock competitors—even those that are larger and better financed—out of attractive markets and with them gain competitive isolation. Such competitive isolation is crucial to enabling the explosive growth sought by venture capitalists. Alternatively, and no less importantly, patents can be used to obtain substantial licensing revenues, and in some cases can be the central components of successful business

models based primarily on licensing technology. Strong patent portfolios can also make companies attractive acquisition candidates, regardless of the viability of their business plans and their potential for
profitability.

Obtaining patents, however, is a time-consuming and expensive
process. As a result, cash-strapped start-ups sometimes seek patent
protection fairly sparingly. Venture capitalists doing intellectual
property due diligence, therefore, often seek to make sure that companies have obtained sufficient patent protection for all things that
can and should be patented.

Patent Value

If the company does hold patents, are they valuable to the company?

Not all patents offer equal value. Just because a company boasts that
it has obtained patent protection, it does not necessarily follow that
the company's patents actually add value to that company. David
Byer explains:

> [I]f one of the company's patents covers obsolete technology, or
> technology different from the company's planned products, then
> its value to the company may be minimal. Similarly, if the com-
> pany has a patent relating to a specific method of making a prod-
> uct, but there are many economically feasible ways of making the
> product without infringing the patent, then the patent may have
> little value, even if the company intends to employ that method.[16]

Therefore, during their due diligence, venture capitalists generally
delve deeply into whether patents held in fact add value to the companies that hold them by materially advancing those companies'
business plans. Investigating this issue involves gaining full understanding of the companies—their patents, their technologies, their
business plans—and all their competitors and each of their competing technologies.

Another issue central to investigations of patent value is that of
"blocking patents." It arises because patents do not actually afford
their owners the right to make, use, sell, offer to sell, or import a

patented invention. Instead, they only afford their owners the right to prevent others from doing the same. This characteristic of patents can cause problems when an invention covered by one patent incorporates and requires the use of someone else's patented invention. Even though the holder of the first patent for an invention can keep anyone from commercializing it, the holder can't commercialize it either unless he or she reaches a licensing agreement with the owner of the second patent or can design around the patent. The second patent in this example is called a "blocking patent," because its owner can block the owner of the first patent from commercializing that invention. The presence of a blocking patent is a crucial piece of information for venture capitalists, because it can significantly diminish the value of an otherwise valuable patent. It can also open a company up to ruinous litigation if the blocking patent is not discovered soon enough. Not surprisingly, venture capitalists are on careful lookout for them during due diligence. When venture capitalists spot blocking patents, they immediately examine the licensing arrangements companies have made with the holders of the patents. (Licensing of intellectual property is discussed in more detail in a later subsection.)

Patent Integrity

If the company holds patents, do they have sufficient legal integrity?

Those venture capitalists interested in performing thorough intellectual property due diligence actually go beyond simply gauging the value of companies' patents and also seek to determine their legal integrity. The issue of legal integrity is inextricably connected with that of value because problems regarding legal integrity can significantly (and often completely) erode the value of a given patent. Not surprisingly, therefore, the legal integrity of patents is also an issue of considerable importance for venture capitalists. David Byer provides some guidance as to how they typically go about investigating legal integrity:

> [A]t a minimum, each IP due diligence investigation should include an examination of the recorded assignments (and any other interests) relating to each patent or patent application in

the company's portfolio to determine whether the company has clear chain of title. In addition to verifying the chain of title for an issued patent, it may be advisable to investigate other aspects of its status. For example, fees must regularly be paid to "maintain" issued patents, and, if the proper maintenance fees have not been paid, or if other formalities have not been followed, patents may lapse and become unenforceable. In addition, issued patents may be invalidated or declared unenforceable, wholly or in part, as a result of court decisions. Alternatively, issued patents may be withdrawn or disclaimed, or may be narrowed or invalidated during "re-issue" or "re-examination" proceedings before the PTO.[17]

Patent integrity is generally researched by venture capitalists (and/or their lawyers) through inquiries to the United States Patent & Trademark Office (PTO) and the PTO's database, or though such other databases as the Delphion Intellectual Property Network.

Copyrights

Are any of the company's intellectual property assets protected by copyright?

Though less commonly utilized by venture-backed companies than other types of intellectual property protection, copyright protection is also sometimes employed to gain competitive advantage. For companies that choose to use them, copyrights can offer fairly valuable protection, allowing them to have exclusive control over certain exploitations of such things as computer programs (including both source code and object code), databases, users' manuals, design documentation, and advertisements. Copyrights protect original works of authorship. A copyright is actually a bundle of rights, which includes the sole and exclusive privilege to reproduce, distribute, and sell the copyrighted material. Others may copy the ideas underlying the copyrighted works, but may not copy the actual forms of expression created by their authors. Most important to venture-backed companies, obviously, is that the specific expression of a software program is protectable through the mechanism of copyright. Copyright protection has traditionally been the most common method of protecting software. This has become less true though as software patents are becoming the method of choice for protecting original software programs. The reason for this shift is that copyrights only protect works in their tangible fixed form. They do not protect the concepts and ideas underlying the works. Therefore, copyright law protects best against the literal copying of software code; protecting ideas, concepts, and other elements from nonliteral copying must be accomplished through patent protection. Nevertheless, copyrights can still be important to early-stage companies if and when literal copying presents a threat. For example, a copyright can be robust protection against a situation where a programmer is incorporating code into the software product of a new company that he or she wrote while still employed by a former company. Therefore, when appropriate, venture capitalists will typically examine companies' copyrights with some level of interest.

Copyright Value

If the company does hold copyrights, are they valuable to the company?

Just as all patents do not have equal value, neither do all copyrights. Merely because a company possesses copyright protection, it does not necessarily follow that the company's copyrights actually contribute value to the company. For example, if a copyright were to cover a specific software product, but that product were to fall outside a particular company's planned product offering and business plan, then its value to the company would be minimal. Or, alternatively, if a copyright were to cover a specific expression of code that had become obsolete, then the value to the company would be minimal as well. Therefore, venture capitalists calculate the value of copyrights against the same standard that they use to determine the value of patents: Will companies' copyrights materially advance the companies' business plans?

Copyright Integrity

If the company does hold copyrights, do they have sufficient legal integrity?

The question of copyright integrity is actually a subpart of the question of copyright value because, all other things being equal, a copyright with questionable legal integrity will be relatively less valuable to its holder than one with solid legal integrity. Therefore, legal integrity is also an important issue for venture capitalists. The first step they (or their intellectual property lawyers who do their intellectual property due diligence) explore is whether companies' copyrights have sufficient legal integrity to verify legal ownership. They accomplish such verification through a review of all copyright registrations filed with the United States Copyright Office and of all licenses and/or agreements regarding transfer of ownership from the actual authors of the particular works. Disputes over copyright ownership can arise in the venture capital context where early-stage companies have used consultants to write software code as a means for controlling costs. David Byer explains:

> *If the author worked for the company while the work was created and created the work within the scope of . . . employment, absent a written agreement to the contrary, the company owns the copyright. But, if an outside consultant was employed to create all or part of the work, a review of the consulting agreement is necessary to determine who owns the copyright. If the consulting agreement does not include an assignment of copyright in the work created by the consultant, the consultant likely will be deemed the owner or joint owner of the work in question. If the work is deemed to be a work of joint-ownership, the company will typically be required to give an accounting of profits to the joint owner.*[18]

Investigations into copyright integrity, just as with investigations into patent integrity, can be significant to venture capitalists, especially if the specific intellectual property covered by copyright figures largely into the business plans of the particular companies. As mentioned, however, it is relatively more rare for venture-backed companies to use copyright mechanisms to protect their key intellectual property than it is for the same companies to use other intellectual property mechanisms such as patents or the trade secret laws.

Trade Secrets

Are any of the company's intellectual property assets protected by the trade secret laws?

A trade secret is generally defined as information that derives economic value from not being generally known to others who can obtain economic value from its disclosure or use. Obviously, therefore, the breadth of subject matter able to be protected by companies under the trade secret laws is wider than that able to be protected by other sources of intellectual property protection. Generally, the trade secret laws cover formulas, compounds, processes, plans, devices, tools, mechanisms, software program code, compilations of information, business plans and strategies, contact information, and customer lists, but they can cover other types of information as well. Companies possessing trade secrets are able to restrict employees and business partners from revealing them and can prevent competitors from using any secrets that have been misappropriated. Furthermore, in contrast to patents and copyrights, which terminate after a specified period, trade secrets can endure indefinitely, if the proper steps are taken to maintain their secrecy and if they do actually remain secret. Trade secrets can also be extinguished when and if the information can be recreated or legitimately obtained such as through reverse engineering.

The protection afforded by the trade secret laws is often of unique and critical importance to venture capitalists and to the early-stage companies in which they invest. According to Byer, such companies "may be financially ill-equipped to obtain patent protection and engage in expensive patent litigation, but . . . may still find it cost-effective to police and enforce . . . trade secrets."[19] Therefore, trade secrets are often the most valuable assets early-stage venture-backed companies own. Not surprisingly, venture capitalists tend to be acutely interested in the subject matter of companies' trade secrets during their due diligence. What is also not surprising, however, is

that entrepreneurs tend to be reticent about revealing their trade secrets to *anyone,* even potential investors. To break this impasse, venture capitalists and companies usually strike agreements whereby the
companies agree to reveal only what is absolutely necessary for due
diligence purposes (this is often called "opening the kimono" among
venture capitalists) and the venture capitalists agree in return to sign
nondisclosure agreements (NDAs), agreeing to keep all information
revealed during due diligence confidential. Some venture capitalists,
however, refuse to sign NDAs. Franklin "Pitch" Johnson and his colleagues at Asset Management Company offer the following guidance
to entrepreneurs:

> *We do not sign Non-Disclosure Agreements (NDAs). We receive
> so many plans each week, that if we signed every NDA request,
> we would quickly be swamped with legal documents. Our repu-
> tation depends on our professionalism and our ability to main-
> tain the trust of the entrepreneurs with whom we work. We will
> take care to keep all of your material confidential.*[20]

Therefore, in some situations entrepreneurs, when opening their ki-
monos, must rely simply on the word and reputation of venture capitalists. On the other hand, some venture capitalists will sign NDAs
when deep into due diligence with companies in which they are very
likely to invest.

Trade Secret Value

*If the company does have trade secrets, are they valuable to the
company?*

Assessing the value of companies' trade secrets is often one of the most
important parts of the entire due diligence process for venture capitalists. The process is virtually the same one used to assess patent value
and copyright value. It involves gaining a full understanding of companies' business plans and as full an understanding as is possible of
companies' trade secrets, and then asking whether the trade secrets
will materially advance the companies' business plans.

Trade Secret Structural Protections

Are structural protections in place to protect the company's trade secrets?

Trade secrets are only afforded legal protection if they are indeed "secrets" of the companies that possess them, and only if those companies have taken sufficient steps to keep the information secret. Some venture capitalists, therefore, make it a part of their routine legal due diligence to ensure that any information claimed by a company to be covered by the trade secret laws will indeed be so covered. Such assurance is generally obtained by identifying trade secrets and evaluating the steps taken by the company to guard their secrecy. Such efforts should, at a minimum, include the following 11 steps:

1. Identifying the company's trade secrets precisely and maintaining detailed and current records of their nature and scope.
2. Allowing access to the company's trade secrets only to those for whom access is absolutely necessary.
3. Ensuring that all employees for whom access to the company's trade secrets is absolutely necessary have signed employment agreements acknowledging their obligation to keep trade secrets confidential.
4. Keeping employees for whom access to the company's trade secrets is absolutely necessary continually aware of their obligation to keep trade secrets confidential.
5. Writing a trade secret protection policy and circulating that policy to all employees on a regular basis.
6. Requiring all business partners, investors, and any other parties for whom access to the company's trade secrets is absolutely necessary, to sign NDAs or confidentiality agreements.
7. Marking all documents containing trade secrets as "trade secret" or "confidential."
8. Monitoring and logging access to documents, areas, filing cabinets, computer files, and databases that contain trade secrets.
9. Conducting exit interviews with departing employees to ensure that no trade secrets are taken, to remind them of their trade secret obligations, and to determine future plans, including future employers or start-up plans.

10. Bringing suit for trade secret misappropriation and promptly requesting injunctive relief, when appropriate.
11. Avoiding disclosure of trade secrets through any of the following: (a) selling products that disclose trade secrets or allow for reverse engineering; (b) publishing and/or distributing technical literature, service manuals, professional articles, press releases, marketing information, or other material that discloses trade secrets; (c) discussing trade secrets with professional colleagues who have not signed NDAs; (d) displaying trade secrets at trade shows; (e) allowing issued patents to disclose trade secrets; (f) leaving nonshredded documents containing trade secrets in garbage cans; (g) disclosing trade secrets in court filings and/or court records, without sealing them; (h) disclosing trade secrets in governmental filings such as filings with the Securities and Exchange Commission.

Intellectual Property Licenses

Is the company licensing intellectual property from another company or licensing technology to another company?

An intellectual property license is an agreement between two parties though which the first party, the "licensor," allows the second party, the "licensee," to make some use of the licensor's intellectual property, which is not otherwise available to the licensee due to patent, copyright, or trade secret protection. Licenses play a key role in the operation of venture-backed companies. Nearly every venture-backed company relies on some sort of licensing to achieve its business plan. Some of them license manufacturing processes from third-party companies to produce their products more efficiently. Others license their own technology to third-party companies to generate revenue. Still others cross-license their intellectual property with competing companies to avoid costly and distracting litigation, or with partners to enable codevelopment efforts. Intellectual property licenses are therefore of great significance to the venture capitalists who back such companies, and they usually examine them carefully during their due diligence.

Intellectual Property License Value

If the company is a licensor or a licensee of technology, are its licenses valuable?

The process used by venture capitalists to calculate the value of intellectual property licenses does not differ much from the process used to calculate the value of any other intellectual property assets, such as patents, copyrights, and trade secrets. Intellectual property licenses typically confer exactly the same rights as would be given to an initial owner of such assets. Therefore, the overriding issue is still whether the licenses materially advance companies' business plans. This typically involves examining the license agreements to understand thoroughly how they relate to companies' business plans and, therefore, how they actually contribute value to the companies.

Some additional issues are associated specifically with licenses, however; and venture capitalists and their counsel examine them to completely round out their due diligence on license value. The most obvious one is whether the licenses companies hold are exclusive or nonexclusive. A license is exclusive if the licensee is the only one to whom the granted rights may be assigned. In contrast, a nonexclusive license is one in which the rights granted may be offered to other licensees, as well. If a particular company is a licensor of technology, venture capitalists generally prefer—all things being equal—that it hold nonexclusive licenses. That way the company can license the underlying technology to multiple companies and, thereby generate revenue from multiple sources. Alternatively, if the company is a licensee of technology, then venture capitalists typically prefer for the company to have secured exclusive licenses. The reason is that exclusive licenses can often be great competitive advantages over companies not able to obtain access to the same technologies.

The next issue has to do with the actual technology underlying the licenses. When the company under due diligence scrutiny is a licensor of technology, venture capitalists delve into the question of whether the company has, as David Byer explains, "out-licensed technology in a way that may interfere with its business plan (e.g., by creating a future competitor or by giving away a future market)."[21] Though entrepreneurs, as a group, are fairly cautious with key technologies and tend to guard them judiciously, such mistakes are not unheard of. On the other side, when the company under scrutiny is a licensee of technology, venture capitalists explore whether the company has obtained sufficient rights to use the technology as is necessary according to its business plan, that is, whether the license has sufficient scope. A license is essentially just a bundle of rights and venture capitalists simply seek to make sure that companies' license agreements afford them enough rights to fully use the technologies as they desire.

The last significant issue has to do with the amount paid (or to be paid) for the license. Revenue generation is typically the primary motivation for licensors to enter into license agreements. Much time, effort, and money may go into the development of technologies underlying licenses, and licensing rights to such technologies is often used to extract value from such expenditures. License payments can be structured many ways; for example, with fees paid completely up front or, alternatively, with periodic royalty payments, which can be based on time or volume. Regardless of the payment structure, the question of revenue (or cost, depending on what side of the license the particular company falls) is important for due diligence purposes. When a particular company is a licensor, venture capitalists examine the terms of the license agreement to ensure that revenue will be generated from the license at a level sufficient to meet the goals set out in the company's business plan. When the company is a licensee, venture capitalists seek to make sure it has not paid too much for a particular license in light of the license's relative value to the company and whether cost of the license is at a level that will still allow the company's business models to function properly.

Intellectual Property Litigation

Is the company involved in or vulnerable to any intellectual property litigation of a material nature?

Early-stage venture-backed companies are particularly vulnerable to legal liability and the dangers of litigation in the area of intellectual property. The reason for this vulnerability is that very often such companies are led by management team members and technologists who have recently exited from competing firms. Such companies run the risk, therefore, of becoming entangled in expensive and disruptive litigation initiated by competitors over trade secret misappropriation, unfair competition, violation of invention assignment agreements, and violation of noncompetition agreements. Whereas individuals are entirely free to leave their employment to start or join a competing company, they are not free to use confidential information and/or trade secrets of their former company, or violate agreements with their former employer, to benefit their new one. Therefore, venture capitalists are fairly vigilant on this issue. Although even the best planning cannot prevent litigation completely, companies can take three steps to avoid getting involved with most legal disputes, and venture capitalists like to see that companies are taking those steps: (1) making sure that no employees have taken trade secrets or confidential information from their former employer; (2) making sure that no employees are violating invention assignment agreements with former employers, for example, by using software code copyrighted by a former employer in software programs written for a new employer; (3) making sure that no employees are violating noncompetition agreements.

Invention Assignment Agreement

Are all of the company's founders and employees covered by invention assignment agreements?

Intellectual property *ownership* is a crucial issue for venture capitalists. Most make it a routine part of their due diligence to dig deeply into this issue. It is not entirely uncommon for key employees to leave their employment after their companies have secured venture funding, either because they have to be replaced or because they leave on their own accord, and venture capitalists have a strong interest in minimizing the risk that any intellectual property might leave with them. Therefore, venture capitalists generally make sure, prior to their investment, that all material intellectual property is owned outright by companies, and not by any individuals associated with such companies. They want to avoid, at all cost, situations where individuals have claims to key intellectual property. There is just too much risk that companies might be left with diminished abilities (or no abilities at all) to commercialize their products.

Sometimes, especially when key intellectual property has been developed by company founders, companies initially have arrangements whereby they simply license their intellectual property from their employees. Venture capitalists take a dim view of these arrangements. Jonathan Cole and Albert Sokol explain, "Structures that anticipate that the founder or entrepreneur or other related party will retain the rights to the basic patents or other intellectual property under a license and royalty arrangement are not favored by the VC community and will often lead to an investment rejection."[22]

Therefore, venture capitalists usually require that full and proper assignments have been made of all material intellectual property assets to companies, even when that intellectual property was developed by company founders, before they will commit funds. Furthermore, they generally also require that all employees, existing and new, are covered by comprehensive invention assignment agreements, whereby any intellectual property developed in the future is immediately and automatically assigned to the companies. These actions ensure that venture capitalists never find themselves in situations where their portfolio companies face the risk of losing key technology or of being hit with costly litigation against claims by employees or consultants to such technology.

Noncompetition Agreements

Are the company's key employees covered by noncompetition agreements?

The risk that a key employee might leave to join a direct competitor is a serious one for early-stage companies. "The flight of the scientific brains of the company into the arms of a competitor can be a death sentence," says Joseph Bartlett.[23] In addition to losing a valuable member of the start-up team (including that employee's knowledge, experience, and ability), companies also risk losing valuable trade secrets. A common way for trade secrets to be misappropriated is for them to travel with individuals leaving one company for a competitor. Therefore, early-stage companies, and the venture capitalists that back them, often ask that noncompetition agreements be executed by any employees who are key to the success of the companies—usually the management team and important technologists. Noncompetition agreements can be structured many different ways, but generally restrict employees from entering into direct competition with their former employers for a reasonable period of time. The courts of some jurisdictions and the legislatures of some states have, however, deemed noncompetition agreements unenforceable (most notably, California); they generally view them as overly burdensome on employees and their ability to make a living in their fields and against public policy due to their anticompetitive nature. Nevertheless, when available, venture capitalists by and large strongly prefer the use of such agreements because they offer strong protection to the companies and their investments in them.

OTHER POTENTIAL PRETRANSACTION ISSUES

Existing Approval Rights

Do any existing investors in the company, those from prior rounds of financing, hold "approval" rights?

Often, as a part of earlier rounds of financing, companies will have granted investors various forms of *approval rights*. These rights afford investors who hold them veto power over certain actions of boards of directors: mergers, acquisitions, or consolidations involving changes of control; liquidations; dispositions of substantial assets; amendments to certificates of incorporation, charters, or bylaws; payments of dividends, distributions, redemptions; dilutive issuances of stock; issuances of additional preferred equity; incurrences of debt over certain levels; and other similar fundamental changes. Veto rights can be structured in several ways. Investors can be granted shareholder voting rights so that they can essentially block certain actions of boards of directors. For example, seed-round equity investors may demand that a company obtain approvals for certain actions from a majority or supermajority of the holders of the class or series of preferred stock sold in the seed round. Alternatively, seed investors may insist that companies agree to a sequence of negative or restrictive covenants, in which the companies agree to obtain approvals from specific investors (or a specific percentage of investors) before the companies' boards of directors may take certain actions.

Venture capitalists themselves use these mechanisms liberally for their own protection, but generally object to them when they have been granted to prior investors. The reason is that investors who have been granted such rights can inhibit the ability of boards to manage and to act in the best interests of their companies (and, thus, in the interests of the newly invested venture capitalists). Investors holding approval rights often have the power to seriously inhibit companies' ability to raise additional capital, if they are for some reason so inclined. Few investors are ever so inclined, but just the possibility that some prior investor or group of investors may inhibit a particular transaction is something venture capitalists find objectionable. When any such grants have been made, venture capitalists typically require that—prior to their committing any funds—investors waive their approval rights, or agree to their removal from companies' organizational documents. And, they are usually successful in obtaining such waivers, because investors have little interest in holding up significant venture financings, just so that they may retain their approval rights.

Existing Rights of First Refusal

Do any existing investors in the company hold rights of first refusal?

Rights of first refusal are often granted to seed-round investors as well. Such rights require that, when seeking further equity financing, companies must first offer newly issued shares to the holders of such rights. Mark C. White, cofounder and partner of the law firm of White & Lee, warns of the dangers of such rights to investors in later rounds:

> *While granting such a right might be critical to completing an early-stage financing, from the company's standpoint the right of first refusal may delay, complicate, and even prevent a subsequent financing. This would be the case where new investors may*

not participate in a financing as a result of delays, or a reduction in securities available for sale if the right of first refusal is exercised. The problem with rights of first refusal is the barrier they potentially present to raising additional working capital that will permit the company to mature to the point where it is an attractive acquisition or IPO candidate. Most investors who do not wish to participate will waive their rights of first refusal in such financings as probably it will be in their best interests to do so. But other investors may exercise their right, and thereby jeopardize the financing.[24]

Therefore, venture capitalists typically request that these terms, and any other unusual provisions granting special rights to prior investors, also be waived or completely removed from companies' organizational documents.

Existing Price-Based Antidilution Rights

Do any existing investors in the company hold price-based antidilution rights?

Price-based antidilution rights are also commonly given by companies in early seed financings. These rights come in a few different forms: full ratchet rights, broad-based weighted average rights, and narrow-based weighted average rights. (Each of these forms is discussed in greater detail later in this chapter.) When going into a new deal, venture capitalists generally prefer that existing investors not hold such rights, in any form, though especially the potentially draconian full ratchet. If and when companies are forced to raise capital at prices lower than those of previous rounds (e.g., when companies stumble in executing their business plans or greatly underestimate their capital requirements), the antidilution rights held by existing investors can result in significant dilution for follow-on venture capitalists, management teams, and employees. In fact, it is often the holders of the common stock (management teams and other employees) who suffer the greatest dilution when price-based antidilution rights are exercised. That is something venture capitalists like to avoid, because of its disincentivizing effect. Therefore, even though they use them quite commonly for their own protection, venture capitalists sometimes request that such rights be waived when held by existing investors, or that the provisions be completely removed from organizational documents.

TRANSACTIONAL LEGAL ISSUES

Richard J. Testa, cofounder and senior partner of the law firm of Testa, Hurwitz & Thibeault and counsel to several venture capital firms, provides the following insight into how venture capitalists properly structure venture capital investment transactions in ways to best foster successful business growth and successful investor/company relationships:

> *Venture capital investing involves a long-term commitment of support for a company. As such, the parties involved in negotiating and implementing the investment transaction must bring to the process a sensitivity to the changing and differing objectives and requirements (financial, legal, personal, etc.) of the business, and it principal participants. A key element in the attainment of a successful relationship between a young business enterprise and its venture capital investors is the careful crafting of the legal structure of the investment transaction. The legal documents must foresee the evolution of the enterprise from a development stage start-up to a publicly held company or viable acquisition candidate. Not only do the investment documents represent a charter of the legal rights of the parties spanning the growth cycle of the business, but they also set the tone of the relationship between the management/entrepreneurs and the financial backers of the enterprise, serving as a model for resolution of their often differing interests. [T]here exists no such thing as the perfect model of legal documentation for the investment transaction. Each set of documents needs to be tailored to reflect the unique combination of styles and interests involved.[25]*

Most venture capitalists do indeed tailor the terms of each investment transaction to each particular company; in some cases, they have little choice but to tailor the terms in certain ways. Some terms common to venture capital transactions are virtually ubiquitous, whereas others are available to venture capitalists only in certain situations; for example when their bargaining power is high because there are few or no competitors for the particular deal. Alternatively, such terms may not be available when venture capitalists' bargaining power is low and entrepreneurs' bargaining power is high because a deal is hot and there are several competing investors.

SECURITY STRUCTURE

Security

What is the nature of the security to be used for the investment?

Assuming the C corporate form because it is so overwhelmingly used among venture-backed companies, venture capitalists have been known to utilize both equity and debt securities for their investments. On the equity side, the securities employed over the years have been common stock and preferred stock (and warrants, as well, but these instruments will be dealt with later). On the debt side, the securities used have been notes and debentures. Venture capitalists have often combined these securities, for example, debentures with warrants; convertible notes; preferred stock with warrants; convertible preferred stock. Which of these securities is actually employed (and in what combinations) is of great importance to venture capitalists because each kind has very different economic characteristics, both for investors and for their portfolio companies. Each of the securities is discussed in the following subsections.

Common Stock   Common stock is the basic unit of corporate ownership. It gives holders ownership, but not much else. Holders are generally afforded no rights other than those associated with basic ownership, such as the right to vote on all matters submitted for shareholder vote. None of the special rights important to venture capitalists are typically given to holders of common stock—antidilution protection, registration rights, and dividend preferences. Most importantly, the holders of common stock are given no liquidation preference. The claims of holders of common stock to companies' earnings and assets are subordinated to all other claims: taxes, secured debt, unsecured debt, subordinated debt, and preferred stock. Common stock, therefore, evidences a residual interest in company earnings and assets; when companies are liquidated (or sold in asset sales) the holders of common stock receive whatever is left after all other claims have been satisfied. Common stock is the form of ownership taken by founders, management team recruits, and all other employees. Venture capitalists almost never buy common stock. Professors Edgar Norton and Bernard H. Tenenbaum explain why:

> *An investment in common stock places investors on the same level as the management team and thus will emphasize the partnership relationship between the venture capitalist and entrepreneurial team. [However, c]ommon stock, by placing investors on the same level as the management team, is not attractive as an investment mode if investors have concerns about control of the firm's cash flows and other potential agency problems. Profits or positive cash flow may be appropriated by the management team rather than properly returned to the investors or reinvested to meet the firm's goals.*[26]

The problems that Professors Norton and Tenenbaum point out— primarily, appropriation of profits by management teams—occur when the interests of venture capitalists (owners or partial owners of companies or principals) and entrepreneurs (the management of companies or "agents" of the principals) diverge, and are commonly called *agency* problems. *Agency risk* is the risk borne by venture capitalists that agency problems will occur—that their agents (the management) will not act as their fiduciaries, but rather will act in their own self-interest (to the detriment of the venture capitalists). Such detrimental actions might include misleading venture capitalists about material aspects of their companies during the due diligence phase, appropriating profits though unreasonable management salaries, and/or dilution of venture capitalists' interests through the issuance of unreasonably large amounts of new shares to themselves at prices below the prices paid by venture capitalists (i.e., issuing themselves "cheap stock"). As Norton and Tenenbaum note, when venture capitalists hold common stock, they are not able to control these agency risks effectively. They generally find this unacceptable and use other securities that better align the interests of investors and entrepreneurs.

Probably the most important reason that venture capitalists prefer not to use common stock, however, is that it is important for tax reasons that entrepreneurs and their employees be able to purchase equity at a price that is significantly lower than that paid contemporaneously by venture capitalists for their equity. Robert V. Gunderson, partner and founder of the law firm of Gunderson Dettmer Stough Villeneuve Franklin & Hachigian, explains this concept using a hypothetical company, Hi-Tech Corporation (the "Company"):

> *Critical to the choice of security decision is usually the fact that founders and key employees of the Company have bought, are buying, or will buy Common Stock from the Company at a cheap price. Hi-Tech Corporation is a typical example. Common Stock is still being sold at $0.30 per share while an outside financing is being discussed at a price of $5.00 per share. If Common Stock were to be sold to the investors at a price of $5.00, the tax consequences to the key employees contemporaneously buying Common Stock could be devastating, as they would be forced to choose between recognizing a very large "bargain" immediately for tax purposes by making an election under Section 83(b) of the Internal Revenue Code or risking recognition of an even larger bargain later under Section 83 as their stock vests. As a result, it may be very much in the interest of the founders and key employees that the investors purchase senior securities that can be valued at a price higher than the Company's Common Stock.*[27]

Therefore, venture capitalists prefer to employ securities that will allow them to have a two-class structure and dual pricing, so that entrepreneurs and employees can pay one price for their equity and venture capitalists can pay a relatively higher price for their equity.

Debt Debt, in the venture capital context, is typically a written promise committing a company to pay an investor a specified sum of money on demand or at a fixed or determinable date in the future, with or without interest. Such debt is usually *unsecured,* meaning that it is not backed by collateral and is typically *subordinated,* meaning that is made junior to other forms of debt (secured debt, trade debt, etc.) in terms of liquidation priority, so that companies are not inhibited from obtaining other debt necessary to their operation. Other possible characteristics of venture capital promissory notes are that they may or may not be redeemable and/or convertible, and may or may not specify events of default and contain affirmative and/or negative covenants. Norton and Tenenbaum explain the implications to venture capitalists of employing debt in venture capital transactions:

> *Debt places the investor in the position of lender, not owner. Debt financing may protect the investors' claim on firm assets and cash flow (to protect the investors' downside) to the detriment of the firm's future viability. Given both the high degree of risk prevalent in most venture capital deals and potential for agency problems, debt may be perceived to be an attractive mode of financing by the venture capitalist. [However, i]n the typical venture capital deal, most assets are intangible growth opportunities. Debt . . . robs the growing entrepreneurial firm of precious cash flow, whereas deals involving common and preferred equity issues are typically structured so that dividends are not paid, nor do they accumulate. Additionally, debt financing may (a) preclude additional debt issues in the future and (b) make future equity issues more difficult to sell as debtholders will have a senior claim on firm cash flow and assets. Thus, even an investment structure such as a zero coupon debt may not generally be attractive in a venture capital setting.*[28]

The two professors neglect to mention the two other disadvantages to venture capitalists of using debt. First, without some sort of equity instrument involved (shares of stock into which the debt is convertible or attached warrants), debt-holding venture capitalists cannot participate in their companies' upside potential (equity appreciation) when and if the companies are successful. Without an opportunity to participate in the upside, venture capitalists cannot justify undertaking the risk associated with investing in early-stage companies. Second, debt-holding venture capitalists are generally much less able (than equity holders) to exert influence on the management of portfolio companies, because debt holders do not typically have the right to vote for directors or to vote on other corporate matters. Therefore, debt as an investment vehicle only makes sense to venture capitalists when transactions and relationships are structured such that they are adequately compensated for the risk they undertake by being allowed to participate in companies' upside potential (when the debt is made convertible into equity or when warrants are attached to the debt) and are able to influence management (when voting agreements and/or proxies are used so that they may participate in the election of directors and affirmative and negative covenants are built in as well). But, even then, companies remain hampered in their ability to issue other types of debt, necessary for their operation. Therefore, except in specific situations, the use of debt in venture capital transactions has become rather rare.

One type of debt security that continues to be used in the venture capital context is the *bridge loan*. Bridge loans are short-term debt financings that fund companies' operations until they can arrange more traditional equity-based venture capital financings; they are "bridges" to traditional financings. Bridge loans can usually be pulled together quickly because of the simplicity of their terms; they usually take the form of promissory notes that are convertible into preferred stock. Say Benton and Gunderson, "Notes convertible into Preferred—rather than Common—Stock are most often used in transactions involving venture capital backed companies, as they preserve the two class (Preferred and Common) structure and pricing."[29] Bridge loans are typically given both by seed-stage investors (e.g., seed-stage venture capitalists and angel investors) and by venture capitalists. Venture capitalists sometimes give companies bridge loans to fund their operations pending the closing of a round of financing (e.g., while the venture capitalists complete their due diligence). Seed-stage investors often prefer to use bridge loans because when they do so, the actual pricing of their investment is determined later by the terms negotiated with more traditional venture capitalists (the bridge promissory notes are converted into preferred stock at the price at which those venture capitalists purchase their preferred stock). This structure is beneficial to seed-stage investors, who often have less bargaining power than do such venture capitalists, because the seed-stage investors can essentially "borrow" their bargaining power by letting the terms of their investment be decided later by those with more bargaining power. However, because seed-stage investors providing bridge loans incur relatively more risk than do the venture capitalists investing at a later point in time, seed-stage investors are often given some sort of "sweetener" to compensate them for the additional risk. (Sweeteners are discussed more fully later in this chapter.)

Preferred Stock　　Preferred stock is an equity security that entitles its holders (usually along with the right to vote with holders of common stock) to certain rights and preferences not generally given to holders of common stock. Most often, preferred stock is given a liquidity preference. Preferred stock, however, can also have preferences with regard to dividends, rights with regard to redemption, conversion, and the receipt of specific financial and operating information about companies, and protective provisions such as affirmative and negative covenants. Norton and Tenenbaum describe the implications to venture capitalists of using preferred stock:

> *The features of preferred equity allow the investors to preserve the advantages of debt and common equity while retaining few of their drawbacks. By investing in preferred stock that has voting rights, investors can exercise some control over the firm and have a priority claim over the management team with respect to cash flow in case of success and with respect to asset liquidation in the case of venture failure. Like debt, preferred equity gives investors protection against selfish managers, but without causing the firm to lose financial flexibility or cash flow. Like common equity, preferred stock allows flexibility to handle crises or meet covenants and has much of the upside return potential of common equity. Unlike common equity, preferred equity places the investors in a senior position, thereby reducing agency concerns inherent with straight common equity. As it provides a means to control risk while maintaining the potential for large returns, preferred equity financing may be especially favored in early stage deals.*[30]

Richard Testa explains that preferred stock offers venture capitalists superior "flexibility . . . in tailoring the critical issues of the investment—principally management control and recovery/return on investment."[31] Furthermore, the use of preferred stock allows companies to use the two-class structure (preferred stock and common stock) and have dual pricing, whereby common stock is sold to entrepreneurs and their employees at relatively low prices and preferred stock is sold to venture capitalists at relatively higher prices. Timothy Tomlinson, cofounder and partner of the law firm of Tomlinson Zisko Morosoli & Maser, explains the two-class structure:

> *In a typical venture investment, venture capitalists provide an amount of cash per share greatly in excess of that paid by the common stockholders. The common holders tend to be the corporation's founders and employees, and their stakes in the company are incentives to make the company a success.*[32]

It is, therefore, not surprising that preferred stock is, by a wide margin, the most popular security among venture capitalists for their investments. The venture capitalists at AVI Capital inform entrepreneurs on their website that their investments "primarily will be made by purchasing Preferred Stock."[33] Simply put, preferred stock best serves the interests of venture capitalists.

Conversion Rights

Will the investment security be convertible into another security, such as common stock?

Nearly all securities used in venture capital financings are convertible. Among venture capitalists, the most popular of the securities that have been discussed—actually, by an overwhelming margin—is convertible preferred stock. And, in the rare situations when debt is used in venture capital transactions, it typically takes the form of convertible promissory notes. Therefore, convertibility is an important characteristic of venture capital securities. Richard Testa explains that "a convertible senior security affords the investor downside protection, in terms of the opportunity to recover the

investment on a priority basis through redemption, repayment or liquidation preferences, with the upside potential of a liquid equity security traded at significantly appreciated values in the public
market."[34] In essence, convertible instruments allow investors to take
full advantage of the protections afforded by preferred stock or debt
until they are no longer necessary, and then allow them to forgo such
protections and to participate in liquidity events (e.g., IPOs, mergers,
or acquisitions) involving the exchange of the common stock. The
protections afforded by preferred stock and debt become unnecessary at such point as the common stock becomes liquid (or is about
to become liquid) and gains a value greater than that of the liquidation value or redemption value of the unconverted preferred stock or
the principal and interest of the unconverted debt. Convertibility affords investors the opportunity to select for themselves the most attractive liquidity options. Therefore, venture capitalists often take
advantage of this characteristic and insist on convertible securities.

Conversion Terms

*If the investment security is convertible, what conversion terms will
be available?*

That a security is convertible is interesting, but exactly *how* it converts is also important to venture capitalists. They (and their lawyers)
have strong opinions about how to accomplish conversion. Typical
conversion mechanisms for each type of security are presented in the
following subsections.

Convertible Preferred Stock   Convertible preferred stock allows holders
to convert their preferred stock into shares of common stock. Mark
White explains that the "conversion of preferred into common stock
is typically calculated by dividing the original per-share purchase
price by a 'conversion price' which is originally set at the purchase
price (for a one-to-one conversion of preferred into common
stock)."[35] The resulting ratio (e.g., one-to-one) is called the *conversion ratio*. Therefore, if a particular investor bought 100,000 shares
of preferred stock at a price of $1, and there was an initial conversion
price of $1, then the conversion ratio would be one-to-one and the in-
vestor could convert the 100,000 shares of preferred stock into

100,000 shares of common stock. The conversion price then may or may not be changed to provide venture capitalists with antidilution protection. (Antidilution protection is discussed later in this chapter.)

The actual timing of conversion is almost as important as how a security converts. Venture capitalists typically require that the conversion terms provide them with both voluntary and automatic conversion rights. Voluntary conversion allows investors to convert at any time, at their option. Automatic conversion forces conversion on the happening of certain events, usually qualified IPOs or majority (or sometimes supermajority) vote of the holders of preferred stock. Providing for automatic conversion on a qualified IPO is a protection measure for venture capitalists, and is used in nearly every venture capital transaction. It is a protection measure because it is virtually impossible for underwriters to take a company public that has more than one class of equity. Underwriters strongly prefer that all of the shareholders of the company have equal standing, as holders of common stock. Therefore, to do an IPO, companies must either obtain the cooperation of their venture capital investors (and get them to convert voluntarily) or they must meet the standards of a qualified IPO. A qualified IPO is typically defined as an underwritten IPO that (1) generates some minimum amount of net proceeds for the particular company, (2) creates a minimum "public float" (makes a sufficient number of shares available for public trading) necessary to provide sufficient aftermarket liquidity, and (3) meets a minimum public offering price that represents some multiple (e.g., 3×) of the per share price paid by venture capitalists for their convertible preferred stock (on an as-if-converted basis). The minimum public offering price corresponds to a specific company valuation. If a company's valuation (as set by the public offering price) meets or exceeds that level, then venture capitalists agree to forgo their preferential status and convert their shares into common stock. This definition of *qualified IPO* ensures that IPOs effected by companies will be of a sufficient size, that there will be sufficient liquidity for the venture capitalists in the public markets after any such IPOs, and that the venture capitalists will achieve some minimum return on their investment before any IPOs may be undertaken.

One additional point should be made about automatic conversion occurring on the vote of some percentage of the holders of preferred stock. Venture capitalists generally prefer that conversion be triggered either by their own actions or by the fact of their portfolio companies going public, but not by the actions of other investors. Other investors may have divergent interests. Gary R. Silverman, partner of the law firm of Kirkland & Ellis, explains:

> *In some deals, conversion is required upon a majority vote of holders of all classes of preferred. Since different classes typically have invested at different prices, this could result in a later (more expensive class) being forced to convert under circumstances that may look very attractive to their earlier (less expensive) classes but much less attractive to such later class. In any event, if the venture capitalist is not itself the holder of the requisite majority voting power, it will need to be comfortable with the controlling holders, since they will have the power to force conversion.*[36]

Convertible Bridge Notes   Convertible bridge notes are typically convertible into preferred stock. Conversion is generally accomplished by applying the aggregate principal amount of the debt securities (with or without accrued interest) to the purchase of the preferred stock, at the preferred stock price. Therefore, if a particular seed-stage investor holds a note with a $1,000,000 face value, and his or her portfolio company manages to close a deal with a venture capital firm whereby the firm purchases preferred stock at a price of $10, the seed-stage investor may convert the note into 100,000 shares of preferred stock. Conversion of bridge notes is typically triggered on the closing of a qualified venture financing. A qualified financing is usually defined as one that occurs before an agreed on date and that results in proceeds in excess of some amount (e.g., $1,000,000).

Simple or Mechanical Antidilution Protection

If the investment security is convertible, will antidilution protection for structural changes in the common stock of the company be available?

Structural changes in the common stock of a company (such as stock dividends or stock splits) can significantly dilute the value of venture capitalists' convertible preferred stock. If a venture capitalist's portfolio company effects a 2-for-1 stock split and the venture capitalist has no antidilution protection, then the value of his or her convertible preferred stock is cut in half. This happens because the total amount of the portfolio company's outstanding shares doubles in a 2-for-1 stock split, but the number of shares into which the investor's convertible preferred stock converts—without antidilution protection—remains unchanged. Such structural changes, however, are merely the result of companies rearranging their capital structure. Therefore, the value of investors' convertible preferred stock should not be disturbed; the value of the stock should be exactly the same both immediately before and immediately after any structural changes. For this reason, venture capitalists who use convertible preferred stock universally require "simple" or "mechanical" antidilution protection in the form of a clause stating that on a structural change in the common stock of their portfolio company, the conversion ratio be immediately adjusted so that the value of their convertible preferred stock is not materially affected by any such structural changes.

When using convertible debt, seed-stage investors typically do not require this type of antidilution protection—or any type for that matter. Because of the manner by which debt is converted into preferred stock, holders of debt are not usually harmed by structural changes in the common stock. However, such investors can be harmed, just like any other holder of preferred stock, if the preferred stock into which they convert their debt does not have sufficient antidilution protection.

Price-Based Antidilution Protection

If the investment security is convertible, will antidilution protection against the company issuing stock at an effective price that is below your conversion price be available?

When companies fail to meet key milestones, they are often forced to raise additional capital at lower valuations than they had expected, and sometimes at valuations that are the same as or lower than those of prior financings. Alan Salzman and John Doerr explain that "achieving a favorable valuation at one stage which is not later justified by performance will result in subsequent valuations being lower than anticipated."[37] In such situations, investors who purchased securities during previous financings can have their ownership percentage *severely* diluted, depending on the size of the new financing. Dilution is generally defined as the reduction of proportionate ownership investors face when new shares (including rights convertible into shares and options to purchase shares) are issued or granted, and can be greatly intensified when the effective prices paid for the new shares are below the prices paid by those investors. Robert M. Johnson, lecturer in entrepreneurship at the London Business School, says, "[I]t is not uncommon in struggling early-stage companies for subsequent rounds of financing to dilute earlier rounds of capital down to insignificant levels of ownership."[38] These severely dilutive rounds of financing are commonly called *smashdown* rounds or simply *down* rounds because they can smash down the ownership percentages of existing investors.

To avoid being smashed down, most venture capitalists require some form of price-based antidilution protection. Such protection shields venture capitalists who hold convertible instruments by allowing them to receive additional shares of common stock when they convert their convertible securities, if down rounds have occurred before such conversion. All price-based antidilution mechanisms are fundamentally based on somehow adjusting the conversion price used to convert preferred stock into common stock. Adjustments of the conversion price automatically change the conversion ratio: They change the number of common shares investors receive in exchange for each share of preferred stock. If a venture capitalist were to buy 1,000,000 shares of preferred stock at a price of $4 (which would have an initial conversion price of $4, because the initial conversion price for a particular shareholder is typically the same as the preferred stock price paid by that shareholder), then the conversion ratio would be one-to-one and the venture capitalist would be able to convert the 1,000,000 shares of preferred stock into 1,000,000 shares of common stock. But, if a down round happened to occur subsequent to the venture capitalist's investment, which resulted in an adjustment of the conversion price down to $2, then the conversion ratio would be two-to-one and the venture capitalists could then convert the 1,000,000 shares of preferred stock into 2,000,000 shares of common stock. These types of adjustment are meant to protect venture capitalists from the dilution that results when companies fail to meet their milestones. The theory behind them is that the responsibility of meeting milestones resides with the holders of the common stock—management team members and employees—and they should bear the brunt of missing those milestones, not the venture capitalists who backed them. The dilutive impact on the common stockholders can be severe when companies must do down rounds and the preferred stockholders have price-based antidilution rights because the impact is concentrated totally on the holders of the common stock. However, the severity depends on the degree of the adjustment to conversion price. There are three primary forms of price-based antidilution protection, and each is distinguished by the degree to which it makes such adjustments.

"Full Ratchet" Antidilution Protection   This type of antidilution protection "ratchets" the conversion price—the denominator in the conversion ratio—down to the lowest price at which any stock is subsequently sold, regardless of the amount of stock sold at that price. Essentially, the full ratchet allows earlier investors to reprice their shares based on the pricing done by later investors. The attorneys at the Venture Law Group (VLG) provide the following example:

> [I]f a company sells 1,000,000 shares of Series A Preferred Stock at $1.00 per share and later is forced to sell 100,000 shares of Series B Preferred Stock at $.50 per share, the conversion rate of the Series A Preferred Stock is adjusted so that such shares are now convertible into 2,000,000 shares of Common Stock (as if the shares of Series A Preferred Stock had originally been sold at $.50 per share).[39]

To continue this example, and to illustrate the full impact of the full ratchet, assume that the management team in VLG's example gave away 40 percent of the company for those first 1,000,000 Series A preferred shares. Therefore, after the Series A round, the management team and the employees would continue to own 60 percent of their company (they would hold 1,500,000 shares of common and the venture capitalists would hold 1,000,000 shares of Series A preferred, which would be convertible into 1,000,000 shares of common). But, after the Series B round (which would technically be considered a down round because the company sold equity at price below that of a previous round, even though such a small amount of equity was sold) they would own, on a fully diluted basis, only 42 percent because of the operation of the full ratchet. After the down round, the management team and employees would continue to hold 1,500,000 shares of common stock, and the Series A venture capitalist would continue to hold 1,000,000 shares of Series A preferred, but those shares would then be convertible into 2,000,000 shares of common. Therefore, on a fully diluted basis, the common shareholders would own 42 percent of the company, the Series A venture capitalist would then own 55 percent, and the Series B venture capitalists would own 3 percent.

The full ratchet treats management teams and employees very harshly when they fail to hit their milestones and are forced to raise equity in down rounds. It can also be of great benefit to venture capitalists who hold rights to such protection, because it allows them to reprice their shares (they get more shares for the same investment, thus decreasing the per share price paid) at a later point in time to put them on equal footing with new investors who were able to price the shares with better information. The venture capitalists at Advanced Technology Ventures explain the rationale behind the full ratchet:

> *Company founders/management often wonder why a ratchet provision is necessary. The simple answer is that the ratchet clause provides early investors some protection. Investors invest based on a company's plan and projections. If the projections are met, investors expect to either see a profitable company that won't need further financing or one that has reached a stage where follow-on financing can be achieved at more attractive prices. The ratchet provides investors some protection if the promises, made by the company, are not met and a follow-on financing must be accepted at less favorable terms.*[40]

The real problem with full ratchet is that it administers its harsh treatment (and its benefits), not only when the amounts of additional equity raised are significant, but also when they are insignificant, as was the case in the earlier VLG example. Sometimes, to soften the impact of full ratchet antidilution provisions, their use is limited to only the first financings that occur subsequent to the dates on which the holders of such rights invested or to those financings that occur within a fixed period of time (e.g., six months to one year) after those dates. Another problem with full ratchet provisions is that later round venture capitalists are often reluctant to hand earlier investors such attractive windfall gains, in terms of equity ownership percentages. Many venture financings have foundered because of their existence.

Not surprisingly, full ratchet antidilution protection has fallen out of favor somewhat. It is generally only used by venture capitalists in situations where they hold a great deal of bargaining power (e.g., when they invest in companies for which there is not much competition) and by those venture capitalists who invest in very early rounds of financing. Early investors bear the greatest risk that companies, at some later point, will have to do down rounds, in which the investors will otherwise be exposed to serious dilution. They bear that risk because it is exceedingly difficult to determine appropriate share prices (company valuations—because share prices are determined by dividing company aggregate valuation amounts by the numbers of shares outstanding) in the very early stages, when realistic financial projections and operational milestones are impossible to verify. Therefore, they face the real risk that a company's projections and milestones will later prove to be overly optimistic, that the valuation agreed initially on will prove too high, and that a subsequent venture capitalist will enter the picture by investing at a lower valuation.

Broad-Based Weighted Average Antidilution Protection   Like the full ratchet, this type of antidilution protection also reprices venture capitalists' shares (it makes adjustments to the conversion price) when companies sell additional stock at prices that are lower than previous rounds of financing. But, unlike the full ratchet, adjustments to the conversion price under the weighted average form of antidilution protection are made according to a formula that takes into account the number of shares sold at those lower prices relative to the number of shares outstanding prior to the financing. A typical broad-based weighted average formula is as follows:

$$NCP = OCP \times \frac{SOB + \dfrac{NS \times NSP}{OCP}}{SOA}$$

where NCP = the New Conversion Price
        OCP = the Old Conversion Price
        SOB = the number of Shares Outstanding Before the new issuance, on a fully diluted basis (i.e., including all shares of common stock that are issuable on conversion of convertible securities and exercise of options)
        NS = the number of Newly issued Shares
        NSP = the New Share Price
        SOA = the number of Shares Outstanding immediately After the new issuance, on a fully diluted basis

To see the broad-based weighted average form of antidilution protection at work, suppose again that the company in the VLG example had a total of 2,500,000 shares outstanding, on a fully diluted basis, before the Series B financing. This time, according to the broad-based weighted average formula, the sale of the 100,000 shares of Series B preferred stock at $.50 per share would cause the 1,000,000 shares of Series A preferred stock to be convertible into 1,019,617 shares of common stock, as opposed to 2,000,000 shares under the full ratchet. The reason for the difference is that the Series B financing was fairly insignificant and resulted in little dilution to the Series A investors. Had the Series B financing been more significant, then the dilutive impact on the Series A investors would have been greater, but so would have been the adjustment to the conversion price. For example, if the Series B financing involved a sale of 2,000,000 shares at $.50 per share, the 1,000,000 shares Series A preferred stock would be convertible into 1,285,727 shares of common stock.

A unique aspect of the weighted average form of antidilution is that the degree of protection against dilutive financings that it provides to early investors depends on their percentage ownership. Says Seth L. Pierrepont, Principal at Sycamore Ventures, "Those investors who have provided a large amount of financial support to the company in the past, and thereby have acquired a large percentage of the company, should receive *proportionately* more protection than other shareholders."[41]

Narrow-Based Weighted Average Antidilution Protection Companies and venture capitalists sometimes agree to narrow the base used in the weighted average antidilution formula somewhat, from the broad base of all shares outstanding, on a fully diluted basis. Sometimes they agree to narrow the base to the number of shares outstanding prior to the financing, ignoring unconverted preferred stock and unexercised options (that is, not on a fully diluted basis). Or, alternatively, sometimes they agree to narrow the base to the number of shares of preferred stock outstanding prior to the financing. A narrow-based weighted average formula based on this second approach follows:

$$NCP = OCP \times \frac{PSOB + \dfrac{NS \times NSP}{OCP}}{PSOA}$$

where NCP = the New Conversion Price
   OCP = the Old Conversion Price
   $PSOB$ = the number of Preferred Shares Outstanding Before the new issuance, on a fully diluted basis
   NS = the number of Newly issued Shares
   NSP = the New Share Price
   $PSOA$ = the number of Preferred Shares Outstanding immediately After the new issuance, on a fully diluted basis

Applying this narrow-based weighted average to the VLG example, the sale of the 100,000 shares of Series B preferred stock at $.50

per share would cause the 1,000,000 shares of Series A preferred stock to be convertible into 1,047,625 shares of common stock, as opposed to 2,000,000 shares under the full ratchet and 1,019,617 shares under the broad-based weighted average formula. Alternatively, if the Series B financing had involved a sale of 2,000,000 shares at $.50 per share, the 1,000,000 shares Series A preferred stock would be convertible into 1,500,015 shares of common stock, as opposed to 2,000,000 shares under the full ratchet and 1,285,727 under the broad-based weighted average formula. Therefore, by narrowing the base, investors can gain some additional protection against dilutive financings.

The preceding descriptions and examples show that the full ratchet form of antidilution protection is the most robust protection for venture capitalists against the dilutive impact of down rounds. However, venture capitalists are aware that the full ratchet can prove extremely harsh for the common stockholders, who are often severely diluted by its operation. As noted, the common stockholders in early-stage companies are essentially the management team members and the employees. Although shrewd venture capitalists are vigilant in protecting their own interests, they are cognizant of the interests and incentives of these groups as well. Venture capitalists certainly do not want for management teams and employees to be so diluted in their ownership percentages that they lose all incentive to succeed, let alone remain with their companies. For this reason, and others previously mentioned, the weighted average forms of antidilution protection are generally viewed as more reasonable and fair to the common stockholders, and are therefore much more commonly used by venture capitalists.

No matter which form is employed, however, it is important to venture capitalists that there be some form of price-based antidilution protection. Even if never used, price-based antidilution protection provides great incentives to management teams and employees. According to Pierrepont, venture capitalists tend to "believe that the threat of this type of protection encourages entrepreneurs to tell all of the truth during the due diligence process, to be very conservative in their projections, and to work extra hard to increase the value of the company."[42]

Carve-Outs

If some form of price-based antidilution is available, what exceptions is the company seeking for issuances that will not trigger adjustments to the conversion price?

Companies and venture capitalists usually agree on *carve-outs* or exceptions for certain types of issuances (because there can be many types) that actually will trigger price-based antidilution protection. First of all, price-based antidilution provisions treat all issuances of convertible securities and options on an as-if-converted or an as-if-exercised basis. And, if the effective purchase price for the common stock underlying these instruments is below the conversion price in effect, then antidilution protection is triggered and the conversion price is adjusted downward. However, antidilution protection is usually not triggered when convertible securities are *actually* converted and options are *actually* exercised. That, therefore, is typically the first carve-out. The following, according to Gary Silverman, are other typical carve-outs:

- Issuances to employees, directors, and other service-providers.
- Issuances to lenders as "equity kickers."
- Issuances to vendors and lessors.
- Issuances as consideration for acquisitions and joint ventures.
- Issuances to "strategic investors."[43]

And, says Silverman, "[a]ny or all of the above exceptions may be limited, individually or in the aggregate, to a maximum number of shares or a fixed percentage of the company, so that the venture capitalist will not be subject to unlimited dilution by reason of such exceptions."[44]

Pay-to-Play Provisions

If some form of price-based antidilution protection is available, will a "pay-to-play" provision be connected with this protection?

Though certainly not ubiquitous, pay-to-play provisions are used in some venture capital deals in conjunction with price-based antidilution protection. According to Leslie E. Davis, partner at Testa, Hurwitz & Thibeault, these provisions actually appear "in fewer than half the deals done."[45] Pay-to-play provisions require that to take advantage of price-based antidilution protection, holders of preferred stock must participate in down rounds, at least to the extent of their pro rata share. Holders who do not participate to the extent of that pro rata share in the down round, forfeit all rights to price-based antidilution protection. There are several ways to accomplish such forfeitures, such as converting the shares of nonparticipants into shares of common stock or into new preferred shares with identical rights as the original shares (except lacking price-based antidilution protection), or through contractual waivers in companies' certificates of incorporation.

Pay-to-play provisions are sometimes included at the request of venture capitalists and sometimes at the request of companies. Some venture capitalists—especially those who commit themselves to supporting their portfolio companies through multiple rounds of financing—advocate their use when they enter into deals alongside other investors (or deals with existing investors) who also hold rights to price-based antidilution protection. Pay-to-play provisions enable venture capitalists to hold their investment syndicates together, even in down rounds—they incentivize each member of the syndicate participating in those rounds. There is also an issue of basic fairness. Many venture capitalists tend to feel that only those investors who continue to support their portfolio companies through the tough times should be rewarded with the windfall gains that price-based antidilution provisions provide. Says Jacqueline A. Daunt, partner of the law firm of Fenwick & West:

I really like pay-to-play provisions. Why should an investor who refuses to support the company when they need capital in a "down" round be entitled to gross up the number of shares they have in the company? It hurts the company, it hurts those investors who do continue to provide support (by diluting their percentage interest in the company) and requires greater option grants to continuing employees (also causing greater dilution). I don't know if it actually changes the investor's behavior, but not letting them benefit from the dilutive offering is the right result.[46]

On the other hand, companies typically request the inclusion of pay-to-play provisions because they provide great incentives to investors to continue to financially support them through all rounds of financing. Companies rarely achieve profitability with only one or two rounds of venture funding. They usually require more like three or four rounds. To reduce their financing risk (the risk that they fail to obtain additional financing through each of these rounds), it is often important that companies obtain as much support from existing investors as they can, at least until they reach profitability, effect a merger or acquisition, or gain access to the public markets. Pay-to-play provisions create strong incentives to existing investors to step up and contribute in each round.

Dividend Preferences

If the investment security is preferred stock, will it have a dividend preference?

Venture capitalists have traditionally required that the shares of preferred stock they purchase contain a dividend preference. Dividend preferences mandate that companies first pay dividends to the holders of preferred stock (the investors) before making payments on the holders of common stock. Venture capitalists have required them even though they virtually never expect that their portfolio companies will pay dividends on a current basis. Says Craig Johnson, "[I]n 22 years of venture capital practice, I have had only one private company actually pay dividends. It was so profitable it couldn't figure out anything else to do with the money!"[47] That is certainly the exception. Says Mark White, "While emerging-growth companies do not usually pay dividends, investors insist on preferential dividends in order to encourage the use of retained earnings for working capital purposes,"[48] and not for the payment of dividends to the management team members and employees—the holders of common stock. Essentially, dividend preferences create strong incentives to management to grow their companies, and not to extract precious capital to the detriment of the investors (and the companies). Dividend preferences are, therefore, a method for venture capitalists to control agency risk, and they generally require them to be a part of most venture capital transactions.

Dividend preferences generally come in several different flavors. First, they can be either mandatory or "when, as, and if" declared. The type typically sought by venture capitalists are the "when, as, and if" type, meaning that portfolio companies are under no obligation to pay the dividends on a current basis, only when, as, and if declared by their boards. Mandatory dividend preferences require that companies pay dividends on a current and regular basis, similar to the requirement that they pay interest on their debt. Mandatory dividend preferences are not typically used by venture capitalists because they rob portfolio companies of precious capital and are significantly dilutive; companies have to issue additional stock to retrieve the capital paid out in the form of dividends.

Dividend preferences can also be either cumulative or noncumulative. Cumulative dividends are ones that, if not paid on a current and regular basis (for example, annually), accumulate from period to period. Cumulative dividend preferences, as Gary Silverman explains, are sometimes used by venture capitalists to guarantee "at least a minimum return."[49] When companies fail to achieve liquidity for their equity holders through the traditional routes (fail to reach successful IPOs or fail to be successfully merged into or acquired by other companies), and venture capitalists are forced to realize liquidity—if they can—through redemption or liquidation, they may still realize a return on their investment if the unpaid dividends that have accumulated since their investment are added to the amount that they are entitled to receive either on redemption or liquidation. Actually, "guarantee" is probably too strong a word. The reality is that venture capitalists rarely harvest much capital when companies are unable to effect IPOs or mergers or acquisitions, even when they have cumulative dividend preferences coupled with redemption rights and/or liquidation preferences. Only when such companies have been profitable enough to have sufficient cash to redeem the preferred stock or hold sufficient assets on liquidation to satisfy liquidation preferences will venture capitalists be able to obtain such a minimum return; both are fairly rare for companies unable to pursue traditional liquidity options.

Beyond guaranteeing a minimum return, venture capitalists also sometimes use cumulative dividend preferences to *enhance* their returns from traditional liquidity events. They do this in two ways. First, when portfolio companies are acquired, venture capitalists are sometimes able to receive their liquidation preference amounts plus all accumulated dividends (as opposed to simply converting their preferred stock into common stock and participating in the sales with the rest of the common stockholders). This is only an option when the initial deals between venture capitalists and their portfolio companies contain provisions defining acquisitions as *deemed liquidations,* thereby allowing investors the option of exercising their liquidation preferences. The second way cumulative dividend preferences can be used to enhance returns is for accumulated dividends to be recognized on conversion. There are a few ways that accumulated dividends can be treated on conversion. Says Frederick Lipman, "Some venture capitalists, in computing the number of shares of common stock into which the preferred stock is convertible, also require that the accrued dividends, as well as the original investment, be convertible."[50] This conversion into common stock can be accomplished at either the conversion price used for the convertible preferred stock, at the public offering price (or the price determined by a merger or acquisition transaction that requires conversion), or at a price determined in good faith to be fair market value by a board of directors. Accumulated dividends can also be paid in cash to venture capitalists before conversion. In fact, some venture capitalists have been known to make automatic conversion contingent on the payment of all accrued but unpaid dividends. It is becoming most common, however, for venture capitalists to forgive or waive all accumulated dividends on conversion. Gary Silverman explains the reasoning behind this trend:

> *The argument advanced for this is that since the dividend is only intended to insure that the venture capitalist achieves a minimum return on investment, and since by definition such return is exceeded if the venture capitalist is converting into common stock (either because it has made the economic decision to do so or*

*because the threshold has been met for a Qualified IPO), the ac-
crued dividends are no longer needed to achieve this result.*[51]

Therefore, the use of cumulative dividend preferences to enhance
venture capital returns from traditional liquidity events is probably
becoming less common than it once was.

There are also several variations on the straight cumulative dividend preference. Dividend preferences can also be what is called *cumulative-if-earned*. Cumulative-if-earned dividends only accumulate
for those periods during which companies generate sufficient earnings. Generally, a company would be said to have generated sufficient earnings if they are greater than or equal to the aggregate
amount of all dividend payments to shareholders eligible to receive
them. If companies' earnings during a particular period are less than
the aggregate dividend amount, then no dividend will accumulate for
that period. Dividend preferences can also be made cumulative only
after a certain period of time has elapsed after investment (e.g., after
three years). Such dividends are noncumulative at the outset, but become cumulative after the agreed on period has elapsed. The lengths
of such periods typically correspond to the periods of time in which
liquidity events (IPOs, mergers or acquisitions) should reasonably
occur. Lastly, default provisions are sometimes attached to cumulative dividend preferences. These default provisions typically state
that if dividends are not paid for some number of periods then a default occurs, upon which the preferred shareholders are sometimes
allowed to gain additional board seats. (These and other change of
control provisions are discussed later in this chapter.)

Probably the most common type of dividend preference, however,
is the noncumulative dividend preference. Under this type, unpaid dividends do not accumulate from period to period. When dividends are
not paid for a particular period, the preferred stockholders have no
claim for their subsequent payment and they are not added to redemption prices or liquidation preference amounts, and are not made convertible into common stock. Therefore, if not paid, the dividends are
essentially gone forever. And, given the scarcity of available cash in
early-stage companies and the need to deploy that scarce cash for
company growth, venture capitalists virtually never assume that they
will ever be paid. In fact, a caveat to the effect that it is "unlikely" that

any dividends will ever be declared is often contained in the disclosure language of a typical preferred stock venture capital financing with a noncumulative dividend preference. Notwithstanding the relative popularity of the noncumulative dividend preference, Mark White suggests that venture capitalists still sometimes require cumulative dividend preferences with "less attractive companies."[52] However, when they do choose to require cumulative dividends, they typically leave boards of directors, or some percentage of the preferred stockholders, a means by which to waive the payment of accumulated dividends. Indeed, the ability to waive payment of accumulated dividends may be necessary to carry out future financings.

Interest

If the investment security is a debt instrument, what will be the interest payment terms?

Bridge loans always contain certain interest rates (e.g., 8%), similar to the dividend rates sometimes contained in preferred stock. As Richard Testa points out, however, the rights of venture investors to receive that interest "are more secure than their rights to receive dividends on preferred stock, inasmuch as payment of dividends may be restricted by state corporate laws relating to legally available funds and by the requirement that dividends must be declared by the board of directors."[53] Interest payment terms on bridge loans can be structured in several different ways. Though exceedingly rare because of the onerous burden that interest obligations can bestow on early-stage companies, venture capitalists can require that interest be paid over the entire term of the debt, at a fixed rate. That allows venture capitalists to realize a current return on their investments by receiving periodic interest payments. Much more commonly, however, bridge loans are structured as *zero coupon* or *split coupon* securities:

■ *Zero Coupon* Zero coupon securities require that companies pay at maturity (1) the amount they borrowed, plus (2) an amount representing the compounded interest that would have been due during the time that the loans were outstanding had they been traditional interest-bearing debt securities. Zero coupon securities are particularly popular in the venture capital context because they allow companies to escape the (usually overwhelming) burden of paying interest on a current basis.

■ *Split Coupon*   Split coupon securities also ease the burden on companies of paying interest on a current basis, but to a lesser degree than zero coupon securities. Typically, they either allow companies to defer their interest obligations for specified periods or specify lower initial rates of interest that increase over time. Deferral provisions are fairly common in venture capital debt transactions.

When negotiating interest payment terms, venture capitalists and seed-stage investors usually are careful not to impose on their portfolio companies debt service obligations that are too overwhelming; they usually negotiate interest payments terms that companies will be able to cover without disturbing their business plans. It is not in their interest to drive their portfolio companies into bankruptcy or to force them to detrimentally scale back their business plans. One term that is rarely negotiated, however, is that all accrued, but unpaid, interest on their bridge loans be convertible (along with the principal debt) into preferred stock. Without the ability to maximize their participation in their portfolio companies' equity upside potential, the potential rewards of bridging seed- or early-stage companies might not be sufficient to justify the risk. To that end, venture investors also often require that warrants be attached to bridge loans, to further maximize their potential upside participation.

Warrants

Will warrants be attached to the investment security?

Warrants are contractual rights, exercisable over specified periods of time, to acquire certain amounts of stock at specified prices. Explains Joseph Bartlett:

> *A warrant is, like an option and a conversion privilege, a derivative security, a right to buy a security at a fixed (or formula) price; the "exercise" or "strike" price. A warrant is, in effect, a*

short-term option and, although often issued in connection with another security—debt with warrants attached—it ordinarily can be, by its terms, traded as an independent security. In contrast, an option, in venture capital usage at least, is usually long term (up to ten years) and personal to the holder because the typical recipient is an employee.[54]

The warrants most often used by venture capitalists are preferred stock warrants, as opposed to common stock warrants. According to Robert Gunderson, preferred stock warrants "preserve the two class (preferred and common) structure and pricing."[55] Also, using preferred stock warrants effectively captures the antidilution provisions of the preferred stock into which the warrants are exercisable.

Warrants are used by venture capitalists for several purposes. First, they are used as sweeteners to compensate them for incurring any unusual risk. Unusual risk can arise in venture financings with multiple closings (when the time period between closings is significant) or in bridge loan situations. In both cases, there are early investors and late investors, and both types invest on essentially the same terms (that is, both receive the same securities at the same prices), even though the early investors incur more risk as a result of investing earlier. One reason early investors incur more risk is that, on top of the usual risks associated with venture capital investments, they also face relatively more financing risk. Financing risk is the risk that companies will not obtain the additional funding they need. For late investors, financing risk is somewhat less significant. Says Craig Johnson, "Early investors bear more risk," so it is appropriate that they be given "additional benefits such as warrants to compensate them for this added risk."[56] Warrants allow such investors to enhance the returns on their investments. Timothy Tomlinson explains:

A warrant usually gives the venture capitalist the right to purchase more of the same class of shares already being purchased for a set period of time, usually three to five years. By acquiring a warrant, the venture capitalist may obtain the gain on a greater number of shares without an increased cash outlay, effectively giving the VC a greater percent of the increase in value of the company per share it buys. For example, if a VC receives

*a warrant to later purchase one share of stock for every share pur-
chased, the effective return can be doubled.*[57]

Therefore, through the use of warrants, *both* early and late investors
can be adequately compensated for the relative risk they undertake.
For that reason, warrants are very often present in venture capital
bridge financings and sometimes in financings with multiple closings.

Venture capitalists sometimes use warrants for a slightly more subtle purpose. They can be employed as a clever means to effect down
rounds of financing, while avoiding the appearance (and therefore
some of the consequences). Tomlinson explains:

> *Venture capitalists can also use warrants to reduce the effective
> share price of their investment without triggering antidilution and
> price protection provisions of previous investors. These antidilu-
> tion formulas typically provide that if the company sells stock at a
> per share price less than the conversion price of the preferred
> stock, then the holder of the preferred stock is entitled to a greater
> number of shares upon conversion of the preferred stock. This re-
> duces the per share purchase price paid by a VC and protects him
> somewhat against a reduction in his percentage holdings of the
> company. These protections, however, are almost universally
> based on the sale of stock at a price less than the venture capital-
> ist paid, or the issue of warrant or options at an exercise price less
> than what the venture capitalist paid for his stock. Using warrants
> with an exercise price greater or equal to the prior investors' pur-
> chase price does not trigger these antidilution formulas. Classes of
> stock with antidilution provisions that are not triggered suffer
> greater dilution. Classes of stock without these protections do not
> suffer as much dilution as if the new investor had not received
> warrants, but instead had paid a lower price for shares of stock.
> This situation most often benefits the common stock, which, in a
> typical venture capital-backed company, is held by employees.
> Reducing dilution of these key contributors is an advantage to the
> new investor since most employees are better motivated if happy
> with their stockholdings in the company.*[58]

Therefore, warrants represent a flexible and attractive mechanism
for venture investors, and they tend to use them liberally.

Warrant Terms

If warrants will be attached to the investment security, what warrant terms will be available?

The warrant terms that are most important to venture capitalists are (1) the warrant exercise price or "strike" price, (2) the warrant's term or duration, and (3) the warrant coverage. The strike price is the per share price venture capitalists will have to pay to purchase the shares covered by a particular warrant or warrants. The term of a warrant specifies the period of time venture capitalists will have to exercise their warrants before they expire. Warrant expiration is also sometimes tied to the happening of certain events, such as initial public offerings or mergers or acquisitions. Warrant coverage expresses how many shares venture capitalists will be able to purchase on exercise. Coverage is typically expressed in percentages and depends on the amount a particular company wants to sweeten its deal. For example, a company issuing 100 percent warrants would give venture capitalists warrants to purchase one additional share of stock for each share of stock purchased. Likewise, a company issuing 20 percent warrants would be giving each investor a warrant to purchase one additional share of stock later for every five shares of stock purchased. Warrant coverage typically ranges anywhere from 100 percent down to 5 percent. Venture capitalists tend to be acutely aware of each of these terms when negotiating with companies. These terms ultimately determine the value of the warrants to the venture capitalists.

CONTROL MECHANISMS

Board Representation

Will you have representation on the company's board of directors?

Control, in the strongest sense of the concept, is the ability to direct a company's actions including both company strategy and the choice of people to carry out that strategy. In the corporate context, this type of control is held (1) by shareholders, with whom the power to elect directors resides, and (2) by boards of directors, which are given the power to define their companies' strategies and to select management teams to carry out those strategies. Venture capitalists do not, as a matter of course, seek complete control of the boards of their portfolio companies, at least not initially. They are focused first and foremost on obtaining high rates of return on their investments, not on how to take control of their portfolio companies. Therefore, they seek control only to the extent that they believe it necessary to protect their investments. Very few venture capitalists are interested in actually running the day-to-day operations of their portfolio companies. The venture capitalists at Woodside Fund state: "The last thing a venture capitalist wants to do is run [a portfolio] company. In fact, Woodside Fund only invests when the entrepreneur has the energy, vision and talent to build a successful company."[59] Says Kevin Fong, "[W]e have no desire to run a company; we have no desire to take control of a company; but we do have a strong desire for the company to succeed and grow."[60] He explains:

> [W]e're not in there trying to be pseudoentrepreneurs or pseudomanagers of the company, and in fact that's a dangerous signal for us when we end up trying to get too involved in tactical decisions about the company, and so we would like to make sure that the management of the company or the entrepreneurs of the company have all of the capabilities and all the leverage and all of the help they need in order to run the company such that we don't need to do that. I mean, we're doing something wrong if we're spending too much time with the company.[61]

Venture capitalists do, however, typically require some board representation. In fact, board representation is of supreme importance to venture capitalists and serves a couple of purposes. It enables venture capitalists to effectively monitor their investments and to protect those investments by influencing the operations and the strategic decisions of their portfolio companies.

Whether venture capitalists can exert influence through boards of directors depends first on their voting rights as investors, and it is usually the choice of investment security that determines those rights. Common stock is the basic unit of corporate ownership and the holders of common stock are the corporate shareholder voting base. A share of common stock is evidence of the right to vote in person or by proxy in the election of directors and on other matters submitted for a vote of the holders of common stock. Holders of common stock are typically given one vote for each share they hold. The voting rights of the holders of preferred stock typically vary. They can be greater than, the same as, or more limited than those of the holders of common. Preferred stock can be voting preferred, nonvoting preferred, or have voting rights on certain issues only, or voting rights on the occurence of certain events. Preferred stock that is convertible into common stock is typically treated, for voting purposes, on an as-if-converted basis: It is treated as if it has already been converted into common stock. Holders of debt securities are rarely, if ever, given the right to vote. Although they are sometimes allowed to hold voting rights under the laws of some states (such as Delaware), it is generally considered that voting rights should be reserved for equity holders (holders of common and preferred stock). Therefore, as Testa explains, when venture capitalists employ debt as their investment security, their "ability to influence management of the company directly is diminished, and they must resort to voting agreements and proxies in order to participate in the election of directors or, alternatively, rely on indirect means of influence such as the affirmative and negative covenants contained in the investment agreement."[62]

Whether venture capitalists can exert influence through boards also depends on the voting arrangements employed by their portfolio companies. A combination of state law and companies' organizational documents typically determines the particular voting methods employed. The simplest voting method is the straight voting method. Under the straight voting method, each director is elected in a separate vote and all shareholders entitled to vote (the common shareholders and any preferred shareholders with voting rights), vote as one class. Therefore, a shareholder or group of shareholders with control of more than 50 percent of the voting shares of a company (commonly called *voting control*) can elect the entire board and any minority shareholders are left essentially unrepresented. This is the default voting method under Delaware law. The cumulative voting method is another voting method that was devised to address this minority shareholder representation problem. The cumulative voting method is the default method under California law. Under this method, minority shareholders holding sufficient amounts of stock may be able to obtain board representation despite their minority status. Cumulative voting permits shareholders to aggregate all the votes they may cast in a particular directorial election (calculated by multiplying the number of shares owned by the number of board seats) and to distribute them as they see fit over one or more director candidates. The following formula is used to determine whether the number of shares owned is sufficient to be able to elect one director under the cumulative voting method:

$$S = D + \frac{VS}{1+1}$$

where S = the Shares needed
VS = the total number of Voting Shares
D = the number of Directors to be elected

The following analogous formula is used to determine the number of shares needed to elect N directors:

$$S = D + \frac{NVS}{1+1}$$

Probably the most common voting arrangement employed by venture-backed companies is the class voting method. This method is actually a departure from the "one share-one vote" principle. Under the class voting method, some or all of the different classes of stock (common stock and any classes of preferred stock) are allocated rights to elect certain numbers of directors as separate groups. For example, the holders of common stock may be allocated the right to elect two directors of a five-member board, and all of the holders of preferred stock may be allocated the right to elect the remaining three directors, voting as a single class. Or alternatively, the holders of common stock could be allocated the right to elect three directors of a five-member board, and the holders of Class A preferred stock and the holders of Class B preferred stock could be allocated the right to elect one director each, voting as separate classes. The classes under the class voting method can be grouped, and the rights of those groups can be allocated many different ways, depending on companies' capital structures. The class voting method is generally preferred by venture capitalists because it gives them some assurance of their ability to elect certain numbers of directors in the future, regardless of what stock issuances occur. Lee F. Benton, managing partner of the law firm of Cooley Godward, and Robert Gunderson add:

> *In the instance in which a class or series of stock is entitled to elect a specified number of directors, it is common to find a related covenant, which limits the size of the board of directors, placed in the certificate of incorporation. The purpose of such a covenant is to prevent the corporation from circumventing the intent of the voting provision by greatly increasing the size of the board.*[63]

The last voting arrangement, the voting agreement method, is typically provided for not in companies' organizational documents, but in separate agreements between venture capitalists and the founders (and any other major holders of common stock). In such agreements, these parties agree how they will vote their shares for the election of directors and what limit they will set on the size of the board of directors. Typically, venture capitalists require that the founders and other holders of common stock agree to vote for a certain number of directors designated by the venture capitalists. The voting agreement method allows venture capitalists to achieve results similar to those of the class voting method, but is generally disfavored compared with that method. Benton and Gunderson explain: "Investor's counsel typically prefers to effect the agreement regarding election of directors in the [certificate of incorporation] rather than through a voting agreement because of the concerns as to the enforceability of voting agreements."[64]

Extraordinary Voting Rights

Will extraordinary voting rights (or "voting switch" rights) be available?

Extraordinary voting rights provisions afford venture capitalists, on the occurrence of some triggering events, the right to elect a majority of their portfolio companies' boards of directors, thereby giving them complete control over such companies. The justification for such provisions is that, while venture capitalists are usually content with minority board representation when things are going well, they may, under certain extreme circumstances, need to assume majority board control. What qualifies as "extreme circumstances" is usually heavily negotiated. According to Lee Benton and Robert Gunderson:

> *The triggers for the voting switch . . . will normally be limited to materially adverse corporate developments such as a missed redemption, a missed dividend payment (or, more commonly, a string of missed dividend payments), insolvency, or bankruptcy. Additional [triggering events] may arise upon the failure of the Company to satisfy the terms of any covenants that may be set forth in the certificate of incorporation, or upon the failure of the Company to meet certain financial tests with respect to: (i) net losses exceeding a certain specified amount during a particular period, (ii) net worth of the corporation falling below a certain specified amount, or (iii) cumulative losses not exceeding a certain specified amount during a particular period.[65]*

Venture capitalists also sometimes require that extraordinary voting rights be triggered when portfolio companies fail to realize their business plans, either by missing specified milestones or by missing revenue benchmarks for multiple quarters. Extraordinary voting rights, therefore, only become operative when investments are put into some sort of jeopardy. Such rights are important to venture capitalists because they enable them to regain control over their jeopardized investments. By assuming control, venture capitalists put themselves in much better positions to influence the timing of liquidity events, such as mergers and acquisitions.

Board Observer Rights

If board representation is neither available nor appropriate, will board observer rights be available?

It is sometimes not possible or appropriate for venture capitalists to take positions on their portfolio companies' boards of directors. This is often true when another venture capitalist or venture capital firm leads the particular round of financing. It is customary that when multiple venture capitalists or venture capital firms coinvest alongside one another that only the lead investor (the investor who performs due diligence, negotiates the deal terms, and puts together the investor syndicate) take a board position. But, whatever may be the reason, when venture capitalists will not have board representation, they often require board "observer" rights. Board observer rights afford venture capitalists the right to have their representatives present at all board meetings of their particular portfolio companies. Although a board observer position is much weaker than a full directorial position because it lacks the power to vote as a director, it can still be an effective control mechanism for venture capitalists. As board observers, venture capitalists can effectively monitor their investments and even as nonvoters, they still can exert varying amounts of influence at board meetings to protect those investments.

Positive and Negative Covenants

To what covenants will the company be subject?

Venture capital investment agreements, whether involving preferred stock or debt, typically include both positive and negative covenants. Such covenants protect venture capitalists from both potential detrimental actions and potential detrimental omissions by their portfolio companies. Richard Testa explains:

> *Affirmative covenants are actions, positions, or results that the company promises to achieve or undertake. Negative covenants are actions, positions, or results that the company promises to avoid. In contrast to affirmative covenants (which generally exhort the company to undertake actions that it would ordinarily choose to take in the normal course), negative covenants contained in the investment agreement have more teeth and serve to limit the company from actions it otherwise might be inclined to take unless the investors have consented in advance. Typically, these negative covenants relate to matters that would affect the fundamental nature of the business in which the investment has*

*been made (e.g., mergers and acquisitions) or would alter the bal-
ance of control between the investors and entrepreneurs reached
in the investment agreement (e.g., controls on stock issuance).*[66]

Testa provides the following examples of typical affirmative
covenants found in many venture capital transactions:

- *Payment of Taxes and Claims*   The company will pay all lawful
  taxes, assessments, and levies on it or its income or property before they become in default. This covenant sometimes provides
  that all trade debt, principal and interest on debt securities acquired by the investor will be paid when due.
- *Property and Liability Insurance*   The company will maintain
  insurance against hazards, risks and liability to persons and
  property to the extent customary for companies engaged in the
  same or similar businesses.
- *Maintenance of Corporate Existence*   The company will maintain its corporate existence and all rights, licenses, patents, copyrights, trademarks, etc., useful in its business and will engage
  only in the type of business described in the business plan.
- *Legal Compliance*   The company will comply with all applicable laws and regulations in the conduct of its business.
- *Access to Premises*   Investors or their representatives will generally be permitted to inspect the company's facilities, books, and
  records. To the extent that confidentiality of corporate business
  information may be compromised by such rights of access, investors generally agree to confidentiality restrictions or to limiting access to lead or major investors.
- *Accounts and Reports*   The company may be asked by the investor to agree to maintain a standard system of accounting in
  accordance with generally accepted accounting principles consistently applied, and to keep full and complete financial records.
- *Repair and Maintenance*   The company will keep all necessary
  equipment and property in good repair and condition, as required to permit the business to be properly conducted.
- *Approval of Budgets*   The investor will frequently require management to produce comprehensive annual operating and capital
  budgets for approval by the investor or by the board of directors.

Revisions of such budgets during the year may also require advance approval.

■ *Protection of Proprietary Rights* The company will agree to take all necessary steps to protect proprietary developments made in the future, including causing all key employees to sign confidentiality and proprietary rights agreements.

■ *Compliance with Key Agreements* The company will enforce its rights under key agreements, such as the stockholders agreement, and will cause future stockholders to join the agreement.

■ *Life Insurance* The investor will often require the company to maintain insurance on the lives of key officers and employees. The face amount in some cases may be as much as the purchase price of the securities, and the insurance proceeds are often payable directly to the investor, particularly if the investor holds debt securities.

■ *Board of Directors* Venture capital firms will generally seek assurances that they will be represented on the company's board of directors. The right to be represented on the board may be backed up by voting agreements with the principal stockholders. If investors are not to be represented on the board, the company may be required to notify investors of the time and place of board meetings, and to permit investors or their representatives to attend such meetings and receive written material disseminated to directors. Frequency of board meetings and financial arrangements may also be covered.

■ *Financial and Operating Statements* The company will invariably agree to provide the investor with detailed financial and operating information. The information to be provided may include annual, quarterly, and sometimes monthly reports of sales, production, shipments, profits, cash balances, receivables, payables, and back log; all statements filed with the Securities and Exchange Commission or other regulatory agencies; notification of significant lawsuits or other legal proceedings; and any other information that investors may need for their own voluntary or involuntary filing requirements. Particularly where investors are acquiring debt securities or preferred stock containing extensive financial and other covenants, financial statements are required to be accompanied by a certificate for the company's chief executive or financial officer and, in the case of audited financial statements, its auditors, to the effect that the company is in compliance with all provisions of the investment agreement. The right to receive financial information is often terminated when the company goes public in order to avoid dissemination of "inside" information. Although companies generally concede the legitimate interests of investors to receive business information, negotiation over the scope and form of this information may be considerable in view of the operational burden and potential liabilities it can impose on management.

- *Current Ratio, Working Capital, or Net Worth*   These covenants normally are included only in debt financings and are agreements to maintain the current ratios, working capital, or net worth, either at a minimum amount or as specified for various time periods.

- *Use of Proceeds*   Often the company will agree to apply the proceeds deriving from the financing to a specified use. The investor will sometimes require that the proceeds be applied within a narrow area of the business in connection with a specific financing plan, or may simply require that the funds be used for working capital.[67]

Testa also provides the following examples of negative covenants that are often found in venture capital transactions:

- *Mergers, Consolidations, and Sale or Purchase of Assets*   Mergers, consolidations, acquisitions, and so forth, with respect to the company or any of its subsidiaries, are generally prohibited without the investor's advance approval. Liquidation and dissolution of the company or any subsidiary and the sale, lease, pledge, or other disposition of substantial assets without consent may also be barred. Restrictions may also be placed on the company's purchase of capital assets.

- *Dealings with Related Parties*   The company will covenant that no transactions between the company and any officers, directors, or stockholders of the company shall be effected unless on an arm's length basis and on terms no less favorable to the company than could be obtained from nonrelated persons. Approval of all transactions with affiliates by either the board or the investors may be required.

- *Change in Business* The company will not change the nature of its business as described in its business plan.
- *Charter Amendments* The investor may prohibit the company from amending its corporate charter or bylaws without the consent of the investor. More narrowly drawn covenants might prohibit only certain specified actions (such as a change in the capital structure) without the investor's consent.
- *Distributions and Redemptions* The company typically agrees not to make any dividend distributions to stockholders. Dividends may be prohibited until a given date or until the completion of a public offering of the company's stock, or may be limited to a fixed percentage of profits above a set amount. In addition, the company may covenant not to repurchase or redeem any of its securities except in accordance with the terms of the securities purchased by the investor (e.g., redeemable preferred stock), employee plans (e.g., forfeiture of stock upon termination of employment), or agreements with stockholders (e.g., right of first refusal).
- *Issuance of Stock or Convertible Securities* The investor may prohibit the company from issuing any securities that would result in dilution of the investor's position. This covenant includes restrictions on the issuance of securities of the type purchased by the investor and any securities convertible into such securities at a price less than that paid by the investor. Alternatively, a formula may be employed so that such an issuance will automatically trigger an improved conversion rate for the securities purchased by the investor. Frequently, these covenants are included in the terms of the securities themselves.
- *Liens and Encumbrances* The investment agreement (generally for debt-oriented securities, including redeemable preferred stock) may provide for restrictions on liens, pledges, and other encumbrances, with exceptions for such liabilities as real estate mortgages. Separate restrictions can be placed on leases of real property or equipment.
- *Indebtedness* The company may agree to restrictions of future indebtedness. Unsecured bank debt is frequently permitted.

Certain dollar limits on other debt is common. This provision is most typical of investments in debt-oriented securities.

- *Investments* Restrictions against investing in other companies may be imposed by the investor. Exceptions are made for investments in wholly owned subsidiaries.
- *Employee Compensation* The company may agree to limit employment and other personal service contracts of management or key personnel to a maximum term and a maximum amount of annual compensation. In addition, the investment agreement may prohibit the acceleration or termination of vesting schedules applicable to stock held by officers, directors and employees.
- *Financial Covenants* Negative financial covenants are frequently imposed upon a company in a debt-oriented investment, such as prohibiting key ratios or financial conditions from exceeding certain limits, or limiting the company from incurring losses in excess of a certain amount. Short of resulting in a default on securities, failure to comply with financial covenants may trigger adjustments in conversion ratios of securities, or give rise to preferential voting or other rights for the investor.[68]

Additionally, if the investment security is a debt instrument, Testa adds, there may be added to these standard covenants "lengthy financial covenants of the variety typical in a commercial lending transaction."[69]

If companies fail to comply with any of the positive or negative covenants to which they have agreed, they typically must get waivers from their venture capital investors (or from some percentage of the holders of the preferred stock, usually two-thirds) to avoid fairly severe consequences, such as triggering extraordinary voting rights or even rescission rights.

Positive and negative covenants are particularly effective control mechanisms and are therefore common in venture capital transactions. They allow venture capitalists to pinpoint potential problematic issues with great accuracy and address them. The actual number of covenants and their rigor are determined by venture capitalists on a case-by-case basis and depend on the particular companies and their situations. When venture capitalists do not take control of companies' boards of directors, the covenants they require tend to be extensive. The duration of covenants also tends to vary. They may endure as long as venture capitalists hold their securities, or they may expire after some period of time or on the occurrence of specific events, such as a company's IPO. Also, according to Lee Benton and Robert Gunderson, sometimes "the concept of a 'floor' percentage (such as 25%) is used. If the number of outstanding shares of Preferred Stock drops below the floor, the covenants are extinguished."[70]

One group of covenants deserves special mention. Some of the negative covenants previously listed cover actions and/or transactions in which virtually all venture-backed companies must engage, at least at some point in their development. Therefore, these covenants give rise to what are called *approval* rights. They require that companies get the approval of their venture capital investors (or the approval of two-thirds of the holders of the preferred stock) before taking certain actions or entering into certain transactions, especially those that might adversely affect the rights of such investors. Approval rights certainly do not allow venture capitalists to wield absolute control over board decisions, but they do give them *blocking positions*. Blocking (or veto) positions can be powerful control mechanisms, allowing venture capitalists to demand that the actions and/or transactions over which they have blocking positions be favorable (or at least not too unfavorable) to their interests.

Repurchase and Vesting Provisions

Will the company's management team members be subject to repurchase and vesting provisions?

One effective method of control for venture capitalists that is almost universally employed is the use of equity incentive provisions. Two incentive provisions commonly used are repurchase provisions and vesting provisions. Repurchase provisions allow companies to buy back from entrepreneurs and key employees the stock owned by them if and when they cease their employment or are terminated for cause. According to Joseph Bartlett, "Typically, an employee will be allowed to purchase at bargain prices shares of stock subject to the company's right to buy them back at the employee's nominal cost if the employee prematurely terminates his employment for reasons other than death or disability."[71] Because of the sometimes harsh effect that repurchase provisions can produce, they are often combined with vesting provisions. Vesting provisions cause repurchase rights to terminate with regard to any *vested* shares of stock. Therefore, companies may only repurchase those shares that have not yet vested. Vesting typically occurs incrementally over three to five years according to vesting schedules. Says Bartlett, "[A] five-year vesting provision will typically provide that one-fifth of the shares issued shall vest in each of the five years following the employee's receipt of stock; that is, they are no longer repurchasable by the corporation at cost."[72] It is typical that stock vest on a monthly basis after a certain period of time, often referred to as a *cliff,* has elapsed. The attorneys at Venture Law Group explain:

> *Usually stock grants have a "cliff" (usually six months or one year). If the employee leaves before the "cliff," he/she gets nothing (no stock has vested). If the employee survives past the "cliff," he/she gets full vesting for the time elapsed . . . and then goes onto normal monthly vesting. Founders don't usually have a "cliff." The rationale is that they've taken a special risk to get the company started and should be rewarded. So they typically start out with monthly vesting from Day One. In fact it's common to give the founders some advance vesting (typically 10% to 20% of their shares). Then if something happens to them, they or their estate still get some benefit from having started the company.[73]*

Repurchase and vesting provisions are attractive to venture capitalists. First, they ensure that entrepreneurs and key employees are committed. They do this by transferring equity gradually and incrementally to entrepreneurs over time, as opposed to giving them full rights to such securities all at once. Essentially, they force entrepreneurs to "earn" their equity by maintaining their employment for certain periods of time. These provisions are therefore often called *golden handcuffs,* as they tie entrepreneurs to their companies. They require entrepreneurs to earn their equity by (1) maintaining their employment with their companies (by not leaving voluntarily) and (2) maintaining satisfactory job performance (so as to avoid being fired). Repurchase and vesting provisions also encourage entrepreneurs to work hard to build the value of their companies, because they benefit directly from any appreciation in the value of their stock. Second, repurchase and vesting provisions control dilution and allow companies to conserve their equity. These provisions free up stock for reissuance to new employees brought in to replace key employees who have left or were terminated prematurely. For example, if a particular individual fails to meet the targets expected of him or her (or is simply no longer contributing value), he or she can be fired—which causes vesting to cease—and replaced. Then, all unvested shares may be repurchased by the particular company and sold to a replacement employee more likely to create value.

By the time venture capitalists become involved with early-stage companies, however, the entrepreneurs and key employees may have already purchased large amounts of equity not subject to vesting requirements or repurchase restrictions. Venture capitalists, therefore, typically require that such persons execute additional agreements, after the fact, with vesting and repurchase provisions. When significant sweat equity (time, effort, and talent) has been contributed, however, Martin H. Levenglick, partner at the law firm of O'Sullivan Graev & Karabell, points out that some entrepreneurs "will often expect their initial equity to be fully invested at inception as compensation for their having come up with the idea behind the company and having provided the early 'sweat' to build it."[74] This is usually a hotly negotiated point between venture capitalists and entrepreneurs, but some venture capitalists are fairly immovable on the subject. Says Fred Dotzler, "While founders may object to vesting, believing that they already have full ownership, investors make this a requirement in order to ensure that the individuals will stay with the company and contribute their skills until significant value is realized."[75] Such venture capitalists simply want to make certain that *all* key employees are fully committed to the growth and success of their portfolio companies on a long-term basis.

Staged Capital Commitments

Will the commitment of capital to the company be staged in several tranches or closings?

Venture capitalists often require that portfolio companies receive staged infusions of capital over time, instead of transferring an entire amount of capital at one time. The venture capitalists at Benchmark Capital state that they typically "invest $2 to $4 million initially and expect to invest $5 to $7 million over the life of a company."[76] The venture capitalists at Weiss, Peck & Greer Venture Partners say that their "initial investments generally range from $2 to $7 million" and that they "expect to support portfolio companies by participating in subsequent financings, which may result in a total investment of as much as $10 million in any one company."[77] These staged infusions are commonly called *tranches,* after the British finance term. Venture capitalists generally prefer to invest in multiple tranches for several reasons.

First, staging the commitment of capital can be a powerful control mechanism for venture capitalists. Timothy Tomlinson explains that the "venture capitalist's obligation to [fund each tranche] is contingent upon the company's achieving certain pre-negotiated milestones. . . ."[78] Because those milestones are usually drawn straight from companies' business plans, says Richard Testa, a "staged investment serves as an incentive to management to proceed diligently with the development of its business, as outlined in its business plan. . . ."[79] Staging the commitment of capital also encourages portfolio companies to spend conservatively while seeking to meet those next milestones. If a particular portfolio company does not work diligently and spend prudently to meet its next milestones, it might be forced to find funding elsewhere, or face more draconian terms from existing investors. Jeffry Timmons explains:

> *Staging the capital . . . provides incentives to the entrepreneurial team. The credible threat to abandon a venture, even when the firm might be economically viable, is the key to the relationship between the entrepreneur and the venture capitalist. By denying capital, the venture capitalist also signals other capital suppliers that the company in question is a bad investment risk.*[80]

It is very much in the interest of venture capitalists to encourage their portfolio companies to use capital wisely. The misuse of that capital can be very costly to them. If capital is squandered, then additional equity financing will likely be required—and that will mean dilution for existing equity holders. The venture capitalists at Sequoia Capital state that dilution is their "greatest enemy."[81] Therefore, venture capitalists also stage their commitment of capital to help companies keep their spending under control and to prevent them from becoming too well endowed. Keeping resources limited at all times has the added benefit of tending to cause companies to be hungry and driven. William Sahlman explains this phenomenon:

> *There is not a more powerful motivator than the knowledge that the enterprise is scheduled to run out of cash in the relatively near future. In the parlance of entrepreneurial finance, the rate at which a company consumes cash is called the "burn rate." Given any level of initial cash and a burn rate, it is possible to calculate the "fume date"—the date on which the company will have exhausted its cash and will be operating solely on fumes. The existence of periodic "fume dates" focuses the energies of management on creating value from limited resources; and this process can accrue to the benefit of both entrepreneur and venture capitalist.*

For precisely this reason, it is often observed that well-endowed companies tend to be less successful in the long run than those whose resources have been limited.

Second, staging the commitment of capital in tranches also maximizes venture capitalists' internal rates of return and reduces their risk. When the commitment of capital is staged, venture capitalists gain the following valuable options before each tranche is invested: (1) to abandon the project and to discontinue further investment, (2) to revalue the project and commit further capital, or (3) to increase the capital committed. Because new information is learned between each tranche—whether the people are working out, whether the technology works, whether the market is accepting the product—venture capitalists are able to make semi-informed decisions about these options. Simply put, these options allow venture capitalists to ensure that the net present value of an investment remains positive before each tranche is put into a company or, if the net present value of the investment ceases to be positive, to abandon their investment. These options are not available if venture capitalists do not stage the commitment of capital. Says Sahlman, successful venture capital firms "generate high rates of return by cutting their losses early, not investing great amounts in early rounds, and letting their winners run by investing larger amounts of money in multiple rounds of financing."[82]

Right of First Refusal

Will you have a right of first refusal (or preemptive right) to participate in future financings of the company?

Venture capitalists almost always insist on having rights to participate in future financings of their portfolio companies. Rights of first refusal guarantee venture capitalists such participation by allowing them to preempt new investors (that is, allowing them the opportunity to invest before the same opportunity is given to any other investors). Mechanically, when venture capitalists hold these rights they are entitled to receive notice of any proposed financings and are then given the right to purchase the securities under precisely the same terms being offered to the new third-party investors.

There are, however, many different versions of these rights. They may afford venture capitalists rights to participate in such financings only to the extent as will maintain their fully diluted percentage equity interests. Or, they may also afford venture capitalists "oversubscription rights" that allow them to take up any of the securities not subscribed for by other investors. Alternatively, rights of first refusal may afford venture capitalists the right to assume future financings in their entirety. They may also be "all or nothing" rights, meaning that venture capitalists must either assume all of a particular financing or their rights terminate. Also, rights of first refusal are typically given carve-outs similar to those given to price-based antidilution rights, so that such things as issuances of stock options to employees do not trigger the rights.

Rights of first refusal are not always exercised by the venture capitalists that hold them, but the options they create can be valuable. The right to participate in future financings can be an effective antidilution mechanism. This protection is of particular importance in down financing rounds. Furthermore, without the right to participate in future financings, investors cannot be sure of reaping the benefits of staging their commitment of capital, discussed previously.

Pay-to-Play Provisions

If you will be given the right to participate in future financings of the company, will a "pay-to-play" provision be attached to that right?

Just as with other types of antidilution provisions, whether a venture capitalist's right to participate in future financings continues from one round to the next is sometimes made contingent on its being used in each round. Pay-to-play provisions mandate that if an investor fails to exercise its right to participate in one round of financing, then the right extinguishes and is not available for the next round. According to Leslie Davis, it is fairly common for "investors to lose their right of first refusal on new issuances if they skip a round."[83] As discussed, pay-to-play provisions are popular among venture capitalists who tend to coinvest alongside other venture capitalists and support their portfolio companies through multiple rounds of financing. For those types of venture capitalists, pay-to-play provisions are attractive because they provide strong incentives to the other investors to step up and contribute their share of the capital to each round of financing. On the other hand, for venture capitalists who do not support each and every one of their portfolio companies through multiple rounds of financing (e.g., seed-stage venture capitalists who do not have the financial resources to do so), pay-to-play provisions are unattractive. They can severely limit their ability to invest in hot deals for which they would otherwise have rights of first refusal.

Redemption Rights

Will redemption rights be triggered if certain milestones are not met?

Whereas redemption provisions are rarely used in venture capital transactions to achieve liquidity, venture capitalists sometimes do use them for control. (Redemption rights—or "put rights"—are discussed later in this chapter.) Frederick Lipman explains:

Another control mechanism utilized by professionally managed venture capitalists is to permit their preferred stock to be redeemable on certain events. Typically, the redemption rights will become effective around the fifth year. However, some venture capitalists add provisions permitting redemption even earlier if certain milestones or projections in the business plan are not met. This redemption right gives venture capitalists an important control mechanism. If they can force the company to repurchase the preferred stock (plus accumulated but unpaid dividends), they can exercise substantial influence over the company, particularly if the company cannot afford to redeem the preferred stock.[84]

Redemption rights, when held by venture capitalists, encourage companies to work diligently to find paths to liquidity for investors. Jonathan Cole and Albert Sokol explain:

On a practical basis, . . . the "put" may not give the investors the ability to receive cash upon exercise, since many growing companies, especially ones that have experienced bumps in the road to success, will likely not be able to finance a buyout of a significant equity partner. Rather, a "put" gives the VCs the power to force the management to find a practical solution to the exit requirements of the investors, the absence of which will give the investors the right to cause the liquidation of the company and forced sale of the company. The "put" rights set the negotiating table far in advance of the exit date and give a strong incentive to management to plan for a liquidity event for the investors in a timely manner.[85]

They become particularly important when portfolio companies begin to go "sideways." Says Leslie Davis, "redemption rights are used to provide leverage in a 'sideways' deal—one where the company is not making progress to a liquidity event but is not totally failing."[86] In such cases, redemption rights provide venture capitalists leverage to force the sale of such companies, so that they might still achieve some liquidity.

HARVEST MECHANISMS

Registration Rights

Will you have registration rights?

Every venture capitalist in every venture capital deal is ultimately looking forward to the day when the investment will become liquid. Nothing is more important to venture capitalists than liquidity. One of the two primary sources of liquidity is the mechanism of the IPO. Registration rights enable venture capitalists to participate in the liquidity that IPOs provide. These rights allow venture capitalists to compel their portfolio companies to register their stock, or to let them piggyback on other registrations. Once registered, venture capitalists are able to sell their stock in the public markets. That ability is what provides them with liquidity. Therefore, registration rights provisions are of great importance to venture capitalists, and are something on which venture capitalists are reluctant to negotiate. Says Richard Testa:

> *The right to register securities for public sale under the Securities Act of 1933 and state securities laws represents the most advantageous vehicle for a venture capital investor to achieve liquidity and realize a return on his investment. The potential of an enterprise to achieve a size conducive to a public offering is an imperative to most venture capital investments; accordingly, the right of the investor to participate in the public market for the company's securities is an area in which the venture capitalist will concede few limitations on his ability of action.*[87]

Although there can be numerous versions of registration rights provisions, the fundamental registration rights principles are present in most venture capital investment transactions.

Demand Registration Rights

Will you have demand registration rights?

Venture capitalists frequently require that they have the right to compel their portfolio companies to register the shares held by them.

Such rights are referred to as *demand* registration rights because they entitle venture capitalists to demand that companies file registration statements covering their shares. Though companies generally view them negatively, demand registration rights are fairly common in major venture capital financings. Demand rights assure venture capitalists access to the public markets. In their unrestricted form, they guarantee liquidity. They are, therefore, the strongest form of registration rights. However, demand registration rights rarely appear in their unrestricted form. They are typically limited in several ways.

They are usually limited in timing. Demands may only be allowed after three to five years following investment or after companies effect their IPOs (and the underwriters' holdback period has expired). Or, demands may only be allowed after some period has elapsed following such IPOs (e.g., 6 or 12 months). Without such limitations, venture capitalists would be able to force their portfolio companies to go public. Therefore, according to Gunderson and Benton, the rationale behind timing limitations "is that, for a reasonable period of time, the decision to go public ought to be made exclusively by . . . Board[s] of Directors and management and that the Investors ought not be able to force [companies] public."[88] The reality is that demand registration rights are seldom used for this purpose. However, their mere presence can influence the decision of a company to go public. Limiting the timing of demands reduces this influence. Another common limit on this influence is that companies may be given the power to delay demand registrations, if in their discretion business conditions are not favorable or if registrations would be seriously detrimental to the companies (e.g., if sensitive information about an upcoming acquisition would be disclosed by such registrations). Companies, however, usually only have the right to delay demand registrations once. Demand registration rights may also be limited in terms of the number of demands that may be made (e.g., no more than one demand in any six-month period) and the number of shares that must be covered by the registrations (e.g., 20%–50% of the registerable securities). The reason for these limitations is the expense involved with the registration process. Companies push for these limitations because they want to avoid having to effect too many registrations and to avoid effecting registrations that cover too few shares. Also, it has become common for demands to be limited to those that will result in offerings of some specific dollar amount (e.g., $5 million to $10 million).

Short-Form Registration Rights

Will you have short-form registration rights?

Venture capitalists nearly always require *short-form* registration rights. These rights entitle investors to cause companies to register their shares using short-form registration statements (SEC Forms S-2 or S-3). When companies initially go public, they must file full-blown registration statements on SEC Form S-1; these are extensive disclosures and expensive to prepare. Once public for a certain period (and once they meet several other technical requirements), companies may effect secondary offerings by filing short-form registration statements. Short-form registrations are relatively less expensive for companies because companies can use information already filed with the SEC under the Securities Exchange Act of 1934, thereby dramatically reducing the costs (both in terms of time and money) of compiling the information required for registration. Venture capitalists are generally given unlimited short-form registration rights, which become effective once companies become eligible to use short-form registration statements. Short-form registration rights can prove valuable because short-form registrations are much less expensive than full registrations and companies are much more willing to use them. For venture capitalists, short-form registrations can turn out to be paths of minimal resistance to liquidity in the public markets.

Piggyback Registration Rights

Will you have piggyback registration rights?

Venture capitalists also usually insist on being given *piggyback* registration rights. Piggyback registration rights obligate companies to let (or sometimes to use their "best efforts" to let) venture capitalists piggyback on the registrations of newly issued shares that companies already intend to make by including under the companies' registration statements the shares owned by venture capitalists. In contrast to demand registration rights, few additional limitations are typically placed on piggyback registration rights. There is usually no need to limit the timing of piggyback registrations because they are already limited by their nature. Say Gunderson and Benton, "the Company is entitled to determine the timing of the registration, and, indeed, whether to complete it at all. The Investors are merely along for the ride."[89] Additionally, as Richard Testa points out, piggyback registration rights "will frequently be unlimited in number on the theory that no significant burden is imposed on the company by requiring it to include additional shares in a registration that it is otherwise undertaking."[90]

One limitation that typically accompanies piggyback registration rights provisions in venture capital transactions is the right of underwriters to exclude the venture capitalists' stock from public offerings. This right is commonly referred to as the *underwriter's cutback*. Testa explains the underwriter's cutback:

> *"Piggy-back" registration rights generally contain provisions enabling the underwriters managing the public offering to cut back the number of shares to be registered by selling security holders on a pro rata basis if, in the underwriters' opinion, such a cutback is necessary or desirable to market the public offering effectively.*[91]

Venture capitalists do sometimes, however, limit the ability of companies to eliminate their shares completely from initial public offerings. They also sometimes limit their ability to cut back their shares in secondary registrations (registrations made subsequent to initial public offerings).

Registration Expenses

Will the company pay the expenses of registration?

Venture capitalists generally prefer to address up front the issue of who will pay the expenses of registration, which can be very high. Because of the enormous cost involved with the registration of securities, venture capitalists usually require companies to agree up front to pay for the registration expenses. However, sometimes venture capitalists will agree to pay their own costs for any short-form registrations, which tend to be much less expensive.

Rule 144 Requirements

Will the company agree to file all necessary reports and take all necessary actions required by Rule 144?

An alternate (and extremely important) method of achieving liquidity for venture capitalists is to sell their securities under Rule 144 of the Securities Act of 1933. Rule 144 allows them to sell their securities in the public markets without having to go through the registration process once their portfolio companies have gone public and if all the other requirements of Rule 144 have been met. One of the requirements of Rule 144 is that portfolio companies be reporting companies under the Securities Exchange Act of 1943 and that they file all reports required by that Act for the specified period of time. Therefore, venture capitalists usually require that companies agree up front that, once they go public, they will indeed file all reports and take all other action necessary to enable investors to sell shares in public markets under the exemption from registration contained in Rule 144.

Drag-Along Rights

Will you have drag-along rights?

The second of the two primary methods by which venture capitalists harvest their investments is through merger and acquisition (M&A) transactions—transactions in which their portfolio companies are acquired by or merged with other companies. Traditionally, entrepreneurs (and venture capitalists, for that matter) have preferred the IPO route to liquidity over the M&A route. However, when particularly attractive M&A opportunities come along, or when companies have failed to effect their IPOs or make redemptions after reasonable periods, venture capitalists generally like to be able to influence their portfolio companies to go ahead and take the M&A route. It is often difficult, however, for them to exert such influence without the full cooperation of entrepreneurs and other major investors, especially when venture capitalists are substantial, but minority, shareholders. Even when venture capitalists are majority shareholders, or are able to convince sufficient other shareholders of the M&A strategy, entrepreneurs and management teams may still inhibit the transactions. The founders may hold veto rights, or the acquirors may seek to purchase a certain percentage of the portfolio companies' equity. The way venture capitalists deal with these situations is through the mechanism of the *drag-along* provision. Drag-along provisions permit venture capitalists to force the sale of their portfolio companies by allowing them to compel entrepreneurs and management team members to also sell their interests if and when the venture capitalists receive acceptable offers for their portfolio companies from corporate acquirors. "The justification for this clause," says Frederick Lipman, "is that the venture capitalists may not be able to sell their interest in the business unless the founder's interest is sold along with their own. . . ."[92] Even though these provisions can be attractive to venture capitalists, they have actually become something of a rarity in venture capital transactions. When they do appear, they are typically limited by becoming effective only after portfolio companies fail to consummate their IPOs or to redeem venture capitalists' stock after specified numbers of years.

Anti-Lockout Rights

Will you have anti-lockout rights?

The venture capitalists at Advantage Capital Partners make use of a legal term that is relatively new to venture capital transactions: *anti-lockout* provisions. These provisions are essentially an alternative to drag-along rights. They require that when portfolio companies receive reasonable M&A offers, and when entrepreneurs and/or management team members are reluctant to participate in the transactions, then they are required to buy out their venture capital investors on the same terms as were offered by the potential acquirors. Anti-lockout provisions, therefore, allow entrepreneurs and management team members to maintain their equity ownership in their companies, but also inhibit them from locking venture capitalists out of attractive M&A harvest opportunities. Says Scott Zajac, principal and managing director of Advantage Capital Partners, "This is a term that we instituted just this year, and, because of incidents we had in the past, we are making it standard."[93]

Tag-Along Rights

Will you have tag-along (or co-sale) rights?

Venture capitalists always face the danger of having the entrepreneurs they back and/or key management team members bail out on them by leaving their employment and selling their shares to third parties. To manage this risk, venture capitalists very often employ *tag-along* or *co-sale* provisions. Tag-along provisions appear frequently in venture capital transactions, often in separate agreements executed by the entrepreneurs and key management team members and the venture capitalists. Tag-along provisions give venture capitalists the right to participate alongside entrepreneurs and/or management team members in any sales of portfolio company shares to third parties. Says Richard Testa, "Although rarely exercised, this co-sale or 'ta[g]-along' right limits the ability of management to bail out of the company leaving the investors at risk to recover their investment."[94] The risk of this happening is especially acute when founders hold such significant percentage equity interests that they can effectively sell control of their companies without the requirement of shareholder votes. Although merger transactions and transactions in which substantially all the assets of companies are sold generally require shareholder votes to become effective, sales of controlling blocks of stock generally do not. This fact can leave venture capitalists vulnerable. Benton and Gunderson explain:

> *Outside parties are frequently willing to pay a premium for a controlling interest in a business. A co-sale agreement allows the venture capital investors to share in this premium. Furthermore, sale of a controlling block to a corporate buyer may eliminate going public or sale to another corporation as a potential avenue of liquidity for the investors. A practical effect of the co-sale agreement may also be to encourage the outside party to offer to*

buy all of the Company's outstanding stock, rather than just a controlling interest.[95]

Therefore, tag-along rights are of great importance to venture capitalists. Mark White explains how they work:

[F]ounders give the investor the right to participate pro rata in any sale of the founders' shares to a third party. The number of shares that the founders can sell is reduced and replaced by the number of shares that the investors elect to sell to the third party.[96]

Most venture capitalists, however, allow entrepreneurs and management team members to sell their shares in limited amounts. According to Fred Dotzler, venture capitalists usually permit them to sell "up to 10 to 15 percent, without restriction."[97] Beyond that range, says Dotzler, "the founders can sell shares only if the investors can also sell their shares."[98]

Redemption Rights

If the investment security is preferred stock, will you have redemption rights?

Venture investors sometimes use redemption rights provisions, not as control mechanisms as discussed previously, but as outright liquidity mechanisms. Redemption rights allow venture capitalists to require their portfolio companies to buy back (or redeem) their stock at an agreed-on price after a specified period of time. According to Lee Benton and Robert Gunderson, however, redemption rights provisions are somewhat rare in venture capital transactions:

In many venture capital financings, there are no redemption provisions with respect to the Preferred Stock. Investors expect to achieve liquidity after the Company goes public or when the Company is acquired. Cash redemption of the Preferred Stock is not viewed as a realistic alternative.[99]

Unless redemption formulas are generous, the returns generated by redemptions generally do not approach those that can be generated by IPOs or M&A transactions. When venture capitalists implement redemption rights provisions for the purpose of liquidity, says Stephen Glover, they use them exits of last resort: "In general, venture capitalists use these exit mechanisms, which work only if the company has sufficient liquidity to satisfy the put or redemption obligation, when the company's performance has been mediocre and an initial public offering or sale of the business is not feasible."[100]

Redemption Prices

If the investment security is preferred stock and you will have redemption rights, what will the redemption price be?

The price at which shares will be redeemed directly determines the value of the redemption rights to venture capitalists. There are two general methods for calculating redemption prices. The first method relies essentially on venture capitalists' liquidation preference amounts, which usually equal the original purchase prices they paid for their stock plus accumulated but unpaid dividends. (Liquidation preferences are discussed in more detail later in this chapter.) A third component, a redemption premium, is sometimes added to this calculation. Redemption premiums, according to Frederick Lipman, can sometimes be large: "[S]ome venture capitalists require a redemption price that is three or more times the original investment. . . ."[101] It should be noted that if premiums are too large, they will be considered "unreasonable" by the IRS and will be treated as a "constructive dividend" under Section 305 of the Internal Revenue Code. If the IRS treats a premium as a constructive dividend, then the premium amount will be taxed at ordinary rates (as opposed to capital gains rates). Mark White tells us, however, that a "safe harbor under applicable regulations provides that a premium of no greater than 10% over five years is reasonable."[102] Because this is quite small, many venture capitalists, according to White, "seek premiums in excess of the safe harbor under the view that the inherent risk of early-stage investments justifies the premium."[103]

The second method by which redemption prices are calculated, according to Cole and Sokol, is based on "the common stock equivalent value of the investment (e.g., the 'as converted value' of the preferred stock as if it had been converted to common stock as shared in the value of the company's common equity on a pro rata basis)."[104] Cole and Sokol explain that some "redemption pricing formulas determine common stock equivalent value by reference to 'fair market value,' usually fixed by appraisal, while others determine such value by reference to a multiple of earnings (usually EBITDA, or earnings before interest, taxes, depreciation and amortization)."[105]

Debt Repayment Terms

If the investment security is debt, what will be the repayment terms?

In bridge loan transactions, where the investment security is debt, the repayment of principal and interest is not typically expected, because most bridge loan notes are convertible into preferred stock. However, such notes typically provide that if conversion has not occurred by a specified date, then the principal and interest become due and payable. Because the purposes of bridge loans are usually to cover companies' short-term financing needs, the periods of time before which they become due and payable are typically short (e.g., 6–12 months).

One issue of concern to bridging seed-stage venture capitalists and angel investors is that of prepayment. Companies often reserve the right to prepay their debt obligations. This can be a problem for venture capitalists holding convertible debt, Richard Testa explains, because "prepayment will have the effect of extinguishing any conversion rights. . . ."[106] Extinguishing conversion rights effectively eliminates any upside participation on the part of the bridging seed-stage investors.

Liquidation Preferences

If the investment security is preferred stock, will you have a liquidation preference?

Another potentially important harvest mechanism for venture capitalists is the liquidation preference. Liquidation of a portfolio company is an unfortunate outcome for venture capitalists, but company failure is a reality of the business and a liquidation preference can enable investors to harvest at least some portion of their investment.

The preferred stock purchased by venture capitalists virtually always contains some sort of liquidation preference. Harold M. Hoffman and James Blakey, partners at the law firm of Kronish Lieb Weiner & Hellman, explain, "Liquidation preferences specify the order in which holders of different classes of securities get paid and how much of the liquidation proceeds they can collect before other investors are repaid."[107] According to Frederick Lipman, the proceeds on liquidation of a corporation are usually paid in the following order of priority:

- *Secured Creditors* Secured creditors will receive the value of the assets that were collateral for the respective secured debts owed to them. To the extent that the collateral is insufficient to satisfy the secured debts, secured creditors are treated as unsecured creditors with respect to the balance of the debt. To the extent the value of the collateral exceeds the amount of secured debt, the next lower level of creditors, namely, unsecured nonsubordinated creditors, receive the benefit of that excess.
- *Unsecured Nonsubordinated Creditors* The class of unsecured nonsubordinated creditors consists of trade creditors (suppliers of goods and services), employees (ignoring the small bankruptcy priority given to certain wage claims), holders of unsecured notes, holders of tort and contract claims, and so forth.
- *Subordinated Creditors* Holders of subordinated debt are paid after the unsecured creditors to which they are subordinated.
- *Preferred Stockholders* If the preferred stock has a liquidation preference over common stock, holders of preferred stock are the next distributees.
- *Common Stockholders* Holders of common stock receive the residue of the liquidation proceeds that remains after all of the other categories have been paid.[108]

If the investment security is debt (such as a bridge loan), therefore, venture capitalists and angel investors will typically receive on liquidation their original investment amount plus any accrued, but unpaid interest, assuming that the liquidation proceeds are adequate to make such payments. The actual type of debt, however, will determine the precise liquidation priority, among the different types of debtholders. The debt purchased in venture capital transactions is typically unsecured. Venture-backed companies rarely have the type of assets by which debt is usually secured: accounts receivable, inventory, equipment, or real estate of sufficient value. Furthermore, in order that their portfolio companies may obtain bank and other institutional lending as well as equipment leasing on favorable terms, venture capitalists often contractually subordinate their rights to receive payments on liquidation to the rights of lenders. Those types of lender are usually reluctant to loan money to early-stage companies that already have debt outstanding. Therefore, subordination facilitates future lending transactions because lenders generally view subordinated debt essentially as equity. Venture capitalists usually only subordinate their debt, however, to that of banks, institutional lenders, and equipment leasing firms, not other types of debt, such as trade debt. Subordination is usually very much in venture capitalists' interest. They certainly benefit when their companies are able to obtain favorable lending. Bank financing and equipment leasing typically has none (or much less) of the dilutive impact that further equity financing would have if companies were not able to secure such financing arrangements.

If the investment security is preferred stock—and if the liquidation proceeds are sufficient—venture capitalists will typically receive a specifically stated amount on liquidation, before any of the proceeds are distributed to the holders of the common stock (entrepreneurs, management team members, and employees). That liquidation preference amount is usually equal to the original purchase price of the preferred stock plus any accrued, but unpaid dividends. Greg Gallo, partner at the law firm of Gray Cary Ware & Freidenrich, and Scott Stanton, associate at the same firm, state that the "basic premise of a liquidation preference is that [those] who undertake large financial risk to invest hard cash (and receive no salaries or bonuses) should receive as much of their original investment as possible if the business fails."[109] Holders of common stock typically pay small fractions (for their common stock) of the per share amounts paid by venture capitalists (for their preferred stock). Additionally, "Where there are multiple classes of preferred stock," explains Gary Silverman, "such classes may be senior to, *pari passu* with, or subordinated to each other upon liquidation."[110]

Deemed Liquidation

Will a merger or acquisition be treated as a deemed liquidation?

Whether M&A transactions in which their portfolio companies are not the surviving entities are treated as *deemed* liquidations is a subtle, but important term for venture capitalists. If they are so treated, then with any M&A transactions, venture capitalists can choose between receiving their liquidation preference as holders of preferred stock or converting their preferred stock into common stock and participating in the transactions as holders of common stock. The "amount available from distribution," Gary Silverman explains, "will dictate which choice will yield the greatest proceeds for the venture capitalist."[111] Because of the option it provides, this is an important term for venture capitalists. Say Greg Gallo and Scott Stanton, "This simple term gives the liquidation preference a significant impact. Instead of being a minimal downside protection, it becomes a negotiated allocation of return on investment in the event the business is sold."[112]

Participation Rights

If the investment vehicle is preferred stock, will there be participation rights that extend beyond any stated liquidation preference?

More and more, venture capitalists are insisting on *participation rights*. Participation rights essentially obviate any need for venture capitalists to choose between participating in liquidations or M&A transactions as preferred stockholders or as common stockholders. Participation rights allow them to do both. According to Gary Silverman, participation rights entitle the venture capitalist "to receive *both* its liquidation preference *plus* accrued and unpaid dividends *plus* the value of its underlying common stock on an 'as-if-converted' basis."[113] Joseph Bartlett describes having participation rights as being able to "have your cake and eat it too."[114] But, the reality is that participation rights only make much of a difference when investments turn out to be mediocre. And, when returns are mediocre, participation rights simply correct for the inequitable results that are sometimes created by straight liquidation preferences. According to

Timothy Tomlinson, relying simply on straight liquidation preferences (without participation rights) "can be unfair to venture capitalists, as it permits common holders to realize gains—sometimes, significant gains—on their investments while depriving preferred holders of any gain whatsoever."[115] Tomlinson offers the following illustration:

> *An example would be a newly formed company in which the venture capitalist invests $5 million for 50 percent of the stock and the common stockholders $1 million for the other half. In a merger valuing the business at $10 million, under a simple liquidation preference, the preferred holder would receive $5 million (its money back) and the common holders $5 million (five times their original investment). The preferred stockholder will have provided almost all the cash that gave rise to the common stockholders' return on investment but will have received no return.*[116]

When investments turn out to be home runs, on the other hand, the fact that venture capitalists first get their liquidation preferences (plus accumulated, but unpaid dividends) before participating with the holders of the common stock (as opposed to simply participating with the holders of the common stock) does not always make a material difference to their returns.

When participation rights are attached to preferred stock, that stock is generally referred to as "participating" preferred stock. Participating preferred stock has become common in venture capital transactions and generally takes one of two forms—full or capped:

1. *Full Participating Preferred*   Under full participation rights, venture capitalists are first paid their specified liquidation preference amount and then preferred and common stockholders share all remaining proceeds on a pro rata basis. In other words, venture capitalists holding participating preferred stock get the additional benefit of "participating" with the common stockholders in the distribution of the residual proceeds on liquidation.
2. *Capped Participating Preferred*   Capped participation rights can take several forms. Gallo and Stanton explain:

> *A typical capped liquidation preference requires the initial payment of the straight liquidation preference to the preferred*

stockholders, after which the preferred stockholders participate pro rata with the holders of common stock until they receive a certain specified return—normally two to five times their original investment, with earlier rounds usually having multiples on the higher end (determined by the appropriate discount rate). After payment of the capped liquidation preference, the common stockholders take all of the remaining assets. A variation on this method is to pay the straight preference, followed by a similar straight liquidation preference to the holders of common stock on a pro rata basis before the preferred stockholders begin to share again on a pro rata basis with the common stock owners up to their cap.[117]

The rationale behind participation rights is the same as that for straight liquidation preferences: Venture capitalists should be entitled to additional returns because they incur substantial financial risk but do not receive salaries and bonuses, which the entrepreneurs, management team members, and employees—the holders of the common stock—do receive. Whether venture capitalists obtain participation rights depends on bargaining power, according to Lee Benton and Robert Gunderson: "The most attractive deals may utilize the simple preference, with no participation, while the corporation struggling for funding will often have to concede to the most extreme form of participation. . . ."[118]

MISCELLANEOUS PROVISIONS

Representations and Warranties

To what representations and warranties will the company agree?

In almost every venture capital transaction, companies are required to make certain representations and warranties. A representation is simply a statement of fact made to induce another party to enter into contract. A warranty is a promise that that statement of fact is true. Therefore, the purpose of requiring companies to make representations and warranties is to get companies to state certain things about themselves and then promise that those things will be true at the time of the actual transaction. Each representation covers a particular issue that is the responsibility of companies to address and which is usually solely within the knowledge of those companies—but which can potentially create problems for venture capitalists. Each warranty creates potential liability for companies if the corresponding representation is false. Thus, investors are protected somewhat if companies mislead them, because they can sue the companies based on their warranties that their representations were correct. Arthur Lipper explains:

> *Investors have a right to believe what entrepreneurs seeking funding tell them. As an extension of this, investors have a right to recover their investment, to the extent lost, if it can be shown that the entrepreneur misstated or failed to bring to the investor's attention information that might have changed the investor's mind about the project.*[119]

Richard Testa provides the following list of specific representations and warranties that are common in most venture capital transactions:

Organization and authority: The company is properly organized, in good standing, and has legal authority to conduct its business.

Corporate action: All necessary actions under state corporate law, and the company's corporate charter and bylaws, have been taken to authorize the transaction and to issue the securities.

Governmental approvals: All consents and approvals of governmental agencies necessary to complete the transaction have been obtained. In particular, this covers compliance with state securities laws and environmental regulations.

Absence of litigations: No litigation or other proceedings exist, or are threatened, which would adversely affect the company's business or the financing transaction.

Employment of key personnel: No restrictions exist relating to employment of key personnel or use of business information, particularly as a result of prior employment of such personnel by another enterprise.

Compliance with other agreements: No violations of the company's corporate charter, bylaws, or other valid agreements exist, or will exist as a result of the financing.

Ownership of properties and assets: The company possesses sufficient ownership rights in its business assets, particularly its patent, copyright, trademark, and other intellectual property rights to conduct its business.

Financial information: Audited, and internal unaudited, financial statements have been prepared in accordance with generally accepted accounting principles and fairly represent the financial position and operating results of the company. Statements as to specific categories of items, such as inventory valuation and status of accounts receivable, may be included. No adverse changes have occurred since the date of the most recent financial statements.

Transactions with insiders: Disclosure is made of any direct or indirect transactions between the company and its directors, officers or stockholders.

Third-party guarantees or investments: Absence of continuing financial involvements with third parties.

Compliance with federal securities laws: Certification that the transaction complies with federal and state securities laws, including the possibility that the transaction may be integrated with other securities sales.

Registration rights: Absence of rights to cause the company to file any registration statement under the federal securities laws or any right to participate in any such registration.

Disclosure: The business plan used to seek financing is accurate and complete and all material disclosures have been made to investors either in the business plan or in legal documents relating to the transaction.

Brokerage: Disclosure of any finder's or broker's fees or commissions payable in connection with the transaction.

Capitalization: Description of the company's authorized capitalization and status of outstanding securities, including warrants, options and convertible securities. Any transfer restrictions, re-purchase rights or preemptive rights are also described.

Insurance: The company has insurance in such amounts and covering such risks as is customarily carried by companies of similar size engaged in similar businesses.

U.S. real property holding corporation: Certification that the company has not now and has never been a "United States real property holding corporation" and that the company has filed with the Internal Revenue Service all statements, if any, with its federal income tax returns that are required under related regulations.

Small business concern: If a member of the investment group is an SBIC, certification that the company, including its affiliates, is a "small business concern" and the information pertaining to the company set forth in any required Small Business Administration form is accurate and correct.[120]

As further assurance that entrepreneurs and management team members are being truthful, venture capitalists sometimes require that they assume personal liability for the representations and warranties made by their companies. Says Testa, "[f]rom the investor's point of view, imposing the specter of personal liability on the insiders can be an effective means of assuring complete and accurate disclosure of all material business information."[121]

CHAPTER 6

Financial Due Diligence

FINANCIAL ANALYSIS

Venture capitalists, because they invest in companies in their nascent stages, find it difficult (and often impossible) to perform financial analysis, at least in the traditional sense. Traditional financial analysis is largely based on historical financial statements and ratio analysis. Although a few early-stage companies may be able to compile meaningful historical financial information, most cannot. Furthermore, many of these companies' most important and most valuable assets—top-notch management teams, brilliant technologists, business relationships, trade secrets—cannot be reflected on their financial statements. Therefore, traditional financial analysis produces little in the way of meaningful results. As Jeffry Timmons points out, "financial ratios are misleading when applied to most private entrepreneurial companies."[1] Instead, venture capital financial analysis tends to be based most heavily on projected, future financial statements (pro forma financial statements, or simply, *pro formas,* as they are commonly called).

Historical Financial Statements

Has the company provided you with any and all historical financial statements?

Because companies seeking venture capital, almost by definition, have little (if any) historical financial information—true seed-stage companies typically have incomplete business plans and management teams, and have not completed their product development—venture capitalists generally do not expect to receive much in the way of historical financial statements from such companies. Virtually none have any history of revenues, but most are also unlikely to have extensive expense histories. Once beyond the seed stage, however, companies start to collect meaningful financial data, beginning with expense information. And, that information can be important to venture capitalists. It provides them with insight into how companies are managing their expenses, whether they are spending too much or too little. At some point, companies will also (hopefully) begin to also accumulate revenue information. When companies can provide both historical expense and revenue information, venture capitalists are generally able to gain good visibility into companies' business models—whether customers are adopting the products or services, whether distribution channels are viable from a financial standpoint, and whether the business models are beginning to function properly.

For these reasons, venture capitalists prefer to see that companies are compiling any historical financial information that is available. And, according to Fred Dotzler, they typically require that companies provide them with all historical financial statements, especially when companies have "been in business for a year or more."[2] Venture capitalists normally request that companies provide balance sheets, income statements, and statements of cash flow. If companies should have prepared financial statements, but have not, that is an unequivocal red flag for venture capitalists. Says David Gladstone,

> *Frequently a small business will try to skimp on financial data by not preparing financial statements. This is a sure sign that the company is not being run by the numbers and should give you a clear indication that the company is not serious about using the financials to guide the management team.*[3]

Furthermore, even when financial statements have been prepared, venture capitalists will make sure that they are accurate, current, and free of material problems. Indeed, says Gladstone, "Old or sloppy financials usually mean business problems."[4]

Pro Forma Financial Statements

Has the company provided you with pro forma financial statements?

Pro forma financial statements are of critical importance to venture capitalists. The projections in such statements constitute one of the fundamental bases on which venture capitalists make their investment decisions. Pro forma financial statements provide venture capitalists with black-and-white pictures of companies' business models and of what those models might look like over subsequent years. They help them answer all of those previously discussed questions surrounding business models: How big are their target markets? What market share will they be able to obtain? How large will their gross margins be? But, most importantly, they give venture capitalists a glimpse of the returns they might generate from their investments. Therefore, it is partially from this information that venture capitalists estimate whether investments are likely to generate the returns they require. Aiming his comments directly at venture capital investors, David Gladstone reiterates this point:

> *[The pro forma financial statements] constitute the numerical forecast that you as an investor are buying. The entrepreneur is saying these projections are possible, and you are purchasing a part of the company on the basis of these projections. Your return on investment, the cash that you will receive back, depends on the company making these projections. Your analysis of these projections is one of the key aspects of your investigation of any business opportunity.*[5]

However, pro forma financial statements are, by definition, speculative. They are based on a set of assumptions about the future, which may or may not turn out to be correct. For that reason, some notable venture capitalists actually have little faith in pro forma financial statements. Arthur Rock states, "Frankly, how anyone can figure out what sales and earnings and returns are going to be five years from now is beyond me."[6] Taking an even more negative view, the venture capitalists at Sequoia Capital state that they "are very skeptical about placing too much faith in detailed financial projections beyond the first 12–18 months of a company's operations and have a jaundiced view of reams of financial data."[7] Others hold that, although it is impossible to come up with exact financial predictions for a company's first five years, it is possible to come up with somewhat realistic estimates. Furthermore, pro forma financial statements can be helpful to venture capitalists in determining whether entrepreneurs have properly thought out the financial implications of their companies' growth plans: whether they have developed financial forecasts that accurately reflect the business goals contained in their business plans.

For these reasons, venture capitalists generally require that companies provide them with a complete and cohesive set of pro formas. According to John Doerr and Alan Salzman, they usually require "balance sheets, income statements and cash flow projections for five years, with the information presented monthly for the first year and quarterly thereafter."[8] Venture capitalists also generally require full footnote sections that explain the assumptions used to develop the projections. Such projections are only as meaningful as the assumptions underlying them. Alan Salzman and John Doerr explain that it "is essential to the credibility of the financial forecasts that the assumptions be realistic, logical, attainable and either consistent with industry norms or any deviation explained.[9] Stanley R. Rich, founder and former chairman of the MIT Enterprise Forum, and David E. Gumpert, former small business editor for the *Harvard Business Review* and former senior editor of *Inc.* magazine, warn that "often, entrepreneurs go to extremes with their numbers" and, therefore, that companies "nearly always fail to achieve their rosy ... forecasts."[10] According to Rich and Gumpert, because of this practice of overstatement, the "[o]fficials of five major venture capital firms ... surveyed said they are satisfied when new ventures reach 50 percent of their financial goals."[11] Many venture capitalists routinely adjust the provided projections down based on assumptions that they feel are more reasonable.

The following is a discussion of what venture capitalists usually look for in the assumptions underlying each of the pro forma financial statements.

Income Statements With regard to sales projections, they generally expect companies to explain precisely the numbers of units they expect to sell during each reporting period, and tend to be skeptical of sales figures that appear contrived. They are especially skeptical of sales figures that increase in a lockstep manner, or those that look simply like the all too familiar "hockey stick." Venture capitalists expect sales projections to include average selling prices per unit, and typically independently confirm that the prices used are in keeping with comparable offerings in the market. For expense projections, venture capitalists want companies to provide accurate unit cost data, including the labor costs (based on competitive compensation figures), the material costs, and the overhead costs necessary to produce each unit.

As discussed, venture capitalists seek to understand precisely where product development stands and what will be required to complete that development. They expect companies to explain exactly what product development costs have been assumed in their expense projections, and make sure that those figures correlate with product introduction schedules. Venture capitalists also want to see that entrepreneurs have included in their projections *all* other expenses, including head count, administrative costs, sales and marketing costs, and real estate costs, and that these expense figures also correlate with industry norms.

Balance Sheets Venture capitalists generally make sure that companies' balance sheets correlate exactly with their income statements and statements of cash flows. They also verify that projected inventory levels and capital expenditure levels are appropriate to support the projected sales figures. Many venture capitalists make sure that companies adequately demonstrate fiscal restraint, such as limiting their capital expenditures to current requirements and renting or leasing capital equipment to conserve cash for expenses that contribute directly to revenue generation, such as sales and marketing expenses.

Statements of Cash Flows Venture capitalists also check to see that companies' statements of cash flows correlate with their income statements and balance sheets and are based on the spending and payment decisions in those statements.

PRACTICAL ANALYSIS

Burn Rate

Is the company keeping its burn rate under control?

According to Ruthann Quindlen, in the lobby of Institutional Venture Partners there hangs a very large picture of a singed $1,000 bill bearing the title, "Burn Rate."[12] A card under the work reads: "In the venture capital industry, in a company that has not as yet reached cash flow break-even, the burn rate is usually defined as the amount of capital consumed each month expressed in thousands of dollars."[13] The burn rate is a significant concept for venture capitalists. Joseph Bartlett explains: "One of the critical elements in venture investing is the rate at which a firm incurs expenses, since most financings occur at a time when the business has insufficient income to cover expenses. The monthly expense burden indicates how long the company can exist until the next financing. . . ."[14] If and when burn rates become too large, companies face significant risk of not surviving until their next financings. Indeed, if their burn rates exceed their ability to generate revenues or their ability to raise additional capital, companies simply run out of cash and must shut their doors. Therefore, says Bartlett, "a higher-than-necessary burn rate is a bad sign, a red flag to the venture-capital community."[15]

Many entrepreneurs, however, have a strong tendency to ramp up their expenses aggressively (especially their head count), with the hope that revenues will ramp up soon thereafter or that they can simply raise more capital from venture capitalists. However, revenues typically build much more slowly than expected and companies can raise only so much capital before venture capitalists will step back and discontinue their financial support. Therefore, venture capitalists seek out entrepreneurs who understand that they need to keep their burn rates (and thus their financial destiny) under their own control, rather than letting aggressive burn rates determine those destinies for them. Spending money is not by itself a bad thing; spending more than is necessary at a given stage of development is. Therefore, venture capitalists look for entrepreneurs who realize that they must hit certain milestones—such as completing their teams, validating their products or services with customers, and/or validating their business models—before they begin to aggressively ramp up their burn rates. Much can usually be accomplished with a small team and a small amount of capital. And, companies that *are* able to accomplish much without a lot of capital usually make for the best investments.

COMPANY FINANCING

Past Financings

How has the company been financed to date?

Venture capitalists nearly always want to understand how the companies they are considering for investment have been previously financed. During due diligence, they usually request information about previous investors in the companies, including whether they have been bootstrapped by the founders, the dates of any investments, the amounts invested, the investment securities employed, the prices paid per unit of the investment securities, and the pre- and post-money valuation amounts given to the companies before and after each round of investment. This information is helpful for several reasons. For example, it can be useful to venture capitalists in the valuation process and in understanding companies' capitalization tables. (Valuation and capitalization tables are discussed in more detail later in this chapter.) Also, as mentioned, venture capitalists are interested in companies that can boast an impressive set of previous investors, such as well-known industry executives or well-regarded seed-stage venture capitalists, especially if those investors are significant investors. Beyond their imprimatur, there is a higher likelihood that such investors will become involved and contribute to the success of the companies when their investments are substantial.

Current Financing

What is the total amount of funding currently being sought by the company?

It is a fairly common (and sometimes fatal) mistake that companies seeking venture capital raise the wrong amounts of capital. Alan Salzman and John Doerr explain, "[S]tart-ups can suffer from raising too much money, as well as too little."[16] Their venture capital backers can suffer, too. For that reason, venture capitalists usually take a hard look at the amounts of money companies are seeking—and then at their actual capital requirements. They seek to make sure that companies raise funds sufficient to proceed with their business plans, toward their next milestones, while also getting them safely to their next round of financing. The venture capitalists at Advanced Technology Ventures explain:

> [I]n evaluating an early-stage investment opportunity [they] spend considerable time analyzing the amount of capital required to reach the next logical milestone, most often the successful completion of beta-product installations. When talking with entrepreneurs, [they] advise them to build some cushion into their financing needs to prepare for unanticipated development delays. If a company runs out of capital between planned financing rounds, the startup will be forced to raise interim financing at less attractive valuations.[17]

It is not uncommon, however, for companies to raise small amounts of money, usually in an attempt to avoid dilution of their ownership percentages; and then they discover too late that those amounts were insufficient to carry them to their next rounds. It usually takes much longer than companies think to close their next rounds of venture financing. As Tim Draper explains, a primary cause of venture failure is that a "company just flat runs out of money."[18] On the other hand, it is also not uncommon for companies to raise too much money. It can be tempting to entrepreneurs to take as much money as they can get, when they can get it. When they do this, however, they and their existing investors suffer unnecessary dilution. That is viewed very negatively by venture capitalists. The partners at Sequoia Capital consider dilution their "greatest enemy" and state that they "like to start companies with relatively small amounts of money. . . ."[19] They explain that they "have discovered that founders and entrepreneurs clever enough to develop a large return from a small investment will frequently build significant companies."[20] Also, as discussed, when companies raise excessive funds, it can be detrimental to the development process of moving swiftly from milestone to milestone. There are few better motivators than the knowledge that your company will run out of money unless the next milestone is met. Says Michael Moritz, "We are big believers in the notion that lesser is better. This approach forces companies to be more disciplined—they are hungrier, they worry about how they spend their pennies."[21]

Use of Proceeds from Current Financing

How will the proceeds from the current financing be used?

Venture capitalists generally like to know precisely how their funds are going to be spent by the companies in which they invest. Indeed, cash is just too precious in the early stage not to examine this issue sufficiently during due diligence. Not only must companies not squander any of their cash, they must also spend that cash wisely. A major determinant of venture success is the *way* companies spend their cash. Very often, venture failure is the result of companies spending their initial money unwisely. It is not surprising, therefore, that venture capitalists generally spend some time during due diligence making sure that companies are planning to strategically focus their cash on those places where it will create the greatest value.

First, venture capitalists usually require entrepreneurs to detail exactly how they plan to direct the funds. Actually, such explanations are common components of any good business plan, but many times those included in business plans are inadequate and insufficiently detailed. So, venture capitalists usually obtain the required detail through additional discussions with the entrepreneurs or by requesting additional refinement of those plans. Also, depending on the venture capitalists, many will bring their own experience and knowledge to bear and will provide their own advice as to how best to direct the funds.

Future Financings

What are the projected future capital requirements of the company?

Before making investments, venture capitalists attempt to project and understand the future capital requirements of the companies they are considering for investment, and they generally prefer companies whose requirements are not too large. The venture capitalists at New Enterprise Associates state that they look for companies with "reasonable capital requirements."[22] They do this for a few reasons. First, they minimize their risk. Large capital requirements translate into higher risk for investors because companies with such requirements face relatively more financing risk—risk that they will not be able to obtain enough funding—than companies with more reasonable capital requirements. In fact, it is generally true (with some narrow exceptions) that the more money companies need the less likely they are to be successful. Therefore, says Michael Moritz, he and his partners at Sequoia Capital "like to start wicked infernos with a single match rather than two million gallons of kerosene."[23] Second, venture capitalists project future capital requirements to minimize their dilution. Dilution is defined as the reduction in proportionate ownership that investors face when their portfolio companies issue new shares. Companies with major funding requirements usually must issue a large number of new shares in exchange for that funding. Therefore, investors in such companies face relatively more dilution than investors in companies with less sizable capital requirements. Third, venture capitalists attempt to project capital requirements simply so that they may set aside portions of their own funds for subsequent follow-on rounds of financing. They must earmark those funds so that they will be available later, when they are needed.

According to Jeffry Timmons, capital requirements are calculated by determining both "(1) operating needs (i.e., working capital for operations) and (2) asset needs (for start-up or for expansion facilities, equipment, research and development, and other apparently one-time expenditures)."[24] Alan Salzman and John Doerr explain:

> *[T]he financial needs of the start-up must be evaluated over time—matching capital requirements with stages of the enterprise's development. It is not that the venture will need $5 million of capital*

over the first three years of its existence, but rather it will need, for example, $300,000 in seed capital to verify the feasibility of its business concept; $1.2 million in three to five months to undertake substantial research and development efforts to establish the technological viability of its products; and $3.5 million in twelve to fifteen months to complete initial product development and initiate manufacturing and sales efforts.[25]

Venture capitalists very much like to get into that type of detail, and sometimes into even greater detail, when projecting funding requirements; and they like to do so with the help of entrepreneurs. Often, however, entrepreneurs drastically underestimate their required resources even when making projections in good faith. It is a commonly held belief among venture capitalists that it will usually take two to three times more work and money than what entrepreneurs project.

Future Financers

Will the company be likely to be able to obtain capital sufficient to meet its future capital requirements?

Venture capitalists almost never fund companies' capital requirements single-handedly. Typically, several venture capital firms will coinvest (at the same point in time and at different points), to fund those needs together. A company might initially do a seed round with a small, boutique seed-stage fund, then later do a larger round with a couple of larger, more traditional venture capital funds, and later still do a very large round with several later-stage funds. So, beyond simply projecting how much capital companies will require, venture capitalists also generally attempt to determine the abilities of those companies to attract and obtain that capital. Venture capitalists want to be confident that, when companies go out for their next rounds of financing, other venture capitalists are likely be there to help meet their capital requirements.

Venture capitalists also generally attempt to judge companies' abilities to obtain debt funding from players other than venture capitalists, such as banks and venture leasing firms. Virtually all venture-backed companies obtain debt financing in one form or another to meet their capital requirements, whether it is through obtaining lines of credit, loans, subordinated debt, or capital equipment leases. Without exposing them to overwhelming debt burdens, venture capitalists generally encourage companies to obtain some level of debt financing because it can significantly reduce their dilution. The requirements for obtaining debt financing range across lenders, but most require that companies have already obtained venture capital financing. Speaking specifically about his venture lending firm, William "Boots" Del Biaggio, cofounder and CEO of Sand Hill Capital, says, "First and foremost, they must have support from a top-tier VC."[26] He explains:

> *The risk in our model is that the company may not raise money as planned, and it's still burning money. So we need the support of investors who will feed the company to pay for the burn rate until it raises the money or they sell it. For a company to get our backing, they have to have top-tier venture support and investment. It has to be a well-known fund that manages a lot of money.*[27]

Beyond support from venture capitalists, lenders typically perform due diligence in much the same manner as venture capitalists do, to determine the ability of companies to repay their debt. Says Del Biaggio: "From there, we look at the market space they're in, their technology and patents, whether they have traction [with customers], and if they have a path to profitability."[28]

OWNERSHIP

Capitalization Tables

Are there any problems with the company's capitalization table?

Entrepreneurs often make mistakes when allocating the ownership of their companies. A common mistake is allocating too much of it to themselves. Entrepreneurs often try to hold on to—sometimes quite determinedly—their sizable ownership percentages, even as such companies are financed with venture capital and begin to grow, when it is clearly appropriate for them to share ownership. Venture capitalists, as a general rule, shy away from entrepreneurs who try to do this. Concentration of ownership is a sure sign of trouble. Refusing to share equity is "not a method for attracting a great management team," says Ruthann Quindlen.[29] In fact, not only does it become difficult for companies to attract top-notch management team members when founders are unwilling to part with their own equity to do so, it becomes difficult to attract any top-notch employees. Another mistake entrepreneurs make is allocating too much stock to early investors ("friends and family" investors, angel investors, and seed-stage venture capitalists). Venture capitalists certainly have no problem with these investors being significantly compensated for the risk they undertake by investing early-on, but they also generally have a strong interest in, as Quindlen explains, putting as much stock as possible "in the hands of executives, employees, and investors who will make the company successful" so that they have sufficient incentive to do so.[30]

To understand how ownership has been allocated, venture capitalists request that entrepreneurs provide them with capitalization tables (or simply "cap" tables). Cap tables detail the equity ownership of companies. The venture capitalists at Softbank Venture Capital state that they require each company to provide them with a cap table describing "the current ownership of the company, including number of shares and percentage," including "the employee option pool."[31] Cap tables also typically detail the type of equity owned by each shareholder (e.g., common stock, preferred stock, stock options, or warrants).

When examining cap tables, venture capitalists strongly prefer that companies have kept ownership simple and have adhered to a basic structure. By the time they approach venture capitalists, company ownership should be divided among only three constituencies: the founders, the seed investors, and future executives and employees (called the "employee option pool"). It is of supreme importance to venture capitalists that companies have allocated sufficient ownership to the employee option pool. According to Quindlen, "[W]e venture capitalists encourage entrepreneurs to set aside 20 to 30 percent of their company in the employee pool—stock reserved for future executives and employees."[32] She explains, "[I]t takes approximately 8 to 10 percent of a company's stock to attract a great CEO and about 2 to

3 percent each for the executive-level marketing and engineering positions. Because they receive commissions, executive salespeople can be hired for about half that—generally 1–1.5 percent."[33] If companies have not allocated sufficient stock for future executives and employees, "and they come to a venture capitalist, we'll insist that they do. If most of the stock in the company has been given to the founder, the local investor, or Cousin Bob, the ratio will have to be changed, and the stock from the employee pool will come out of their percentages."[34]

Additionally, some venture capitalists use the allocation process to do further due diligence on entrepreneurs. How entrepreneurs allocate ownership among themselves, among early investors, and to the employee option pool can be revealing about them, as people. Kevin Fong explains:

> How they go through that process of thinking about and evaluating each individual's own self . . . worth to the corporation or the business that they're thinking about forming is really a telling exercise to have them go through, so we have them watch that very carefully as well. We try and give them some guidelines, and try and tell them how to think about it, because sometimes they don't even have a structure to how to think about it, but I would say that that process is a very revealing process.[35]

Some entrepreneurs simply do not know that they need to think in terms of such percentages, but are actually willing to release some of their equity to attract top talent. In those cases, venture capitalists simply request that capitalization be restructured, reducing the founder's ownership percentage to some reasonable level and increasing the size of the employee pool. Other times, however, entrepreneurs are unwilling to share ownership. Venture capitalists generally avoid those types.

VALUATION METHODS

After venture capitalists have decided that they would like to invest in a particular company—once they have convinced themselves of management's qualifications and competence, convinced themselves of the attractiveness of the target market and the viability of the business model, and once their gut tells them to invest—they then turn to the issue of valuation. They value companies to determine whether they will be able to obtain ownership percentages sufficient (and thus returns sufficient) to justify the risk of investing. The "pre-money" valuation (the valuation of a company before any money has been invested, as opposed to the "post-money" valuation, which is the valuation immediately after investment) placed on a company determines the percentage ownership venture capitalists receive in return for the funds they invest (and vice versa). For example, if a company has a pre-money valuation of $10 million and venture capitalists invest $10 million, they will then own 50 percent of that company immediately following that particular round of financing (and the company will have a post-money valuation of $20 million). Alternatively, if a company has a pre-money valuation of $20 million and venture capitalists invest $10 million, they will own 33 percent of that company immediately following the particular financing (and the company will have a post-money valuation of $30 million). Thus, venture capitalists have a strong interest in obtaining the lowest pre-money valuations possible. Doing so maximizes their percentage ownership as well as the returns on their investments. Their intent (and hope) is that by pushing for low pre-money valuations they will be able to own larger (and more valuable) percentages of those companies when they are subsequently successful and command valuations that are many multiples of those pre-money valuations. Most venture capitalists, however, are also careful not to drive pre-money valuations down so low that entrepreneurs lose their incentive. They realize that entrepreneurs must retain sufficient ownership to maintain their drive to make their companies successful. On the other side of the coin, entrepreneurs have a strong interest in obtaining the highest pre-money valuations possible. The higher the valuations they obtain, the less ownership they must give up in return for the venture funding they receive. Ultimately, pre-money valuations are determined through negotiations between venture capitalists and entrepreneurs. There are semiobjective methods of calculating them, but because they are somewhat imprecise, these methods are primarily used as negotiation tools to justify each party's negotiation position. Says Mark White, "[T]he valuation process is a negotiation between buyer and seller. Value is not set by plugging numbers into a formula (though, admittedly, this is part of the process)."[36]

The Venture Capital Method

What is the company's pre-money value according to the Venture Capital Method of valuation?

There are essentially two methods by which venture capitalists determine pre-money valuations. The first is known (quite appropriately) as the *Venture Capital Method*. The Venture Capital Method employs a methodology similar to that used to value public companies. For that reason, William Sahlman explains, it is popular among venture capitalists: The Venture Capital Method involves the "application of a price/earnings ratio (PER) to projected net earnings. This is the measure commonly used in the public stock market, which is where the VC generally hopes to harvest the venture by means of an initial public offering or an acquisition in the terminal year."[37]

The Venture Capital Method has multiple steps and involves making several estimations and then simply plugging the estimated numbers into some basic formulas. The first step in the process is determining a company's terminal value. A terminal value is a company's total value in its terminal year. A *terminal year* is defined as the year in which a venture capitalist expects to have the option of terminating his or her investment in the particular portfolio company— that is, the year in which the venture capitalist expects to achieve liquidity. Therefore, venture capitalists generally estimate terminal years by choosing years that correspond to the liquidity events that have already been projected for the particular companies. Sahlman explains, however, that choosing a terminal year based on the timing of a projected liquidity event "does not necessarily imply an intention to harvest . . . the investment at that time. Such a decision would be based on a number of factors like market pricing, marginal tax rates, and the company's performance trends. However, it is very useful to estimate what the consequences are of selling shares at some future point in time."[38]

Most venture capitalists expect to achieve liquidity in less than seven years from the date of their investment, and some expect it sooner than that. The venture capitalists at Draper Fisher Jurvetson state that they prefer "an exit after a five- to seven-year holding period,"[39] while the venture capitalists at Crosspoint Venture Partners state that they prefer "liquidity in a three to five year period."[40]

The second required estimation necessary for calculating a company's terminal value is a net income figure for the terminal year selected. William Sahlman states that this "estimate of net income is typically based on a 'success scenario,' that is, one in which the company attains its sales and margin projections."[41] Therefore, venture capitalists generally just lift the net income figures contained in companies' pro forma financials (making any adjustments to those figures they deem necessary). As discussed, venture capitalists are always wary of inflated projections. Sahlman explains that it "is very easy for the entrepreneur to develop a forecast designed to justify a desired valuation: knowing the required investment, the desired ownership to be sold, and the VC's discount rate, the necessary earnings and sales can then be calculated and presented as forecasts."[42]

The last estimation required for calculating a company's terminal value is an appropriate price-to-earnings ratio. A price-to-earnings ratio is defined as the current market price of a public company's publicly traded stock divided by its current annual earnings per share amount. Because the companies valued by venture capitalists are private companies, without publicly traded stock, venture capitalists are forced to do some extrapolation. Stanley C. Golder, general partner of Golder, Thoma & Cressey and former president of the Equity Group of First Chicago, explains the question venture capitalists ask about price-to-earnings ratios: "How attractive will the company and industry be in the stock market, and what kind of price-earnings multiple will it be able to command in the marketplace . . . in the years when the investors become interested in liquidating?"[43] However, because the price-to-earnings ratio that the market would place on a particular company three to five years down the road is essentially unknowable, Sahlman offers instead the following advice on how to estimate an appropriate ratio:

> [A] price-to-earnings ratio (PER) is determined that is deemed appropriate for a company that has achieved the measure of success implicit in the forecasted income. Often, this PER is estimated by

studying current *multiples for companies with similar economic characteristics (e.g., size, profitability, growth rate, capital intensity, risk).*[44]

Armed with these items—an estimated terminal year, an estimated net income amount for that terminal year, and an estimated price-to-earnings ratio—venture capitalists can then estimate the terminal value of a company. Terminal values are calculated simply by multiplying companies' projected terminal year net income amounts by the appropriate estimated price-to-earnings ratios.

The next step required by the Venture Capital Method is to calculate the particular company's discounted terminal value, by means of a *required rate of return.* A required rate of return is the discount rate used by venture capitalists to convert companies' terminal values into present values—what those companies are worth today, based on their estimated future values. Required rates of return vary across venture capitalists; however, some general rules of thumb do exist. Mark White explains:

> *Venture investors typically determine their required compounded rate of return based on commitments the VCs have made to their limited partners in the venture funds that the VCs manage. The yardstick followed by many venture capital firms is that they are looking for investments in companies in which they will multiply their investment (a) by 5 times in 3 years (resulting in a compounded annual ROI of 71%), or (b) by 10 times in 5 years (resulting in a compounded annual ROI of 58%).*[45]

The rates of return required by venture capitalists tend to be quite high, which means that venture capitalists put fairly low present values on the companies in which they consider investing. The higher the particular discount rate used, the lower the present value. These high discount rates are, however, usually justified for the following reasons:

■ *High Risk*   Venture capital investments involve a great deal of risk. And, much of that risk is the type for which venture capitalists should be compensated. Such compensation comes partially from high discount rates. As companies mature—as they hit milestones and move through the seed stage, start-up stage, and into the first stage—this risk decreases somewhat, and the discount rates applied by venture capitalists generally decrease as well. The following are, Sahlman explains, typical discount rates by stage of development:

Discount Rates Applied by Venture Capitalists*

Company Stage	Discount Rates
Seed stage	Over 80%
Start-up stage	50% to 70%
First stage	40% to 60%

*William A. Sahlman, "A Method for Valuing High-Risk, Long-Term Investments: The Venture Capital Method," Harvard Business School 7-8 (June 1989).

■ *Illiquidity* Illiquidity, defined by Sahlman as "the inability to convert the holdings to cash at their full value in a reasonable period of time," is another justification for the use of high discount rates.[47] He explains:

A publicly traded stock can be sold at the market and cash received almost immediately. Stock in a privately held company cannot be sold so easily for a number of reasons: first, the amount of credible information available (e.g., audited statements) is far less; second, there are legal restrictions on the sale of unregistered securities; and, finally, there are a relatively small number of potential buyers. These factors suggest that, holding all other things constant, a buyer should pay less for the private stock. This prediction is borne out in the markets. Typically unregistered stock that is sold commands a price well below that for registered shares.[48]

■ *Value Added* Another justification for the use of high discount rates is that venture capitalists often contribute significant value to the companies in which they invest. They contribute start-up advice, strategic business advice, strategic financing advice, mentoring, and assistance in recruiting top-quality management team members and forging relationships with suppliers, partners, customers, and acquirers. Because of their ability to add value, says Sahlman, the high discount rates "demanded by venture capitalists could be viewed partly as compensation for services rendered."[49]

■ *Adjustment of Projections*   A last justification for the use of high discount rates, according to John Willinge, partner at Thomas Weisel Partners, and Josh Lerner, professor at Harvard Business School, is that venture capitalists tend to "believe that projections presented by entrepreneurs tend to be overly optimistic."[50] Therefore, Willinge and Lerner explain, "the large discount rate compensates for these inflated projections."[51] Adds Sahlman: "By experience, the venture capital community has learned that applying high discount rates to forecasted performance can compensate for the fact that earnings forecasts often are not realized."[52]

Simply put, venture capitalists use high discount rates because they work. They ensure that they can incur enormous risk, suffer illiquidity, work very hard personally, expend their resources, endure overstated projections, and still be successful investors.

Once a required rate of return and a terminal value have been calculated, venture capitalists estimate a company's discounted terminal value by employing the following equation:

$$DTV = \frac{TV}{(1+R)^Y}$$

where DTV = the Discounted Terminal Value
TV = the Terminal Value
R = the particular venture capitalist's Required Rate of Return
Y = the number of Years until the terminal year

The third step required by the Venture Capital Method is for venture capitalists to calculate their required ownership percentages—the percentages they decide they must own of the particular companies being considered for investment. Venture capitalists calculate those percentages for the purpose of determining whether they will be able to obtain percentages sufficient to achieve their required rates of return. The first percentage they typically calculate is their *required final ownership percentage.* A required final ownership percentage is that percentage of a company that investors deem they must be left with in the company's terminal year to achieve the required rate of return. Having calculated a company's discounted terminal value, determining the particular required final ownership percentage is not at all difficult. Venture capitalists simply divide the amount being invested in the particular company by that company's terminal value. Willinge and Lerner explain:

> *The venture capitalist uses the discounted terminal value and the size of the proposed investment to calculate her desired ownership interest in the company. For example, if the company's discounted terminal value is $10 million, and the venture capitalist intends to make a $5 million investment, she will want 50% of the company in exchange for her investment.*[53]

Venture capitalists then translate their required final ownership percentages into required *current* ownership percentages; they calculate the percentages they must own immediately after their investment for them to be able to hit their required final ownership percentages later, when companies reach their terminal years. This translation takes into account the dilution that is likely to occur during the time between when venture capitalists initially make their investments and when they achieve liquidity. Sahlman explains:

> *As new stock is issued to later-round investors or to new key employees, the early-round investors can expect to suffer dilution, a loss of ownership due to the issuing of additional shares. As a result, the early round investor will have to purchase a higher ownership percentage as of the financing, in order to achieve a given terminal or final ownership after the future financings.*[54]

Willinge and Lerner offer the following to clarify how venture capitalists account for future dilution:

> To compensate for the effect of dilution from future rounds of financing, [the venture capitalist] needs to calculate the Retention Ratio. The Retention Ratio quantifies the expected dilutive effect of future rounds of financing on the venture capitalist's ownership. Consider a firm that intends to undertake one more financing round, in which shares representing an additional 25 percent of the firm's equity will be sold, and then to sell shares representing an additional 30 percent of the firm at the time of the IPO. If the venture capitalist owns 10 percent today, after these financings her stake will be $10\%/(1 + .25)/(1 + .3) = 6.15\%$. Her retention ratio is $6.15\%/10\% = 61.5\%$.[55]

The method by which venture capitalists calculate retention ratios is to estimate the subsequent rounds of venture financing that a particular company will require, both their timing and their size, and to estimate the discount rates that will likely be used by investors in those subsequent rounds. As discussed, discount rates generally decrease as companies mature and move from milestone to milestone. Once these estimations have been made, venture capitalists are then able to calculate the required final ownership percentages that the subsequent investors in those rounds are likely to demand, and they do that in the same manner with which they calculate their own required final ownership percentages. Additionally, venture capitalists estimate the final ownership percentage to be granted to future management and key employees and the ownership percentage (if any) to be sold in the company's IPO. Then, venture capitalists aggregate each of these percentages and use the following formula to calculate the retention ratio:

Retention ratio = 1 − (Aggregated final ownership percentages)

With an estimated retention ratio in hand, venture capitalists then calculate their required current ownership percentages. The following formula is the one with which they do this:

$$RCOP = \frac{RFOP}{RR}$$

where $RCOP$ = the Required Current Ownership Percentage
$RFOP$ = the Required Final Ownership Percentage
RR = the Retention Ratio

No matter the results of the formula, however, venture capitalists rarely take current ownership percentages lower than 20 percent. The venture capitalists at VantagePoint Venture Partners state that they prefer "to take a position of some substance (typically a minimum of 20%) in [their] Portfolio Companies."[56] This 20 percent minimum current ownership percentage has become a virtually ubiquitous floor among venture capitalists. Although they often assume ownership percentages that are much greater than 20 percent—sometimes greater than 50 percent—venture capitalists, as discussed, usually refrain from demanding ownership percentages that are too large. Doing so would remove entrepreneurs' incentives to make their companies successful (or even to remain with their companies); entrepreneurs' ownership percentages necessarily get smaller as the percentages held by venture capitalists get bigger.

Once venture capitalists have calculated their required current ownership percentage, and they know how much they are going to invest in a particular company, they know roughly what percentage ownership of that company to demand at the time of investment, in return for that investment. They also have all the information they need to calculate the company's pre-money valuation. Indeed, a company's pre-money valuation is implied by those items. First, however, venture capitalists must calculate the company's post-money valuation using the following formula:

$$\text{Post-money valuations} = \frac{I}{RCOP}$$

where I = the Investment amount
$RCOP$ = the Required Current Ownership Percentage

Because of the relationship of post-money valuations to pre-money valuations (discussed previously), pre-money valuations are determined simply by subtracting the amounts to be invested by venture capitalists from the resulting post-money valuations:

Pre-money valuation = Post-money valuation − Investment

The Venture Capital Method of valuation gives the appearance that pre-money valuations can be calculated with some precision. That is not at all the case. The inputs to the Venture Capital Method cannot be precisely determined, they may only be estimated. Therefore, according to Mark White, venture capitalists use the method, not to determine *exact* pre-money valuation amounts, but rather as a tool "for setting a range of valuations that, from their perspective, make sense."[57] To generate such ranges, venture capitalists vary each input slightly. The inputs that are typically varied are the discount rate, the estimated price-to-earnings ratio, the terminal year, and the terminal year net income projections.

The Comparables Method

What is the company's pre-money value according to the Comparables Method of valuation?

The second method by which venture capitalists calculate pre-money valuations is the "Comparables Method." Actually, the Comparables Method is probably the most commonly used valuation method among venture capitalists. It involves simply observing the venture capital transaction market—what other pre-money valuations are currently being given by venture capitalists to companies with similar characteristics. Says Jeffry Timmons, "Knowledgeable . . . venture capitalists make it their business to know the activity in the current market place for private capital and how deals are being priced."[58] Robert Johnson explains, "Over time . . . regular investors see lots of deals and learn that there are acceptable ranges of values that work for them in certain instances and/or industries. Rules of thumb emerge to guide an investor through the maze of valuation issues for such companies."[59] Says Johnson, "[E]ventually investors develop a 'feel' for what an early-stage business is worth at a specific stage."[60] Additionally, venture capitalists keep abreast of valuations being given in the public securities markets and the M&A markets, to estimate the valuations that might be appropriate for the companies in which they invest. All such information is collected and complied by such firms as VentureOne and Venture Economics, and

TABLE 6.1 Median Pre-Money Valuations for Venture-Backed Companies (1995–2001)[1]

Industry	Round Class[2]	1995	1996	1997	1998	1999	2000	2001[3]
Information technology	Seed	$ 2.10[4]	$ 2.04	$ 2.95	$ 3.00	$ 4.00	$ 6.00	$ 3.38
	First round	5.33	7.03	6.95	7.50	10.00	13.50	9.45
	Second round	13.00	18.34	19.28	22.00	34.25	48.03	25.00
Products and Service	Seed	NS[5]	2.50	3.03	3.85	4.45	4.50	NS
	First round	4.33	5.00	6.20	5.99	10.00	12.50	7.00
	Second round	12.35	9.32	15.60	14.52	35.00	39.50	16.00
Healthcare	Seed	0.90	2.44	2.46	3.23	2.48	3.00	3.60
	First round	4.00	6.20	5.97	5.35	7.40	7.65	8.50
	Second round	10.15	11.91	13.50	17.10	17.00	22.00	15.00

[1] Data provided by VentureOne Corporation.
[2] VentureOne's financing round classes (seed, first, and second) roughly correspond the William Sahlman's stages of company development (seed, start-up, and first), discussed previously.
[3] The 2001 figures only include data through the third quarter.
[4] Amounts are in millions of dollars.
[5] "NS" in the table stands for "not significant."

most venture capitalists make great use of their databases. Table 6.1 shows pre-money valuations compiled by VentureOne.

Once venture capitalists have determined a reasonable pre-money valuation based on current comparables and have decided how much they are going to invest in a particular company, they can then easily calculate their Required Current Ownership Percentage by employing the following formula:

$$RCOP = \frac{I}{PV + I}$$

where $RCOP$ = the Required Current Ownership Percentage
I = the Investment amount
PV = the Pre-Money Valuation

As with the Venture Capital Method, once venture capitalists have calculated their required current ownership percentage, they then know roughly what percentage ownership of that company to demand in return for their investment.

epilogue

The benefits to venture capitalists of performing thorough due diligence are unquestionable. The time and effort invested by them up front almost always results in higher returns to them later on. The very best venture capitalists never lose sight of the importance of adequate due diligence. It is important to note, however, that venture capital due diligence is, by its nature, an imperfect process because it has no clear end. Certainty is unattainable. It is easy, therefore, for some venture capitalists to drag the process out, grasping and hoping for something certain. Precious time and effort is often wasted performing due diligence on irrelevancies. But, there is no way venture capitalists can ever say, with absolute certainty, that a particular deal will make a great investment or will turn out to be a dog. Good venture capitalists simply accept that due diligence must be imperfect, gather as many relevant facts as they can, and then just trust their gut feelings. This book explains how venture capitalists obtain those relevant facts; the gut feelings are supplied by them.

notes

Introduction

1. Woodside Fund, *Venture Speak* (visited June 16, 2001), www .woodsidefund.com/f_visionary.htm.
2. U.S. Venture Partners, *Quality of the People* (visited January 21, 1999), www.usvp.com/html/phqual.html.

Chapter 1 Screening Due Diligence

1. Geoff Baum, Interview with Kevin Fong, *Garage.com* (visited February 8, 1999), www.garage.com/soapboxArchive/1998.10.19.kevinFong1.shtml.
2. Michael S. Malone, John Doerr's Startup Manual, *Fast Company* (visited July 14, 1999), www.fastcompany.com/online/07/082doerr.html.
3. Russ Siegelman, Diary, *Slate.com* (visited June 15, 2001), slate.msn .com/Diary/98-11-16/Diary.asp?iMsg=1.
4. C. Gordon Bell, *High-Tech Ventures: The Guide for Entrepreneurial Success* 35 (1991), Addison Wesley.
5. @Ventures, Submitting a Business Plan (visited July 1, 2001), www .atventures.com/contact/bizplan.html.
6. Alan E. Salzman and L. John Doerr, The Venture Funding Process, in *Start-Up and Emerging Companies: Planning, Financing and Operating the Successful Business* § 7.03[1] (1998), Law Journal Seminars Press.
7. Accel Partners, *Challenges in Building World Class Technology Companies* (visited May 27, 1999), www.accel.com/entrepreneurs /world_class.html.
8. Christopher Schaelpe, Structuring a Winning Venture Capital Deal, *American Venture Magazine,* July–September 1999, at 25.
9. Jeffry A. Timmons, *New Venture Creation: Entrepreneurship for the 21st Century* 341 (4th ed., 1994), Irwin McGraw-Hill.
10. Oak Investment Partners, *Oak's Focus* (visited October 12, 1999), www.oakinv.com/body_investq2.html.
11. Robert G. McNeil, Why VCs Have Left Biotech, *Venture Capital Journal,* August 1999.

12. El Dorado Ventures, *FAQs* (visited May 10, 1999), www .eldoradoventures.com/ faqs/answer5.htm.
13. Ibid.
14. Draper Fisher Jurvetson, *Operations and Strategy* (visited May 7, 1999), www.drapervc.com/Operations.html.
15. William A. Sahlman, A Method for Valuing High-Risk, Long Term Investments: The "Venture Capital Method," *Harvard Business School* 22 (June 1989).
16. Kleiner Perkins Caufield & Byers, *Keiretsu* (visited April 14, 1999), www.kpcb.com/ keiretsu/index.html.
17. Alex Gove, American Keiretsu, *Red Herring* (visited October 1, 1999), www.redherring.com/mag/issue51/american.html.
18. @Ventures, *Frequently Asked Questions* (visited April 28, 2000), www.atventures.com/faq/index.html.
19. Tyzoon T. Tyebjee and Albert V. Bruno, A Model of Venture Capitalist Investment Activity, in Mike Wright and Ken Robbie, *Venture Capital* 108–109 (1997); Sahlman, A Method for Valuing High-Risk, Long - erm Investments, Ashgate Publishing Company.
20. Ibid.
21. Sahlman, A Method for Valuing High-Risk, Long-Term Investments.
22. AVI Capital, *Focus* (visited August 7, 1999), www.avicapital.com/.
23. Benchmark Capital, *Our Strategy* (visited August 7, 1999), www .benchmark.com/about/strategy.html.
24. Sequoia Capital, *Frequently Asked Questions* (visited May 9, 1999), www.sequoiacap.com/sequoia/other/faq.htm.
25. Oak Investment Partners, *Strategy* (visited August 7, 1999), www .oakinv.com/.
26. Battery Ventures, *The Battery Advantage* (visited August 7, 1999), www.battery.com/advantage.html.
27. U.S. Venture Partners, *Investment Process* (visited September 26, 1999), www.usvp.com/approach/process.html.
28. El Dorado Ventures, *FAQs*.
29. Ibid.
30. Flatiron Partners, *Investment Philosophy* (visited August 8, 1999), www.flatironpartners.com/index_philosophy.html.
31. See Robert A. Mamis, *Risky Business, Inc. Online* (visited September 29, 1999), www.inc.com/documents/finance/03900291.
32. Baum, Interview with Kevin Fong.
33. Jeffrey Zygmont, *The VC Way: Investment Secrets from the Wizards of Venture Capital* 64 (2001), Perseus Publishing.
34. Ibid.

35. New Enterprise Associates, *Investment Philosophy/Criteria* (visited May 10, 1999), www.nea.com/phil.htm.
36. Rich Karlgaard, Dollars from Heaven, Rich Prospects: *garage.com* (visited January 17, 1999), www.garage.com/richProspectsArchive /1998.06.29.nuggest.shtml.
37. Fred Dotzler, What Percent of a Medical Company Should Founders Sell for Seed/Start-Up Venture Capital, *Medicus Venture Partners* (visited September 30, 1991), www.medicusvc.com/.
38. Draper Fisher Jurvetson, *Operations and Strategy.*
39. John R. Van Slyke and Howard H. Stevenson, Pre-Start Analysis: A Framework for Thinking about Business Ventures, *Harvard Business School* 14 (September 16, 1985).
40. Seth Fineberg, To Sell or Not to Sell, *Venture Capital Journal,* June 1998, at 41.
41. Ibid.
42. Hummer Winblad Venture Partners, *Frequently Asked Questions* (visited May 9, 1999), www.humwin.com/faq.html.
43. Fineberg, To Sell or Not to Sell, at 43.

Chapter 2   Management Due Diligence

1. Alan E. Salzman and L. John Doerr, The Venture Funding Process, in *Start-Up and Emerging Companies: Planning, Financing & Operating the Successful Business* § 7.03[4] (1998), Law Journal Seminars Press.
2. Arthur Rock, Strategy v. Tactics from a Venture Capitalist, *Harvard Business Review,* November–December 1987, at 5.
3. Geoff Baum, Interview with Kevin Fong, *Garage.com* (visited February 8, 1999), www.garage.com/soapboxArchive/1998.10.19.kevinFong1.shtml.
4. Ibid.
5. Ibid.
6. Ibid.
7. Jim Swartz, How to Win a Venture Capitalist, *Accel Partners* (visited May 27, 1999), www.accel.com/entrepreneurs/how_to_win.html.
8. Ibid.
9. Rock, Strategy v. Tactics, at 1.
10. Michael S. Malone, John Doerr's Startup Manual, *Fast Company* (visited July 14, 1999), www.fastcompany.com/online/07/082doerr.html.
11. Baum, Interview with Kevin Fong.
12. Jeffrey Zygmont, *The VC Way: Investment Secrets from the Wizards of Venture Capital* 64 (2001), Perseus Publishing.
13. Zygmont, *The VC Way.*

14. Rock, Strategy v. Tactics from a Venture Capitalist.
15. Accel Partners, *Advice for First Time Entrepreneurs* (visited May 27, 1999), www.accel.com/entrepreneurs.
16. Jim Jubak, Do You Kick Your Dog? *Venture,* June 1987, at 42.
17. Ruthann Quindlen, *Confessions of a Venture Capitalist* 116 (2000).
18. Soledad O'Brien, Interview with Ann Winblad (visited October 5, 1999), ww.womenswire.com/plug.spotlight/d0721winbladTrans.html.
19. Draper Fisher Jurvetson, *Operations and Strategy* (visited May 7, 1999), www.drapervc.com/Operations.html.
20. Ibid.
21. Arthur Lipper, *Venture's Financing and Investing in Private Companies* 78–80 (1988), Missouri Innovation Center Publications.
22. Ibid.
23. Baum, Interview with Kevin Fong.
24. Ibid.
25. Karl H. Vesper, *New Venture Strategies* 56 (1990), Prentice Hall.
26. Hummer Winblad Venture Partners, *Frequently Asked Questions* (visited May 9, 1999), www.humwin.com/faq.html.
27. Vincent Ryan, High Roller: C. Richard Kramlich, Upside, April 1999, at 74.
28. Baum, Interview with Kevin Fong.
29. Jeffrey Zygmont, *The VC Way: Investment Secrets from the Wizards of Venture Capital* 76 (2001), Pereus Publishing.
30. Floyd Kvamme, Remarks at Silicon Valley Learning Adventure (December 3–5, 1998), in *Leadership Network* (visited October 6, 1999), webu7108.ntx.net/leadnetinfo/kvamme.html.
31. Draper Fisher Jurvetson, Operations and Strategy.
32. Venture Capitalists Kevin Fong of the Mayfield Fund, *theSite.com* (visited May 12, 2000), www.zdnet.com/zdtv/thesite/0897w5/work/work811jump1_082597.html.
33. Ibid.
34. Michael S. Malone, John Doerr's Startup Manual, *Fast Company* (visited July 14, 1999), www.fastcompany.com/online/07/082doerr.html.
35. Norwest Venture Partners, *Investment Size and Style* (visited January 17, 1999), www.norwestvc.com/business/overview/index.html.
36. Rock, Strategy v. Tactics, at 3.
37. Draper Fisher Jurvetson, *Operations and Strategy.*
38. Ibid.
39. Hummer Winblad Venture Partners, *Frequently Asked Questions.*
40. Venture Capitalists Kevin Fong of the Mayfield Fund.

41. Quindlen, *Confessions.*
42. The Mayfield Fund, *For Entrepreneurs* (visited January 17, 1999), www.mayfield.com/second/entrefrset.html.
43. Ann Winblad, Keynote Speech, *VentureNet99* (visited September 8, 1999), www.dsm.com/venturenet99/venturenet99june1st.htm.
44. Swartz, How to Win a Venture Capitalist.
45. Malone, John Doerr's Startup Manual.
46. Robert C. Perez, *Inside Venture Capital: Past, Present, and Future* 115 (1986), Praeger Publishers.
47. Ibid., 115–116.
48. Ibid.
49. Rock, Strategy v. Tactics, at 3.
50. Zygmont, *The VC Way* 72.
51. Malone, John Doerr's Startup Manual.
52. Jeffry A. Timmons, *New Venture Creation: Entrepreneurship for the 21st Century* 217 (4th ed., 1994), Irwin McGraw-Hill.
53. Karen Southwick, *Silicon Gold Rush* 47 (1999), John Wiley & Sons.
54. Baum, Interview with Kevin Fong.
55. Rock, Strategy v. Tactics, at 3.
56. Ibid.
57. Sequoia Capital, *Frequently Asked Questions* (visited May 9, 1999), www.sequoiacap.com/sequoia/other/faq.htm.
58. Ibid.
59. Draper Fisher Jurvetson, *Operations and Strategy.*
60. Zygmont, *The VC Way* 64.
61. Ibid.
62. Venture Capitalists Kevin Fong of the Mayfield Fund.
63. Draper Fisher Jurvetson, *Operations and Strategy.*
64. Fred Dotzler, Hiring an Effective Chief Executive to Run a Start-Up Company, Medicus Venture Partners (July 1994), www.medicusvc.com/.
65. Ibid.
66. Sequoia Capital, *Frequently Asked Questions.*
67. Baum, Interview with Kevin Fong.
68. Ibid.
69. Draper Fisher Jurvetson, *Operations and Strategy.*
70. William H. Davidow, *Marketing High Technology: An Insider's View* 12 (1986), The Free Press.
71. David A. Kaplan, *The Silicon Boys* 195 (1999), William Morrow & Company.
72. Karl H. Vesper, *New Venture Strategies* 39 (1990), Prentice Hall.

73. Baum, Interview with Kevin Fong.
74. Fred Dotzler, Hiring an Effective Chief Executive.
75. Shawn Neidorf, Serial Entrepreneurs: Are They Worth it? *Venture Capital Journal,* February 1998, at 38.
76. Draper Fisher Jurvetson, *Operations and Strategy* [emphasis added].
77. Neidorf, Serial Entrepreneurs.
78. Baum, Interview with Kevin Fong.
79. Vincent Ryan, High Roller: Douglas Leone, Sequoia Capital, *Upside,* May 1999, at 70.
80. Kaplan, *Silicon Boys* 311.
81. Hambrect & Quist Venture Capital, What We Look For (visited January 17, 1999), www.hamquist.com/venture/look.html.
82. Dotzler, Hiring an Effective Chief Executive.
83. Ruthann Quindlen, *Confessions* 49.
84. Ibid.
85. Venture Capitalists Kevin Fong of the Mayfield Fund.
86. Quindlen, *Confessions.*
87. Venture Capitalists Kevin Fong of the Mayfield Fund.
88. Laurence J. Peter and Raymond Hull, *The Peter Principle: Why Things Always Go Wrong* (1969), William Morrow & Company ("In a hierarchy, every employee tends to rise to his level of incompetence").
89. Zygmont, *The VC Way* 77.
90. Ibid.
91. Ibid., 67.
92. Dotzler, Hiring an Effective Chief Executive.
93. Ibid.
94. Quindlen, *Confessions* 53.
95. Christine Comaford, How to Build Effective Management Teams (visited May 19, 1999), www.artemisventures.com.
96. Dotzler, Hiring an Effective Chief Executive.
97. Alexander L. M. Dingee et al., Characteristics of a Successful Management Team, in *Pratt's Guide to Venture Capital Sources* 27 (1997), Venture Economics.
98. Baum, Interview with Kevin Fong.
99. Quindlen, *Confessions* 42.
100. Ibid., 126.
101. Swartz, How to Win a Venture Capitalist.
102. Rock, Strategy v. Tactics, at 4.
103. Malone, John Doerr's Startup Manual.
104. Ibid.

105. C. Gordon Bell, *High-Tech Ventures: The Guide for Entrepreneurial Success* 119 (1991), Addison Wesley.
106. Ibid.
107. Dingee et al., Characteristics of a Successful Management Team 26–27.
108. Ibid.
109. Ibid., 27.
110. Ibid.
111. Rock, Strategy v. Tactics, at 3.
112. Winblad, Keynote Speech.
113. Dingee et al., Characteristics of a Successful Management Team.
114. Ibid.
115. Ibid.
116. Floyd Kvamme, Remarks at Silicon Valley.
117. Fred Dotzler, Should I Hire A Vice President of Marketing or a Vice President of Sales into My Start-Up Medical Company? Medicus Venture Partners (visited October 3, 1997), www.medicusvc.com/.
118. Ibid.
119. Ibid.
120. Ibid.
121. Dingee et al., Characteristics of a Successful Management Team 26.
122. Ibid.
123. Ibid.
124. Ibid.
125. Ibid.
126. Ibid.
127. Ibid.
128. Ibid.
129. Ibid.
130. Ibid.
131. El Dorado Ventures, How to Build a Board (visited May 8, 2000), www.eldorado.com/build.html.
132. Ibid.
133. Bell, *High-Tech Ventures* 28.
134. Advanced Technology Ventures, How to Build Your Board of Directors, *Garage.com Venture Capital Forum* (visited January 10, 1999), www.garage.com/forums/ventureCapital/articles.shtml.
135. Ibid.
136. Ibid.
137. Ibid.

138. Ibid.
139. Jeffry A. Timmons and Harry J. Sapienza, Venture Capital: More Than Money? in Pratt's Guide to Venture Capital Sources 58–59 (1997), Venture Economics.
140. Advanced Technology Ventures, How to Build Your Board of Directors.
141. Ibid.
142. Bell, High-Tech Ventures.
143. Darlene Mann, What's Your Business Model? Onset Ventures (visited May 10, 1999), www.onset.com/news/news_fram.html.
144. Bell, High-Tech Ventures 32.
145. Accel Partners, *Advice for First Time Entrepreneurs*.
146. Oak Investment Partners, Oak's Philosophy (visited April 29, 2000), www.oakinvestment.com/fs_about.html.
147. Accel Partners, *Advice for First Time Entrepreneurs*.

Chapter 3   Business Opportunity Due Diligence

1. Regis McKenna, Why High-Tech Products Fail, in *Customer-Driven Marketing: Lessons from Entrepreneurial Technology Companies* 5 (Raymond W. Smilor ed., 1989), Lexington Books.
2. Ibid.
3. William H. Davidow, *Marketing High Technology: An Insider's View* 140 (1986), The Free Press.
4. Geoff Baum, Interview with Kevin Fong, *Garage.com* (visited February 8, 1999), www.garage.com/soapboxArchive/1998.10.19.kevinFong1.shtml.
5. See Robert A Mamis, *Risky Business, Inc. Online* (visited September 29, 1999), www.inc.com/documents/finance/03900291.
6. Davidow, *Marketing High Technology* 38.
7. Karen Southwick, *Silicon Gold Rush* 97 (1999), John Wiley & Sons.
8. Ibid.
9. Jeffrey Zygmont, *The VC Way: Investment Secrets from the Wizards of Venture Capital* 156 (2001), Perseus Publishing.
10. Southwick, *Silicon Gold Rush* 143.
11. David A. Kaplan, *The Silicon Boys* 193 (1999), William Morrow & Company.
12. Fred Dotzler, Market Research Basics for the Start-Up Biomedical Company, *Medicus Venture Partners* (visited January 13, 1994), www.medicusvc.com/.
13. Southwick, *Silicon Gold Rush* 143.

14. Ibid.
15. Ibid.
16. Ibid.
17. Accel Partners, *Advice for First Time Entrepreneurs* (visited May 27, 1999), www.accel.com/entrepreneurs.
18. Kaplan, *The Silicon Boys.*
19. Ruthann Quindlen, *Confessions of a Venture Capitalist* 79 (2000), Warner Books.
20. Draper Fisher Jurvetson, *Operations and Strategy* (visited May 7, 1999), www.drapervc.com/Operations.html.
21. Regis McKenna, *Relationship Marketing* 15 (1991), Addison Wesley.
22. ComVentures, *Criteria* (visited October 5, 1999), www.comven .com/strategy/criteria-content.html.
23. Sequoia Capital, *Frequently Asked Questions* (visited April 30, 2000), www.sequoiacap.com/faq.htm.
24. On the Record: Venture Capitalists Meet the Press, *Redherring.com* (visited October 18, 1999), www.redherring.com/mag/issue20/otrecord. html.
25. Alan E. Salzman and L. John Doerr, The Venture Funding Process, in *Start-Up and Emerging Companies: Planning, Financing & Operating the Successful Business* § 7.03[4] (1998).
26. Zygmont, *The VC Way* 120.
27. Accel Partners, *Advice for First Time Entrepreneurs.*
28. Quindlen, *Confessions* 67.
29. Albert Bruno, Marketing Lessons from Silicon Valley for Technology-Based Firms, in *Customer-Driven Marketing; Lessons from Entrepreneurial Technology Companies* 40 (Raymond W. Smilor ed., 1989), Lexington Books.
30. Quindlen, *Confessions.*
31. Guy Kawasaki, *Rules for Revolutionaries* 46–63 (1999), Harper Business.
32. Darlene Mann, What's Your Business Model? *Onset Ventures* (visited May 10, 1999), www.onset.com/news/news_fram.html.
33. Shawn Neidorf, Choose Your Weapon, *Venture Capital Journal,* June 1998, at 39.
34. McKenna, *Relationship Marketing* 155.
35. Ibid., 155–156.
36. Ibid.
37. Ibid.
38. Mann, What's Your Business Model? *Onset Ventures.*
39. Ibid.

40. Draper Fisher Jurvetson, *Operations and Strategy* (visited May 7, 1999), www.drapervc.com/Operations.html.
41. Quindlen, *Confessions* 115.
42. Bay Partners, *Investment Philosophy* (visited February 17, 1999), www.baypartners.com/philosophy.html.
43. Mann, Raising Money: Some Tips on Working with Venture Capitalists, *Onset Ventures* (visited May 5, 1999), www.onset.com/pdfs /whitepaper.pdf.
44. Mann, What's Your Business Model?
45. Quindlen, *Confessions* 85.
46. Mann, Raising Money.
47. Quindlen, *Confessions* 92.
48. Lawrence Aragon, The Smart VC at Mayfield, *Redherring.com* (visited February 9, 2000), www.redherring.com/vc/2000/0126 /vc-vcps012600.html.
49. Geoffrey A. Moore, *Crossing the Chasm* 90 (1991), Harper Business.
50. C. Gordon Bell, *High-Tech Ventures: The Guide for Entrepreneurial Success* 206–207 (1991), Addison Wesley.
51. Moore, *Crossing the Chasm* 90.
52. Ibid.
53. Leonard M. Lodish et al., *Entrepreneurial Marketing: Lessons from Wharton's Pioneering MBA Course* 5 (2001), John Wiley & Sons.
54. Ibid.
55. Baum, Interview with Kevin Fong, *Garage.com* (visited February 8, 1999), www.garage.com/soapboxArchive/1998.10.19.kevinFong1 .shtml.
56. *The Spotlight: Venture Capital: Ann Winblad* (visited October 5, 1999), www.newmedianews.com/122697/ts_venturecap.html.
57. Quindlen, *Confessions* 61.
58. Ibid.
59. Fred Dotzler, What Percent of a Medical Company Should Founders Sell for Seed/Start-Up Venture Capital, *Medicus Venture Partners* (visited September 30, 1991), www.medicusvc.com/.
60. Quindlen, *Confessions* xiv.
61. John R. Van Slyke et al., The Start-Up Process, in *The Entrepreneurial Venture* 82 (William A. Sahlman and Howard H. Stevenson eds., 1992), Harvard Business School Press.
62. Bob Zider, How Venture Capital Works, *Harvard Business Review*, November–December 1998, at 133–134.
63. George S. Day, Assessing Competitive Arenas: Who Are Your Competitors, in *Wharton on Dynamic Competitive Strategy* 45 (George S. Day and David J. Reibstein eds., 1997), John Wiley & Sons.

64. Robert C. Perez, *Inside Venture Capital: Past, Present, and Future* 116 (1986), Praeger Publishers.
65. Mann, Raising Money.
66. Karl A. Vesper, New Venture Strategies, 183 (1990), Prentice Hall.
67. William A. Sahlman, A Method for Valuing High-Risk, Long Term Investments: The "Venture Capital Method," *Harvard Business School* 19 (June 1989).
68. El Dorado Ventures, *FAQs* (visited May 10, 1999), www .eldoradoventures.com/ faqs/answer5.htm.
69. William H. Davidow, *Marketing High Technology: An Insider's View* 25 (1986), The Free Press.
70. Mann, Raising Money.
71. Quindlen, *Confessions* 96.
72. Ali Asadullah, High Roller: Yogen K. Dalal, Mayfield Fund, *Upside,* February 1999, at 70.
73. Hirotaka J. Takeuchi, Strategic Issues in Distribution, *Harvard Business School* 2 (February 27, 1987).
74. Lodish et al., *Entrepreneurial Marketing* 81.
75. Todd Dagres, *Battery Ventures* (visited October 7, 1999), www .battery.com/press/masshightech.htm.
76. Takeuchi, Strategic Issues in Distribution.
77. Quindlen, *Confessions* 99–99.
78. Mann, What's Your Business Model?
79. Sequoia Capital, Process (visited November 23, 2001), www.sequoiacap .com/process/stepone_market.asp.
80. Mann, What's Your Business Model?
81. John Barry, Prospecting for Ventures, *American Venture Magazine,* April–June 1999 (visited November 23, 2001), www.avce.com/files /editorial/199904/barry.html.
82. Jeffry A. Timmons, *New Venture Creation: Entrepreneurship for the 21st Century* 99 (4th ed., 1994), Irwin McGraw-Hill.
83. Ibid.
84. Draper Fisher Jurvetson, *Operations and Strategy.*
85. Anthony B. Perkins, The Young & the Restless of Technology Finance, *Redherring.com* (visited October 6, 1999), www.redherring.com/mag /issue06/young.html.
86. Hummer Winblad Venture Partners, *Frequently Asked Questions* (visited May 9, 1999), www.humwin.com/faq.html.
87. Accel Partners, *Advice for First Time Entrepreneurs.*
88. El Dorado Ventures, *FAQs.*
89. Ibid.
90. Michael E. Porter, *Competitive Strategy* 232 (1989), The Free Press.

91. Fred Dotzler, What Percent of a Medical Company Should Founders Sell for Seed/Start-Up Venture Capital, *Medicus Venture Partners* (visited September 30, 1991), www.medicusvc.com/.

92. Elton B. Sherwin, Jr., *The Silicon Valley Way* 37 (1998), Prima Publishing.

93. Floyd Kvamme, Remarks at Silicon Valley Learning Adventure (December 3–5, 1998), in *Leadership Network* (visited October 6, 1999), webu7108.ntx.net/leadnetinfo/kvamme.html.

94. Trinity Ventures, *Our Investment Objectives* (visited February 1, 1999), www.trinityventures.com/objectives.htm.

95. Sherwin, *Silicon Valley Way* 107.

96. Hummer Winblad Venture Partners, *Frequently Asked Questions*.

97. Lodish et al., *Entrepreneurial Marketing* 18.

98. Hambrect & Quist Venture Capital, *What We Look For* (visited January 17, 1999), www.hamquist.com/venture/look.html.

99. Lodish et al., *Entrepreneurial Marketing* 3.

100. Pankaj Ghemawat, Sustainable Advantage, *Harvard Business Review*, September–October 1986, at 55.

101. Ibid.

102. Ibid.

103. Lodish et al., *Entrepreneurial Marketing* 3–4.

104. Sequoia Capital, *Frequently Asked Questions* (visited May 9, 1999), www.sequoiacap.com/sequoia/other/faq.htm.

105. Ann Winblad, Keynote Speech, *VentureNet99* (visited September 8, 1999), www.dsm.com/venturenet99/venturenet99june1st.htm.

106. Steve Jurvetson & Tim Draper, *Viral Marketing, Draper Fisher Jurvetson* (visited September 8, 1999), www.venture-capital.com /ViralMarketing.html.

107. Winblad, Keynote Speech.

108. Lodish et al., *Entrepreneurial Marketing* 9.

109. Ibid., 1.

Chapter 4   Due Diligence on Intangibles

1. Elton B. Sherwin, Jr., *The Silicon Valley Way* 2 (1998), Prima Publishing.

2. Ruthann Quindlen, *Confessions of a Venture Capitalist* 57 (2000), Warner Books.

3. Oak Investment Partners, *Oak's Focus* (visited October 12, 1999), www.oakinv.com/body_investq2.html.

4. Jeffrey Zygmont, *The VC Way: Investment Secrets from the Wizards of Venture Capital* 162 (2001), Perseus Publishing.
5. Oak Investment Partners, *Oak's Focus.*
6. Venture Capitalists Kevin Fong of the Mayfield Fund, *theSite.com* (visited May 12, 2000), www.zdnet.com/zdtv/thesite/0897w5/work /work811jump1_082597.html.
7. Jim Jubak, Do You Kick Your Dog? *Venture,* June 1987, at 40.
8. Ibid.

Chapter 5   Legal Due Diligence

1. John Steel, *Choice of Entity: Corporations vs. LLCs* (visited February 2, 2001), www.gcwf.com/articles/vcp/vcp_sum00_1.html.
2. Ibid.
3. Jonathan E. Cole and Albert L. Sokol, Structuring Venture Capital Investments, in *Pratt's Guide to Venture Capital Sources* 31–32 (1997), Venture Economics.
4. Steel, *Choice of Entity.*
5. Ibid.
6. Sequoia Capital, *Frequently Asked Questions* (visited May 9, 1999), www.sequoiacap.com/sequoia/other/faq.htm.
7. Joseph W. Bartlett, *Fundamentals of Venture Capital* 52 (1999), Madison Books.
8. Ibid.
9. Cole and Sokol, Structuring Venture Capital Investments 32.
10. Ibid.
11. Frederick D. Lipman, *Financing Your Business with Venture Capital* 35–36 (1998), Prima Publishing.
12. David J. Byer et al., Intellectual Property Assets: Development and Assessment for Value, *Venture Capital Review,* Spring 1998, at 26–27; see also David L. Hayes, *Acquiring and Protecting Technology: The Intellectual Property Audit* 3 (1992).
13. Michael Lytton, *Advice of Counsel* (visited June 28, 2001), www .palmerdodge.com/frmFindArticle.cfm.
14. Ibid.
15. Jeffry A. Timmons, *New Venture Creation: Entrepreneurship for the 21st Century* 48 (4th ed., 1994), Irwin McGraw-Hill.
16. Byer et al., Intellectual Property Assets, at 28–29.
17. Ibid., at 28.
18. Ibid., at 28–29.
19. Ibid., at 32–33.

20. Asset Management Company, Submitting a Business Plan (visited March 18, 2001), www.assetman.com/contact /submitting_business_plans.htm.
21. Byer et al., Intellectual Property Assets, at 28.
22. Cole and Sokol, Structuring Venture Capital Investments 32.
23. Bartlett, *Fundamentals of Venture Capital* 129.
24. Mark C. White, The Investor-Friendly Startup Company, *Law Firm of White and Lee* (visited January 21, 1999), www.whiteandlee.com /invfrend.htm.
25. Richard J. Testa, The Legal Process of Venture Capital Investment, in Arthur Lipper, *The Guide for Venture Investing Angels* 340 (1998), Missouri Innovation Center Publications.
26. Edgar Norton and Bernard H. Tenenbaum, The Effects of Venture Capitalists' Characteristics on the Structure of the Venture Capital Deal, in Mike Wright and Ken Robbie, *Venture Capital* 151 (1997), Ashgate Publishing Company.
27. Robert V. Gunderson, Hi-Tech Corporation: Series B Preferred Stock Warrant, in *Venture Capital and Public Offering Negotiation* 6–7 (Michael L. Halloran ed., 1999), Aspen Law & Business.
28. Norton and Tenenbaum, The Effects of Venture Capitalists' Characteristics, 151–152.
29. Gunderson, Hi-Tech Corporation: Series B Preferred Stock Warrant, in *Venture Capital and Public Offering Negotiation* 6–3 (Michael L. Halloran ed., 1999), Aspen Law & Business.
30. Norton and Tenenbaum, *Effects of Venture Capitalists' Characteristics* 151–152.
31. Testa, Legal Process of Venture Capital Investment 357.
32. Timothy Tomlinson, Venture Capital Attornies Should Plan for a Merger, *Tomlinon Zisko Morosoli & Maser* (visited June 15, 2001), www.tzmm.com/articles/nlj_b11.htm.
33. AVI Capital, *Focus* (visited August 7, 1999), www.avicapital.com/.
34. Testa, Legal Process of Venture Capital Investment 356.
35. Mark C. White, Venture Capital Financings: Process and Issues, *Law Firm of White and Lee* (visited January 21, 1999), www .whiteandlee.com/ventrcap.htm.
36. Gary R. Silverman, Venture Capital Investing in the New Economy, *Venture Capital Review,* Spring 2000, at 4, footnote 3.
37. Alan E. Salzman and L. John Doerr, The Venture Funding Process, in *Start-Up and Emerging Companies: Planning, Financing & Operating the Successful Business* § 7.02[5] (1998).

38. Robert M. Johnson, Valuation Issues in Start-Ups & Early-Stage Companies: The Venture Capital Method, *London Business School* 6 (December 1997).
39. Venture Law Group, Law Q&A Forum, *Garage.com* (visited February 8, 1999), www.garage.com/forums/law/qandaArchive.shtml.
40. Venture Law Group, Venture Capital Forum, *Garage.com* (visited May 12, 2000), www.garage.com/forums/venturecapital/qandaArchive .shtml#Q15.
41. Seth L. Pierrepont, Antidilution Protection, a Standard Term, in Arthur Lipper, *The Guide for Venture Investing Angels* 436 (1998), Missouri Innovation Center Publications.
42. Ibid.
43. Silverman, Venture Capital Investing, at 5.
44. Ibid.
45. Counsellors to Rising Start-Ups, *National Law Journal* (visited April 16, 2001), www.ljx.com/practice/corporate/forum.html.
46. Ibid.
47. Ibid.
48. White, Venture Capital Financings.
49. Silverman, Venture Capital Investing, at 4.
50. Frederick D. Lipman, *Financing Your Business with Venture Capital* 89 (1998), Prima Publishing.
51. Silverman, Venture Capital Investing, at 4.
52. White, Venture Capital Financings.
53. Testa, Legal Process of Venture Capital Investment 360.
54. Bartlett, *Fundamentals of Venture Capital* 82–83.
55. Gunderson, Hi-Tech Corporation 10-12.
56. Craig W. Johnson, How to Close Investors, *garage.com: Venture Law Group Forum* (visited January 10, 1999), www.garage.com/forums/law /1998.12.21.article.shtml.
57. Timothy Tomlinson, Tips to Enhance Venture Capital Returns, *Venture Capital Journal,* May 1998, at 40.
58. Ibid.
59. The Woodside Fund, Popular Misperceptions about Venture Capitalists (visited June 15, 2001), www.woodsidefund.com/f_visionary.htm.
60. Venture Capitalists Kevin Fong of the Mayfield Fund, *theSite.com* (visited May 12, 2000), www.zdnet.com/zdtv/thesite/0897w5/work /work811jump1_082597.html.
61. Ibid.
62. Testa, Legal Process of Venture Capital Investment 359–360.

63. Lee F. Benton and Robert V. Gunderson, Jr., High-Tech Corporation: Restated Certificate of Incorporation, in *Venture Capital and Public Offering Negotiation* 8–25 (Michael L. Halloran ed., 1999), Aspen Law & Business.

64. Ibid., 8-26.

65. Ibid., 8-29.

66. Testa, Legal Process of Venture Capital Investment 346, 349–350.

67. Ibid., 347–349.

68. Ibid., 345–352.

69. Ibid., 360.

70. Benton and Gunderson, Hi-Tech Corporation: Restated Certificate 8-46.

71. Bartlett, *Fundamentals of Venture Capital 59*.

72. Ibid.

73. Venture Law Group, Law Forum, *Garage.com* (visited May 12, 2000), www.garage.com/forums/law/qandaArchive.shtml#Q13.

74. Counsellors to Rising Start-Ups.

75. Fred Dotzler, What Percent of a Medical Company Should Founders Sell for Seed/Start-Up Venture Capital, Medicus Venture Partners (visited September 30, 1991), www.medicusvc.com/.

76. Benchmark Capital, Our Strategy (visited August 7, 1999), www.benchmark.com/about/strategy.html.

77. Weiss, Peck & Greer Venture Partners, Investment Objective (visited September 13, 1999), www.wpgvp.com/investme.htm.

78. Tomlinson, Tips to Enhance Venture Capital Returns, at 41.

79. Testa, Legal Process of Venture Capital Investment 334.

80. Jeffry A. Timmons, *New Venture Creation: Entrepreneurship for the 21st Century* 517 (4th ed., 1994), Irwin McGraw-Hill.

81. Sequoia Capital, *Frequently Asked Questions*.

82. William Sahlman, Aspects of Financial Contracting in Venture Capital, in *The Entrepreneurial Venture* 237 (William A. Sahlman and Howard H. Stevenson eds., 1992), Harvard Business School Press.

83. Counsellors to Rising Start-Ups, National Law Journal (visited April 16, 2001), www.ljx.com/practice/corporate/forum.html.

84. Frederick D. Lipman, Financing Your Business with Venture Capital 96–97 (1998), Prima Publishing.

85. Jonathan E. Cole and Albert L. Sokol, Structuring Venture Capital Investments, in *Pratt's Guide to Venture Capital Sources* 38 (1997), Venture Economics.

86. Counsellors to Rising Start-Ups.

87. Testa, Legal Process of Venture Capital Investment 352.

88. Robert V. Gunderson, Jr. and Lee F. Benton, Hi-Tech Corporation: Investors' Rights Agreement, in Venture Capital and Public Offering Negotiation 9-12 (Michael L. Halloran ed., 1999), Aspen Law & Business.
89. Ibid.
90. Testa, Legal Process of Venture Capital Investment 353.
91. Ibid.
92. Lipman, Financing Your Business 118.
93. Seth Fineberg, Coming to Terms, *Venture Capital Journal,* October 1998, at 40.
94. Testa, Legal Process of Venture Capital Investment 362.
95. Gunderson and Benton, Hi-Tech Corporation: Co-Sale Agreement, in Venture Capital and Public Offering Negotiation 12–2 (Michael L. Halloran ed., 1999), Aspen Law & Business.
96. Stephen I. Glover, Recapturing Short-Term Investments, *National Law Journal,* February 17, 1997, at B09.
97. Fred Dotzler, What Percent of a Medical Company Should Founders Sell for Seed/Start-Up Venture Capital, Medicus Venture Partners (visited September 30, 1991), www.medicusvc.com/.
98. Dotzler, What Percent of a Medical Company Should Founders Sell?
99. Benton and Gunderson, Hi-Tech Corporation: Restated Certificate of Incorporation 8-16.
100. Glover, Recapturing Short-Term Investments.
101. Lipman, Financing Your Business 93-94.
102. White, Venture Capital Financings: Process and Issues.
103. Ibid.
104. Cole and Sokol, Structuring Venture Capital Investments 37–38.
105. Ibid.
106. Testa, Legal Process of Venture Capital Investment 360.
107. Harold M. Hoffman and James Blakey, You Can Negotiate with Venture Capitalists, *Harvard Business Review,* March–April 1987, at 7.
108. Frederick D. Lipman, *Venture Capital and Junk Bond Financing* § 2.01(b) (1996), American Law Institute and American Bar Association.
109. Greg Gallo and Scott Stanton, What's Your Preference, *Newsroom: garage.com* (visited January 13, 1999), www.garage.com/galloAndStanton.shtml.
110. Silverman, Venture Capital Investing, at 3.
111. Ibid.
112. Gallo and Stanton, What's Your Preference.
113. Silverman, Venture Capital Investing.
114. Bartlett, *Fundamentals of Venture Capital* 89.

115. Tomlinson, Venture Capital Attornies Should Plan.

116. Ibid.

117. Gallo and Stanton, What's Your Preference.

118. Benton and Gunderson, Hi-Tech Corporation: Restated Certificate of Incorporation 8-12.

119. Arthur Lipper, *Venture's Financing and Investing in Private Companies* 72 (1988), Probus Publishing Company.

120. Testa, Legal Process of Venture Capital Investment 345–346.

121. Ibid.

Chapter 6   Financial Due Diligence

1. Jeffry A. Timmons, *New Venture Creation: Entrepreneurship for the 21st Century* 450 (4th ed., 1994), Irwin McGraw-Hill.

2. Fred Dotzler, Raising Venture Capital: Managing the Process for a Medical Start-Up, *Medicus Venture Partners* (visited May 9, 1990), www.medicusvc.com/.

3. David Gladstone, *Venture Capital Investing* 110 (1988), Prentice Hall.

4. Ibid.

5. Ibid., 118.

6. Arthur Rock, Strategy v. Tactics from a Venture Capitalist, *Harvard Business Review,* November–December 1987, at 2.

7. Sequoia Capital, *Frequently Asked Questions* (visited May 9, 1999), www.sequoiacap.com/sequoia/other/faq.htm.

8. Alan E. Salzman and L. John Doerr, The Venture Funding Process, in *Start-Up and Emerging Companies: Planning, Financing & Operating the Successful Business* § 7.03[9] (1998), Law Journals Seminars Press.

9. Ibid.

10. Stanley R. Rich and David E. Gumpert, How to Write a Winning Business Plan, in *The Entrepreneurial Venture* 133 (William A. Sahlman and Howard H. Stevenson eds., 1992).

11. Ibid.

12. Ruthann Quindlen, *Confessions of a Venture Capitalist* 106 (2000), Warner Books.

13. Ibid.

14. Joseph W. Bartlett, *Fundamentals of Venture Capital* 7 (1999), Madison Books.

15. Ibid., 23.

16. Salzman and Doerr, Venture Funding Process § 7.02[2].

17. Advanced Technology Ventures, *Venture Capital Forum, Garage.com* (visited May 12, 2000), www.garage.com/forums/ventureCapital /qanda.shtml.

18. Geoffrey Moore, The Anatomy of Failure, *Red Herring Magazine,* September 1999, at 86, 92.
19. Sequoia Capital, *Frequently Asked Questions.*
20. Ibid.
21. Anthony B. Perkins, The Young & the Restless of Technology Finance, *Redherring.com* (visited October 6, 1999), www.redherring.com/mag /issue06/young.html.
22. New Enterprise Associates, *Investment Philosophy/Criteria* (visited May 10, 1999), www.nea.com/phil.htm.
23. Perkins, *Young & Restless of Technology Finance.*
24. Jeffry A. Timmons, *New Venture Creation: Entrepreneurship for the 21st Century* 450 (4th ed., 1994), Irwin McGraw-Hill.
25. Salzman and Doerr, Venture Funding Process § 7.02[2].
26. Lawrence Aragon, Getting into Debt, *Redherring.com* visited June 29, 2001), www.redherring.com/index.asp?layout=story& channel=40000004&doc_id=1080017708&rh_special_report_id=.
27. Ibid.
28. Ibid.
29. Ruthann Quindlen, *Confessions of a Venture Capitalist* 50 (2000), Warner Books.
30. Quindlen, *Confessions* 176.
31. Softbank Venture Capital, *Funding Process* (visited June 30, 2001), www.sbvc.com/pageload.asp?pagename=funding.
32. Quindlen, *Confessions* 177.
33. Ibid.
34. Ibid.
35. Venture Capitalists Kevin Fong of the Mayfield Fund, *theSite.com* (visited May 12, 2000), www.zdnet.com/zdtv/thesite/0897w5/work /work811jump1_082597.html.
36. Mark C. White, The Valuation of Newly-Formed Technology Companies, *Law Firm of White & Lee* (visited September 11, 1999), www.whiteandlee.com/valuatn.htm.
37. William A. Sahlman, A Method for Valuing High-Risk, Long Term Investments: The "Venture Capital Method," *Harvard Business School* 19 (June 1989).
38. Ibid., 21.
39. Draper Fisher Jurvetson, *Operations and Strategy* (visited May 7, 1999), www.drapervc.com/Operations.html.
40. Crosspoint Venture Partners, *Investment Profile* (visited October 21, 1999), www.cpvp.com/investments/profile.html.
41. Sahlman, Method for Valuing High-Risk, Long Term Investments 1.
42. Ibid., 19.

43. Stanley C. Golder, Structuring and Pricing the Financing, in *Pratt's Guide to Venture Capital Sources* 47, 51 (1984), Venture Economics.

44. Sahlman, Method for Valuing High-Risk, Long Term Investments 1 [emphasis added].

45. White, Valuation of Newly-Formed Technology Companies.

46. Sahlman, Method for Valuing High-Risk, Long Term Investments 7–8.

47. Ibid., 13.

48. Ibid.

49. Ibid., 7–8.

50. John Willinge and Josh Lerner, A Note on Valuation in Private Equity Settings, *Harvard Business School* 8 (September 1998).

51. Ibid.

52. Ibid., 16–17.

53. Willinge and Lerner, Note on Valuation 7.

54. Sahlman, Method for Valuing High-Risk, Long Term Investments 23.

55. Willinge and Lerner, Note on Valuation 7–8.

56. VantagePoint Venture Partners, Investment Philosophy (visited July 20, 2001), www.vpvp.com/.

57. White, Valuation of Newly-Formed Technology Companies.

58. Timmons, *New Venture Creation* 515–516.

59. Robert M. Johnson, Valuation Issues in Start-Ups & Early-Stage Companies: The Venture Capital Method, *London Business School* 4 (December 1997).

60. Ibid., 4–5.

Printed and bound by CPI Group (UK) Ltd, Croydon, CR0 4YY

28/08/2023

08105310-0001